HENRY FIELDING

TOM JONES

Henry Fielding

TOM JONES

[A Complete Study Guide including Textual Analysis, Interpretations and Criticism]

Aditya Nandwani
B.A. English (Hons) , Delhi University;
M.A. (English), IGNOU; Print Journalism (English) YMCA

ANMOL PUBLICATIONS PVT. LTD.
NEW DELHI - 110 002 (INDIA)

ANMOL PUBLICATIONS PVT. LTD.

H.O.: 4374/4B, Ansari Road, Darya Ganj,
New Delhi-110 002 (India)
Ph.: 23278000, 23261597

B.O.: No. 1015, Ist Main Road, BSK IIIrd Stage
IIIrd Phase, IIIrd Block
Bangalore - 560 085 (India)
Visit us at: www.anmolpublications.com

Tom Jones

First Published, 2009

PRINTED IN INDIA

Printed at Mehra Offset Press, Delhi.

Contents

Preface

The History of Tom Jones, a Foundling, often known simply as Tom Jones, is a comic novel by the English playwright and novelist Henry Fielding. First published on February 28, 1749, Tom Jones is arguably one of the first prose works describable as a novel. The novel is divided into 18 smaller books. Both Joseph Andrews and Tom Jones are 'epic' insofar as they contain extended and comprehensive action. In contrast to say, Samuel Richardson, the reader is presented with a sweeping picture of eighteenth-century society in all its variety, and not simply a detailed close-up of a tiny social group. As the intricate plot of Tom Jones reveals, there is a much larger circle of incidents. Fielding also refers to the element of 'burlesque' in his comic romance and this manifests itself in the mock-heroic diction and reveals yet again the ambiguous attitude of an age which admired the ancient classics yet parodied their technique for satirical purposes. Fielding's classical education also meant that he was seeking to achieve a more dignified literary reputation than was possible at the time when novelists were not held in high regard.

The following book presents a critical approach to Fielding's Tom Jones useful for students of both graduate and postgraduate level. We thus look forward to your response and wish that book proves to be a useful study aid.

Author

Chapter 1

Introduction

Henry Fielding's Tom Jones is both one of the great comic masterpieces of English literature and a major force in the development of the novel form. By 749, the year Tom Jones appeared, the novel was only beginning to be recognized as a potentially literary form. Samuel Richardson's novel Clarissa had appeared only the year before, and for the most part in intellectual circles prose fiction was not considered a worthy pursuit. Despite the publication by Jonathan Swift, a member of the literary elite surrounding Alexander Pope, Joseph Addison and Richard Steele, of Gulliver's Travels in 1726, the sanctioned genres of the first half of the eighteenth century were verse and drama. The novels of Daniel Defoe, seen by many as purely adventure tales, were not regarded as worthy of serious consideration. They were, however, instrumental in the development of a suitable reading public, without which Fielding probably would not have attempted any form of sustained prose fiction.

But while Defoe still followed the seventeenth century tradition of claiming his fiction was fact, and Richardson professed that his tales were moral tracts, emphasizing the instructional rather than the fictional aspect, Fielding was the first major novelist to unabashedly write fiction. At the same time, he undertook an initial critical theory of the new fictional form he was creating: together with the preface to Joseph Andrews (1742), the introductory chapters preceding the individual books in Tom Jones constitute the first extended body of work in English which attempts to define and explain the novel as a literary genre. In the preface Joseph Andrews, Fielding described his own fictional form as "a comic romance" or a "comic epic poem in prose," and in Tom Jones as a "heroically, historical prosaic poem"; a form of "prosai-comi-epic writing". In defining the novel as an epic genre, Fielding emphasized its function in presenting a broad picture of an era, but one, unlike verse epic, in which primarily the weaknesses of humanity are put on display.

Although he termed his new style of writing "history," his definition of the budding genre still influences our understanding of novelistic fiction. According to Fielding, the appropriate subject of the novel is human nature (often in its more ridiculous guises) rather than ghosts and fairies; he sees no excuse for the "modern" writer to introduce supernatural agents. His insistence on conforming to the rules of probability rather than mere possibility is integral to the development of the novel as we know it. Fielding knew what he wanted to do in prose fiction and understood the novelty of his undertaking in a way many of his predecessors had not. He is not modest about pointing this out either:

> [...] I shall not look on myself as accountable to any court of critical jurisdiction whatever; for as I am, in reality, the founder of a new province of writing, so I am at liberty to make what laws I please therein. (II, 1)

Although these claims to originality are largely justified, Tom Jones contains many conventional narrative elements as well which Fielding had already made use of in Joseph Andrews (1742), including an ostensibly picaresque form, inserted narrative and the discovery of true identity. But while the character Joseph, with his origins in parody, suffers from an element of the ridiculous, Tom emerges as a deeper character who even goes through a certain amount of superficial moral development. Tom Jones exemplifies serious aspects of Fielding's concept of benevolence and good nature, his generous personality reflecting Fielding's moral philosophy. At the same time, it is from his impulsive and affectionate nature that many of his troubles spring. He is contrasted to the inhibited, self-seeking hypocrite Blifil, his opposite and, as it turns out, his half-brother. Fielding frequently uses this method of contrasting pairs to manage his huge cast of characters: Tom is opposed to Blifil, Sophia to Molly and later Lady Bellaston, and Allworthy to Squire Western. The same technique is used with the minor characters: the tutors of Tom and Blifil are Thwackum, representing blind respect for authority, and Square, representing abstract ethics.

Despite Fielding's insistence on realism, for the most part the figures in Tom Jones are recognizably indebted to stock theatrical types. Like his predecessor Aphra Behn, Fielding was a dramatist before he was a novelist, but while this dramatic training primarily lead Behn to introduce the rhythms of spoken language to prose fiction, the influence of drama on Fielding's novels was in formal structural elements. For example, he employs concrete "visual" symbols such as Sophia's muff to anchor the reader and focus his or her attention in a way similar to the use of stage properties. The most obvious influence of drama on Tom Jones is in the intricacies of the plot, which are the typical confusions of comedy.

The neatly constructed plot reflects a basic eighteenth century faith in the order of the world, which Fielding, despite skeptical overtones, displayed in this huge but far from sprawling novel. Samuel Taylor Coleridge saw the plot of Tom Jones as one of the three most perfectly planned plots in literature. Even seemingly random details have a place, and at the end of the tale the reader notices that elements which might have appeared superfluous are necessary to round off the story.

The role of the lawyer Dowling is a case in point. In his original appearance he seems only to contribute to the busy atmosphere of the scene, but at the end he is revealed to have been instrumental to the development of events. The scene at the inn in Upton, exactly halfway through the novel, is a plot node of great complexity: here all of the major actors and plot threads come together, and actions and misunder-standings occur which will be crucial for the climax and denouement. Despite the involved construction and numerous plot twists, the author is at great pains to provide adequate motivation for these machinations, creating an appearance of causality usually lacking in the monumental prose romances popular in his day.

Not only is the plot of Tom Jones famous for its intricacy, it is also highly symmetrical in design. The novel has eighteen books, six for the beginning, six for the middle, and six for the end, conforming to the three parts recommended by Aristotle. The first six books give the cause of the action: Tom's open, sensual nature; the conflict with Blifil; the misunderstanding with Squire Allworthy; Tom's love for Sophia and their separation.

The next six contain both the consequences of the first six and the incidents and details which will bring about a resolution. The last six books plunge Tom into disastrous circumstances through his actions and get him out of them again. When he is in prison about to be hanged, he hears that Sophia has refused to speak to or see him again as a result of his affair with Lady Bellaston. As if this were not enough, he even has to face the possibility that he might have committed incest. But it is this last misfortune which also brings about his change of fortune: it is through Jenny Jones, Tom's purported mother who is now known as Mrs. Waters, that the truth of Tom's birth emerges. This brings about a reconciliation with Squire Allworthy and Sophia, and the downfall of Blifil.

The formal tidiness displayed by Tom Jones is more the exception than the rule in the history of the novel: Clarissa or Oliver Twist do not display this kind of neatness. And at times, Tom Jones might seem almost too well-made, since the elaborate construction is not calculated to give the reader a sense of real, unpredictable, day-to-day life. On the other hand, part of Fielding's originality is precisely in the honesty and exuberance with which he creates his fictional world: by drawing attention to the nature of the artifice, the authorial intrusions into the narrative prevent the novel from ever taking on the appearance of a true chronicle of events. This admittance of artifice is not common in the novel either. For the most part, the legacy of Tom Jones was not in any influence on structure; it was to make the English novel until the late nineteenth century primarily a comic genre.

The most original and memorable element of Tom Jones, however, is the narrative voice informing the action and discoursing on the philosophy of writing to the reader in the introductory chapters. Fielding controls the reader's response thorough the urbane, tolerant presence of the figure of the omniscient author, a polished and rational gentleman with a pronounced sense of the ridiculous who emerges as the true moral focus in the novel.

While this technique sacrifices to a certain extent the sense of identification and verisimilitude provided by the first-person or epistolary forms used by Defoe and Richardson, the reading experience is enriched by the analysis of the all-knowing 'author.' On the other hand, the wry narrative voice accounts for various comic effects Fielding achieves in this remarkable novel; it is often the detached description which transforms a melodramatic situation into a comic one.

This authorial presence, an integral element of Fielding's aesthetic undertaking, is a very recognizably masculine presence; an all-knowing male author figure who rules over his fictional world for the good of his readers:

[...] these laws my readers, whom I consider as my subjects, are bound to believe and to obey; with which that they may readily and cheerfully comply, I do hereby assure them that I shall principally regard their ease and advantage in all such institutions; for I do not, like a jure divino tyrant, imagine that they are my slaves or my commodity. I am, indeed, set over them for their own good only, and was created for their use and not they for mine. Nor do I doubt, while I make their interest the great rule of my writings, they will unanimously concur in supporting my dignity and in rendering me all the Honour I shall deserve or desire. (II, 1)

Fielding's implied author demonstrates a very paternal attitude towards both his readers and his characters, displaying a humourous tolerance to all, but ruling over them implacably.

While Fielding's aesthetics are frankly masculine, the moral assumptions exhibited in the novel are also frankly sexist by today's standards. The characterization of Tom Jones displays a tolerance for virile young manhood: he is a sensual youth, easily succumbing to temptation of a sexual nature. This tolerance doesn't work the other way around, however; the heroine Sophia is virginal and pure, while the women who indulge in sensual pleasures are either tramps like Molly or hypocrites like Lady Bellaston (the lowest of the low in Fielding's moral universe).

An exception to this can be found in the portrayal of Jenny Jones (Mrs. Waters), who was originally betrayed into living an "immoral" life and once having lost her virtue had no choice but to continue in her sinful ways. Fielding's frank acceptance of (male) sensuality was regarded by many contemporaries with disapproval. The more puritan Richardson criticized outright what he saw as a "very bad tendency" in Fielding's work, and with Sir Charles Grandson (1753) he attempted to create a hero as virtuous as any heroine.

It has become commonplace in literary history to recognize masculine and feminine traditions in the novel going back to Tom Jones and Clarissa. This can be misleading in more than just the fact that both of the seminal works in these supposedly gender specific novelistic modes were written by men: Sophia, for example, has more spirit than Richardson's feminine ideal, Clarissa. In addition, the omniscient, "masculine" authorial voice developed by Fielding was used to great effect by that female master of the Victorian novel, George Eliot. For most of the next century, however, it did remain true that the wise, god-like author-figure Fielding created was not a role that could easily be played by women writers. Social restrictions requiring them to deal with emotions or domestic affairs made the form of the novel developed by Richardson much more suitable for women than the social panorama of a novel like Tom Jones. As Fielding also asserted that authors should have some experience of what they write about (XIV, 1), it would seem to follow that women would not be able to write in the epic fictional mode he established.

The god-like omniscience of the authorial narrator in Tom Jones needs to be taken with a grain of salt, however. The authorial narrator is portrayed as all-knowing and all-seeing, but a reader who relies exclusively on the expressed judgment calls of the narrator will be deceived: one of Fielding's techniques is to introduce important details that are given very little attention by the narrative voice, lulling the reader into ignoring them. The omnipotent role is somewhat tongue-in-cheek, as is much of Tom Jones. Take for example one of the introductory chapters in which Fielding lays down the rules of the new genre:

> Peradventure there may be no parts in this prodigious work which will give the reader less pleasure in perusing than those which have given the author the greatest pains in composing. Among these, probably, may be reckoned those initial essays which we have prefixed to the historical matter contained in every book, and which we have determined to be essentially necessary to this kind of writing, of which we have set ourselves at the head.
>
> For this our determination we do not hold ourselves strictly bound to assign any reason, it being abundantly sufficient that we have laid it down as a rule necessary to be observed in all prosai-comi-epic writing. Who ever demanded the reasons of that nice unity of time or place which is now established as so essential to dramatic poetry? (V, 1)

Here the game Fielding is playing with his readers becomes obvious, especially when he compares his prefaces to the rule of dramatic unity; the comments following this passage make it abundantly clear that he scorns the convention. Of course, the inclusion of prefaces is one rule set down in Tom Jones which has found next to no imitation, and it appears likely that Fielding would not have been disappointed by that fact.

What Fielding did establish with Tom Jones, however, was the role of the novel as the modern epic form. And many of the other "rules" he put forth — plausibility over possibility, for example — still exert a strong influence on novelistic fiction today.

Chapter 2

Henry Fielding: Life and Works

BIOGRAPHY

Henry Fielding, the eldest of seven children, was born on April 22, 1707, at Sharpham Park, in Somerset, England. He was the son of General Edmund Fielding, His mother, Sarah Gould Fielding, was the daughter of a judge. Their marriage had been highly disapproved of by Sarah's parents on the grounds that Edmund was too poor and could not even manage what little money he did have.

When Henry was two, his father 'retired' to an estate near East Stour in Dorset, where he was unsuccessful as a gentleman farmer and where Sarah Gould Fielding died when Henry was just ten years old.

Henry had been raised by his father to dislike Catholics, so it is ironic that when two years later his father remarried a woman to kept an eating-house she was an Italian

Henry's father and his maternal grandmother, Lady Gould, battled for custody of the children. His grandmother eventually sued for custody of Henry and his siblings, and won.

Edmund eventually died in a debtor's prison, leaving behind an estate valued at five pounds. Apparently his wife's parents were on to something. It should be noted that Edmund spelled his name Fielding in the belief that it was the more aristocratic form.

Under the influence of Lady Gould Henry was sent to school at Eton in 1719 where he reputedly enjoyed his time. Henry worked hard and made lifelong friends of his contemporaries Lyttleton, who later became a generous patron, and Pitt the Elder. Upon graduation in 1724, Fielding went to London were he was to spend the next several years as a man-about-town and writer.

In the summer of 1725 Henry was to be found in Lyme Regis, ostensibly for a holiday, but more likely to visit his distant cousin Sara Andrews, with an eye on her fortune and to win her as a wife. (Sara at the age of 15 had just become a rich heiress on the early death of her father.) Henry, accompanied by several friends and a servant named James Lewis was soon involved in a drunken brawl. On September 2nd he was brought before the town's magistrates on a charge of assault against Joseph Cannon a servant of the town miller. Although the outcome is not known it is thought that the attack may have been at the instigation of Sara's guardian Andrew Miller who had hopes that Sara would marry his own son John.

It seems that Henry was having some success in his pursuit of Sara, since he was still in Lyme two months later. On Sunday 11th November matters came to a head when Henry assisted by his servant attempted to abduct Sara as she was walking to church with Andrew Tucker and his family. The attempt failed and the same day Tucker laid a charge before the magistrates against Fielding and his servant for an attack on his person. His servant was soon captured, but Henry eluded capture by the constables and left the town the following day, but not before putting up a hand written poster ridiculing the Tuckers.

In 1728 his first comedy, 'Love in Several Masques', was staged. It was not a success, and at the age of 21 he left to study at the University of Leaden in The Netherlands where it was much cheaper than any of the London schools. Eventually, even Leaden was more than he could afford and about a year later he returned to England with all kinds of unpaid debts behind him. Henry began writing plays again, many of them ridiculing the society and politics of the time. Probably his best play, completed in 1731, was 'The Tragedy of Tragedies; or, The Life and Death of Tom Thumb the Great'. It was a spoof of heroic stage plays that took themselves too seriously.

Henry still couldn't manage his money and was never well off. In 1734, aged 27, he married Charlotte Cradock of Salisbury, one of the beauties of the city. Charlotte brought a settlement of £1,500 to the marriage and with the money they planned to live in Dorset as 'County' folk. Thus in 1735 the newly married couple took up residence in a small manor house at East Stour, settled into their comfortable lifestyle and produced a daughter Amelia. In the process becoming extremely popular with there neighbours. However within a year due to a combination of Henry's spendthrift ways and poor budgeting the Fielding's were stony-broke, the estate sold, and the penniless young couple left Dorset to return to London, taking with them Charlottes maid Mary McDaniel.

In London Fielding became the manager and chief playwright of the Little Theatre in the Haymarket. Even though he was rumored to be a terrible drunkard and something of a womanizer, Henry was a hard worker. He wrote several new plays a year, until the theatre was forced to close by the stage Licensing Act was of 1737 which provided that only plays licensed by the government could be performed. The act having been introduced largely as a result of Fielding's plays ridiculing the politics of the day.

By this time, Henry and Charlotte had two children needed another source of income. Henry took up the study of law and turned to writing for the newspapers, becoming editor of The Champion in 1739, and graduated as a lawyer in 1740. It was at this time that he developed gout, which was to get worse as he grew older.

Henry Fielding's novel 'Joseph Andrews' was published in 1742. It was a comic takeoff on Samuel Richardson's 'Pamela,' but the success of 'Joseph Andrews' was made less sweet for Henry by the death of his daughter, Charlotte and a serious illness which afflicted his wife.

'Miscellanies', published in 1743, included the novel 'Jonathan Wild', a mock biography of a criminal hero.

The death of his wife in 1744 was a great blow, exasperating his already bad health. He took comfort largely in the company of his daughter Harriet, his sister Sarah, and his wife's maid, Mary Daniel. Sarah had followed in her fathers literary footsteps and did some writing but none of it was very memorable; however her book for educating girls, 'The Governess, or Little Female Academy', was used well into the next century.

It was about a year before Fielding went back to newspaper writing, where he continued to work on various politically oriented newspapers and publish many political and satirical pamphlets, some of which the government actually approved of, and even distributed. These were often published anonymously, which unfortunately led to Henry being blamed for some atrociously mean pamphlets that he had nothing to do with.

In 1747 defying convention Fielding married Mary McDaniel, who was around six months pregnant with their son William at the time. The following year, Henry was appointed a judge at Middlesex. Over the next few years, Henry's wife had four more children and Henry himself became increasingly angry with the state of the law and law enforcement.

'Tom Jones', Fielding's comic masterpiece and best known work was published in 1749. It was a novel for all time. The life and robustness of 'Tom Jones' were recreated in a 1963 movie, which featured perhaps the most sensuous meal ever filmed.

The heroine is Sophia Weston, and it is claimed that Fielding based this character on Sara Andrews, his 'first love'.

Fielding's last novel 'Amelia' was published in 1751. Allegedly a biography of his former wife Charlotte in which she is portrayed as the heroine. It was not up to his other work. Perhaps, because by this now he was a very sick man, suffering from asthma and jaundice in addition to his gout. The plot was contrived, the heroine conveniently inherits a large sum of money, and if indeed it was a biography, contained several factual errors.

Also in 1751, Henry published a pamphlet entitled 'An Inquiry into the Causes of the late Increase of Robbers, etc.,' which called for sweeping changes in the laws and in the way they were enforced. Today these proposals would not appear to be anything special but by 1753, several of these reforms had been put into practice and Henry helped break up several large gangs by offering money and immunity to those who turned in their fellow criminals.

Perhaps the most important result of his ideas was the reform of the police. It was as a direct consequence of this pamphlet that Home Secretary, Sir Robert Peel, was to form the Bow Street Runners, Britain's first professional police force.

Henry was directly responsible for improvements in record keeping, founding what was later to become the Criminal Record Office of Scotland Yard.

Due to ill health, Henry reigned as a Judge in 1752 and in the hope that a warmer climate would be beneficial he sailed to Lisbon in 1754. Unfortunately he had contracted jaundice, and this combined with dropsy was to cause his death on 8 October 1754 just two months after his arrival in Portugal. Published after his death, his final work, Journal of a Voyage to Lisbon, has been described as a classic example of the horrors of traveling.

CHRONOLOGY

- 22 April 1707: Henry Fielding is born to Edmund Fielding, a retired army lieutenant colonel, and Sarah Gould, daughter of Sir Henry Gould, a judge of the Queen's Bench.
- September 1715-February 1716: The first Jacobite Rebellion.
- *14 April 1718*: Fielding's mother dies.

- 1719-1724: Fielding goes to Eton. Important friends include George Lyttleton, William Pitt, and Sir Charles Han bury Williams.
- April 1721: Robert Walpole begins his 21-year tenure as Prime Minister.
- 28 October 1726: Swift's Gulliver's Travels published.
- 10 November 1727: Fielding's first works published.
- 1728-1729: Fielding attends Leaden University, studying the classics. He leaves in April 1729.
- 29 January 1728: The Beggar's Opera, Gay's famous opera, opens at Lincoln's Inn Fields.
- 30 January 1728: The Masquerade, a satirical poem by Fielding, is published.
- 16 February 1728: Love in Several Masques, Fielding's first comedy, is performed at Drury Lane.
- 26 January 1730: Fielding's comedy The Temple Beau performed at Goodman's Fields.
- 30 March 1730: The Author's Farce begins a run of 42 performances at the New Theatre in the Haymarket.
- 24 April 1730: Tom Thumb begins a run of 41 performances at Haymarket.
- 23 June 1730: Fielding's comedy Rape upon Rape: or The Justice Caught in His Own Trap performed at the Haymarket.
- 24 March 1731: The Tragedy of Tragedies: or The Life and Death of Tom Thumb the Great first performed at the Haymarket.
- 22 April 1731: Fielding's satirical ballad opera The Welsh Opera: or The Grey Mare the Better Horse performed at the Haymarket.
- 1 January 1732: Fielding reappears at Drury Lane with The Lottery.
- 14 February 1732: The Modern Husband, a dark comedy by Fielding, is published and acted for 14 nights.

- 18 May 1732: Pope's Dunciad published.
- 1 June 1732: The Covent Garden Tragedy and The Old Debauches performed together.
- 23 June 1732: Fielding's adaptation of Moldier, The Mock Doctor: or The Dumb Lady Cur'd, opens on stage.
- 3 August 1732: Fielding's first prose essay "The Benefit of Laughing" anonymously published in Mist's Weekly Journal.
- 17 February 1733: First performance of The Miser at Drury Lane.
- 6 April 1733: Deborah: or A Wife for You All, a ballad opera by Fielding, plays at Drury Lane for one night.
- May 1733: A mutiny is led by Theophilus Cibber at the Drury Lane. Most of the performers end up at the Little Haymarket Theatre. Fielding sides with the management at Drury Lane.
- 15 January 1734: Fielding's play The Author's Farce is performed at Drury Lane.
- 5 April 1734: Don Quixote in England is performed at the Haymarket.
- 28 November 1734: Fielding marries Charlotte Cradock in Bath.
- 6 January 1735: Fielding's An Old Man Taught Wisdom: or The Virgin Unmask'd appears at Drury Lane.
- 10 February 1735: The Universal Gallant is not well received.
- 5 March 1736: Fielding's satire Pasquin appears at the Little Haymarket Theatre.
- 29 April 1736: Tumble Down Dick opens at the Haymarket Theatre.
- 27 May 1736: Fielding stages Lillo's Fatal Curiosity.
- 19 February 1737: Eurydice: or the Devil Henpeck'd is despised when it opens at Drury Lane.

- 21 March 1737: The Historical Register for the Year 1736 plays at the Haymarket Theatre.
- 23 May 1737: Fielding's final play at the Haymarket – the end of an era.
- 21 June 1737: The Licensing Act becomes law.
- 1 November 1737: Fielding is admitted to the Middle Temple in preparation for becoming a barrister.
- 13 May 1738: Fielding uses an alias to publish an essay in Common Sense.
- 15 November 1739: The Champion published for the first time with essays by Fielding.
- 6 November 1740: Richardson publishes Pamela.
- End of 1740: Fielding's contributions to The Champion cease.
- 22 January 1741: The Veroniad is published.
- 6-20 March 1741: Debts catch up to Fielding, and he is confined.
- 2 April 1741: Fielding publishes his parody of Pamela, An Apology for the Life of Mrs.Shamela Andrews.
- 18 June 1741: Fielding's father dies.
- 15 December 1741: Fielding satirizes his former friends in The Opposition: A Vision.
- February 1742: Walpole resigns and is created Earl of Orford.
- 22 February 1742: The History of the Adventures of Joseph Andrews and of His Friend Mr. Abraham Adams is published.
- 2 April 1742: A Full Vindication of the Duchess Dowager of Marlborough is published.
- 6 May 1742: Miss Lucy in Town is produced at Drury Lane.
- 31 May 1742: Fielding and William Young's translation of Aristophanes' Plutus, the God of Riches appears.

- 5 June 1742: Fielding apologizes to subscribers of the Daily Post for being unable to publish the Miscellanies because he has been ill.
- 16 February 1743: Publication of Some Papers Proper to be Read before the Royal Society Concerning the Terrestrial Chrysipus, Golden-Foot or Guniea... Collected by Petrus Gualterus, Fielding's satire of the Philosophical Transactions of the Royal Society.
- 17 February 1743: Fielding's comedy The Wedding Day performed at Drury Lane.
- 7 April 1743: Publication of Fielding's Miscellanies in three volumes, including The Wedding Day, A Journey from This World to the Next, and The Life of Mr. Jonathan Wild the Great.
- 14 November 1744: Fielding's wife Charlotte dies.
- December 1744: Formation of the "Broad-Bottom" government, which includes Fielding's friends Lyttleton, Dodington, the Duke of Bedford, and Pitt.
- July 1745: Charles Edward Stuart (The Young Pretender) lands in Scotland and raises his standard at Glenfinnan.
- 3 October 1745: Fielding publishes A Serious Address to the People of Great Britain on the possible dangers of the Jacobite Rebellion.
- October 1745: A Dialogue between the Devil, the Pope, and the Pretender appears.
- 5 November 1745: Fielding's first contribution to The True Patriot: and The History of our Times, an anti-Jacobite journal published every Tuesday until 17 June 1746.
- 14 April 1746: Fielding appointed as High Steward of the New Forest and of the Manor of Lyndhurst, Hampshire by the Duke of Bedford.
- 16 April 1746: The Jacobites are defeated at the Battle of Culloden, ending their rebellion.

- 17 June 1746: The True Patriot ceases publication.
- 25 February 1747: Fielding's Ovid's Art of Love Paraphrased and Adapted to the Present Times published.
- 7 November 1747: Fielding marries his former cook Mary Daniels, who is six months pregnant with their child.
- December 1747: Fielding's Jacobites Journal begins its run as a publication.
- 28 March 1748: Fielding stages a puppet show with the help of his wife and a puppeteer.
- July-December 1748: Fielding is appointed as a magistrate and takes up his post in November 1748, establishing himself at Bow Street, Covent Garden by December.
- 3 February 1749: The History of Tom Jones is published. 10,000 copies are printed in this year.
- 21 July 1749: Charge delivered to the Grand Jury is published. Fielding is chosen to be the chairman of the Westminster Sessions in March and writes a "bill" suggesting ways to improve the police force of the city.
- January-February 1750: Fielding organizes the Bow Street Runners into the first modern police force.
- 19 February 1750: Fielding and his brother John announce the opening of the Universal Register Office.
- 19 December 1751: Publication of Fielding's last novel, Amelia.
- 4 January 1752: The first number of The Covent-Garden Journal appears.
- 25 November 1752: The last number of The Covent-Garden Journal.
- 19 March 1754: The revised version of Jonathan Wild appears.

- 26 June 1754: Fielding leaves London by ship for Lisbon.
- 8 October 1754: Fielding dies. His body is buried in Lisbon, Portugal in the English Cemetery.
- 10 February 1755: Fielding's books go on sale.
- 25 February 1755: Fielding's Journal of a Voyage to Lisbon and A Fragment of a Comment on L. Bolingbroke's Essays are published together.
- 1762: Arthur Murphy publishes the first collected edition of Fielding's works in eight volumes with a portrait of the novelist by Hogarth on the first page.
- 30 November 1778: The Fathers: or, The Good-Natured Man, thought to be Fielding's lost comedy, is performed at Drury Lane.

LIST OF WORKS

- Love in Several Masques - play, 1728
- Rape upon Rape - play, 1730. Adapted by Bernard Miles as Lock Up Your Daughters! in 1959, filmed in 1974
- The Temple Beau - play, 1730
- The Author's Farce - play, 1730
- The Tragedy of Tragedies; or, The Life and Death of Tom Thumb - play, 1731
- Grub-Street Opera - play, 1731
- The Modern Husband - play, 1732
- Pasquin - play, 1736
- The Historical Register for the Year 1736 - play, 1737
- An Apology for the Life of Mrs. Shamela Andrews - novel, 1741
- The History of the Adventures of Joseph Andrews and his Friend, Mr. Abraham Abrams - novel, 1742
- The Life and Death of Jonathan Wild, the Great - novel, 1743, ironic treatment of Jonathan Wild, the most notorious underworld figure of the time.

- Miscellanies - collection of works, 1743, contained the poem Part of Juvenal's Sixth Satire, Modernized in Burlesque Verse
- The Female Husband or the Surprising History of Mrs Mary alias Mr George Hamilton, who was convicted of having married a young woman of Wells and lived with her as her husband, taken from her own mouth since her confinement - pamphlet, fictionalized report, 1746
- The History of Tom Jones, a Foundling - novel, 1749
- A Journey from this World to the Next - 1749
- Amelia - novel, 1751
- The Covent Garden Journal - 1752
- Journal of a Voyage to Lisbon - travel narrative, 1755
- Tom Thumb N.D.

Chapter 3

Historical Context

To understand the natural world and humankind's place in it solely on the basis of reason and without turning to religious belief was the goal of the wide-ranging intellectual movement called the Enlightenment. The movement claimed the allegiance of a majority of thinkers during the 17th and 18th centuries, a period that Thomas Paine called the Age of Reason. At its heart it became a conflict between religion and the inquiring mind that wanted to know and understand through reason based on evidence and proof.

Reflections of the Age in Cultural Expression

The eighteenth century, when Newtonian science exerted its greatest impact, was exceptionally noteworthy for European cultural expression. This was most evident in philosophy, which sought to find in human affairs natural laws similar to those sciences had discovered in the physical universe. This approach, with its optimistic utopianism, found some expression in literature, but it was much more obscured in the visual arts and barely noticeable in music. Because they were largely affected by tradition, individual feeling, and patronage, the arts were less responsive to scientific influence. They were, nevertheless, quite rich and varied, reflecting the increasing wealth, widening perspectives, and rising technical proficiency of European life.

Reflections of the Age in Literature

More than in art, neoclassicism in literature came closer to voicing the eighteenth century's fascination with reason and scientific law. Indeed, the verbal media of poetry, drama, prose, and exposition were commonly used to convey the new philosophic principles.

A typical poetic voice of the Age of Reason in England was Alexander Pope (1688-1744). In his most famous work, An Essay on Man (1733), Pope expressed the optimism and respect for reason that marked the era. He described a Newtonian universe in the following often quoted lines:

All are but parts of one stupendous whole,
Whose body nature is, and God the soul...
All nature is but art, unknown to thee;
All chance, direction, which thou cannot see.
All discord, harmony not understood;
All partial evil, universal good
And, spite of pride, in erring reason's spite,
One truth is clear: Whatever is, is right.

Two other poetic voices deserve mention here. One belonged to the English Countess of Winchelsea (1661-1720), who extolled reason and feminine equality in her verse. The other was that of a Massachusetts slave girl, Phyllis Wheatley (1753-1784), whose rhyming couplets, in the style of Pope, pleaded the cause of freedom for the American colonies and for her race.

Reflecting the common disdain for irrational customs and outworn institutions were such masterpieces of satire as Candide (1759), by the French man of letters, Francois-Marie Arouet, better known as Voltaire (1694-1778). Another famous satirist, England's Jonathan Swift (1667-1745), ridiculed the pettiness of human concerns in Gulliver's Travels (1726), wherein Captain Gulliver, in visiting the fictitious land of Lilliput, found two opposing factions: the Big-endians, who passionately advocated opening eggs at the big end, and the Little-endians, who vehemently proposed an opposite procedure.

The novel became a major literary vehicle in this period. It caught on first in France during the preceding century and was then popularized in England. Robinson Crusoe (1719), by Daniel Defoe (1659-1731), is often called the first modern English novel. The straight prose of the novel satisfied a prevailing demand for clarity and simplicity; but the tendency in this period to focus on middle-class values, heroic struggle, and sentimental love foreshadowed the coming romantic movement. Writing along these lines Samuel Richardson (1689-1761) produced Pamela (1740-1741), the story of a virtuous servant-girl, and Henry Fielding (1707-1754) wrote the equally famous Tom Jones (1749), the rollicking tale of a young man's deep pleasures and superficial regrets. Each novel, in its own way, defined a natural human morality.

In both France and England women found a uniquely promising outlet for their long-ignored talents in the romantic novel, with its accent on personal feminine concerns and domestic problems. Two among the multitude of able French women novelists were Madame de Graffigny (1695-1758), whose Lettres D'Une Peruvienne (1730) became a best-seller, and Madame de Tencin (1682-1749), who wrote The Siege of Calais, a historical novel of love and danger. In England, Fanny Burney (1753-1840) was universally acclaimed after publication of her first novel, Eveline (1778), about "a young lady's entrance into the world." Aphra Behn (1640-1689) was an early playwright whose novel, Oroonoko (1688), was a plea for the natural person, long before the works of Defoe and Rousseau.

The Enlightenment and the Age of Reason in Philosophy

Western Europe's worship of reason, reflected only vaguely in art and literature, was precisely expressed in a set of philosophic ideas known collectively as the Enlightenment. It was not originally a popular movement. Catching on first among scientists, philosophers, and some theologians, it was then taken up by literary figures, who spread its message among the middle classes. Ultimately, it reached the common people in simplified terms associated with popular grievances.

The most fundamental concept of the Enlightenment were faith in nature and belief in human progress. Nature was seen as a complex of interacting laws governing the universe. The individual human being, as part of that system, was designed to act rationally. If free to exercise their reason, people were naturally good and would act to further the happiness of others. Accordingly, both human righteousness and happiness required freedom from needless restraints, such as many of those imposed by the state or the church. The Enlightenment's uncompromising hostility towards organized religion and established monarchy reflected a disdain for the past and an inclination to favor utopian reform schemes. Most of its thinkers believed passionately in human progress through education. They thought society would become perfect if people were free to use their reason.

Before the eighteenth century, the Enlightenment was confined to Holland and England. Its earlier Dutch spokesmen were religious refugees, like the French Huguenot Pierre Bayle (1674-1706), whose skepticism and pleas for religious toleration were widely known in France. Baruch Spinoza (1632-1687), a Jewish intellectual and Holland's greatest philosopher, was a spokesman for pantheism, the belief that God exists in all of nature. Spinoza's influence, along with Newton's, profoundly affected English thinkers. Mary Astell (1666-1731), perhaps the earliest influential English feminist, lauded rational thinking and cited Newton as proof of an ordered universe. Such ideas were given more credibility by John Locke (1632-1704), the famous English philosopher. Back home from exile in Holland after the Glorious Revolution of the 1680s, Locke applied Newton's recently published principles to psychology, economics, and political theory. With Locke, the Enlightenment came to maturity and began to spread abroad. After the Peace of Utrecht (1713), the Enlightenment was largely a French Phenomenon. Its leading proponents were known as the philosophes, although the term cannot in this instance be translated literally as "philosophers." The philosophes were mostly writers and intellectuals who analysed the evils of society and sought reforms in accord with the principles of reason. Their most supportive allies were the salonnieres, that is, the socially conscious and sometimes learned women who regularly entertained them, at the same time sponsoring their discussion of literary works, artistic creations, and new political ideas. By 1750, the salonnieres, their salons, and the philosophes had made France once again the intellectual centre of Europe.

A leading light among the philosophes was the Marquis de Montesquieu (1688-1755), a judicial official as well as a titled nobleman. He was among the earliest critics of absolute monarchy. From his extensive foreign travel and wide reading he developed a great respect for English liberty and a sense of objectivity in viewing European institutions, particularly those of France. Montesquieu's Persian Letters (1721), which purported to contain reports of an Oriental traveller in Europe, describing the irrational behaviour and ridiculous customs of Europeans, delighted a large reading audience. His other great work, The Spirit of Laws (1748), expressed his main political principles.

It is noted for its practical common sense, its objective recognition of geographic influences on political systems, its advocacy of checks and balances in government, and its uncompromising defence of liberty against tyranny. More than any of the philosophes, Voltaire personified the skepticism of his century toward traditional religion and the injustices of the Old Regimes. His caustic pen brought him two imprisonments in the Bastille and even banishment to England for three years. On returning to France, Voltaire continued to champion toleration. He popularized Newtonian science, fought for freedom of the press, and actively crusaded against the church. In such endeavors, he turned out hundreds of histories, plays, pamphlets, essays, and novels. His estimated correspondence of 10,000 letters, including many to Frederick the Great and Catherine the Great, employed his wry wit in spreading the gospel of rationalism and reform of abuses. Even in his own time, his reputation became a legend, among kings as well as literate commoners.

Voltaire had many disciples and imitators, but his only rival in spreading the Enlightenment was a set of books - the famous French Encyclopedie, edited by Denis Diderot (1713-1784). The Encyclopedie, the chief monument of the philosophes, declared the supremacy of the new science, denounced superstition, and expounded the merits of human freedom. Its pages contained critical articles, by tradesmen as well as scientists, on unfair taxes, the evils of the slave trade, and the cruelty of criminal laws.

More than has been widely understood, the Encyclopedie, and many other achievements of the philosophes were joint efforts with their female colleagues among the salonnieres. Madame de Geoffrin (1699-1777) contributed 200,000 livres (roughly $280,000 equivalent) to the Encyclopedie and made her salon the headquarters for planning and managing it. Mademoiselle de Lespinasse (1732-1776), the friend and confidential advisor of Jean d'Alembert (1717-1783), who assisted Diderot in editing the work, turned her salon into a forum for criticizing prospective articles. Most of the philosophes relied upon such assistance. Voltaire was coached in science by Madame du Chatelet; and the Marquis de Condorcet (1742-1794), the prophet of progress and women's rights among the philosophes, was intellectually partnered by his wife, Sophie (1764-1812), who popularized their ideas in her own salon. Even Madame de Pompadour aided the philosophes in 1759, when she presuaded Louis XV to allow sale of the Encyclopedia.

Perhaps the best-known of all the philosophes was that eccentric Swiss-born proponent of romantic rationalism, Jean-Jacques Rousseau (1712-1778). Although believing in the general objectives of the Enlightenment, Rousseau distrusted reason and science. He gloried in human impulse and intuition, trusting emotions rather than thought, the heart rather than the mind. His early rebuffs from polite society encouraged his hatred for the Old Regime. He also professed admiration for "noble savages," who lived completely free of law, courts, priests, and officials. In his numerous writings, he spoke as a rebel against all established institutions. The most famous of these works, The Social Contract (1762), was Rousseau's indictment of absolute monarchy. It began with the stirring manifesto: "Man is born free, But today he is everywhere in chains."

The French Enlightenment exerted a powerful influence on English thought. Many young upper-class Englishmen visited France to complete their education. Among them were three leading English thinkers: Adam Smith (1723-1790), the Scottish father of modern economics; David Hume (1711-1766), the best-known English skeptic; and Jeremy Bentham (1748-1832), the founder of utilitarian philosophy. Another famous English rationalist was the historian, Edward Gibbon (1737-1794), whose Decline and Fall of the Roman Empire markedly criticized early Christianity. Among English political radicals after 1770, Joseph Priestley, Richard Price (1723-1791) and Thomas Paine (1737-1809) were also very much affected by French thought. Paine, who figured prominently in the American and French revolutions, was also a leader in English radical politics.

The Enlightenment also affected English women. Hannah Moore and a coterie of lady intellectuals, known as "bluestockings," maintained a conservative imitation of the French salons after the 1770s. One atypical "bluestocking" was Catherine Macaulay (1731-1791), a leading historian who published eight widely acclaimed volumes on the Stuart period. A republican defender of the American and French Revolutions, Macaulay exerted a decided influence on Mary Wollstonecraft (1759-1797), whose life symbolized the Enlightenment and the emerging English feminist movement. Born in poverty and burdened by a dependent family, Wollstonecraft became a teacher and a successful professional writer. She was personally acquainted with leading English radicals, including Richard Price, Thomas Paine, and William Godwin (1756-1836), whom she later married. Her Vindication of the Rights of Man (1790) was the first serious answer to Edmund Burke's diatribe against the French Revolution, which

Wollstonecraft personally observed and ardently supported. The reforming rationalism of the Enlightenment spread over Europe and also reached the New World. A leading spokesman in Germany was Moses Mendelssohn (1729-1786), who wrote against dogmatism and in favor of natural religion. In Italy, the Marquis of Beccaria (1738-1794) pleaded for humanitarian legal reforms. The Enlightenment was popular among the upper classes in such absolutist strong-holds as Prussia, Russia, Austria, Portugal, and Spain. French ideas were read widely in Spanish America and Portuguese Brazil. In the English colonies, Locke and the philosophes influenced such leading thinkers as Benjamin Franklin, Thomas Jefferson (1743-1826), Mercy Otis Warren (1728-1814), and Abigail Adams (1744-1818).

The Reaction against Reason

The eighteenth century was primarily an "Age of Reason," but in the latter decades there was a general reaction against rationalism. One form of the reaction came in philosophy with a new idealism, in opposition to the materialism of the early Enlightenment. Another form was an emotional religious revival, which won back many wavering Protestants and Catholics. A third form of reaction replaced reason with religion as the justification for humanitarian reforms. These movements stressed emotion over reason but continued the Enlightenment's accent upon individual liberty.

Idealistic Philosophy

Immanuel Kant (1724-1804), a kindly and contemplative professor of philosophy at the German University of Konigsberg, was thoroughly aroused by the skeptical and materialistic extremes of the Enlightenment. While appreciating science and dedicated to reason, he determined to shift philosophy back to a more sensible position without giving up much of its newly discovered "rational" basis. His ideas, contained primarily in the Critique of Pure Reason (1781), ushered in a new age of philosophic idealism.

Kant agreed with Locke on the role of the senses in acquiring knowledge but insisted that sensory experience had to be interpreted by the mind's internal patterns. This meant that certain ideas - the mind's categories for sorting and recording experience - were "a priori", that is, they existed before the sensory experience occurred. Typical innate ideas of this sort were width, depth, beauty, cause, and God; all were understood yet none were learned directly through the senses. Kant concluded, as had Descartes, that some truths were not derived from material objects through scientific study. Beyond the material world was a realm unapproachable by science. Moral and religious truths, such as God's existence, could not be proved by science yet were known to human beings as rational creatures. Reason, according to Kant, went beyond the mere interpretation of physical realities.

In Kant's philosophic system, pure reason, the highest form of human endeavor, was as close to intuition as it was to sensory experience. It proceeded from certain subjective senses, built into human nature. The idea of God was derived logically from the mind's penchant for harmony. The human conscience, according to Kant, might be developed or be crippled by experience, but it originated in the person's thinking nature. Abstract reason, apart from science and its laws, was a valid source of moral judgment and religious interpretation. Thus Kant used reason to give a philosophic base back to mystical religion.

The Religious Reaction

Religious rationalism, despite its appeal to intellectuals, provoked considerable religious reaction. Part of this came from theologians such as Bishop Joseph Butler (1692-1752) and William Paley (1743-1805) in England, both of whom defended Christianity and challenged deism on its own rational grounds. Even more significant was a widespread emotional revival, stressing religion of the heart rather than the mind.

The new movement, known as pietism, began in England after 1738, when the brothers John (1703-1791) and Charles (1708-1788) Wesley began a crusade of popular preaching in the Church of England. The Anglican pietists discarded traditional formalism and stilted sermons in favor of a glowing religious fervor, producing a vast upsurge of emotional faith among the English lower classes. "Methodist," at first a term of derision, came to be the respected and official name for the new movement. After John Wesley's death in 1791, the Methodists officially left the Anglican church to become a most important independent religious force in England.

On the continent, Lutheran pietism, led by Philipp J. Spener (1635-1705) and Emanuel Swedenborg (1688-1772), followed a pattern similar to Methodism. Swedenborg's movement in Sweden began as an effort to reconcile science and revelation; after Swedenborg's death it became increasingly emotional and mystical. Spener, in Germany, stressed Bible study, hymn singing, and powerful preaching. The Moravian movement sprang from his background. Under the sponsorship of Count Nicholaus von Zinzendorf (1700-1760), it spread to the frontiers of Europe and to the English colonies in America.

The "Great Awakening," a tremendous emotional revival sustained by Moravians, Methodsts, Baptists, and Quakers, swept the colonial frontier areas from Georgia to New England in the late eighteenth century. Women played prominent roles in this activity, organizing meetings and providing auxiliary services, such as charities and religious instruction. Among the Quakers, women were often ministers and itinerant preachers. One was Jemima Wilkinson (1752-1819), leader of the Universal Friends; another was Ann Lee (1736-1784), who founded Shaker colonies in New York and New England. By the 1780s, religious rationalism and pietism stood in opposition to each other. Proponents of each disagreed passionately on religious principles though they agreed on the issue of religious freedom. Both rationalists and pietists were outside the state churches, both feared persecution, and both recognized the flagrant abuses of religious establishments. The two movements were therefore almost equally threatening to state churches and the old regimes.

The New Humanitarianism

One dominant characteristic of the early Enlightenment - the concern for individual human worth - received new impetus from religion in the reaction against reason. The demand for reform and the belief in human progress were now equated with traditional Christian principles, such as human communality and God's concern for all people. Religious humanitarianism shunned radical politics and ignored the issue of women's rights, despite the movement's strong support among women. It did, however, seek actively to relieve human suffering and ignorance among children, the urban poor, prisoners, and slaves. This combination of humanitarian objectives and Christian faith was similar in some ways to the Enlightenment but markedly different in its emotional tone and religious justifications.

Notable among manifestations of the new humanitarianism was the antislavery movement in England. A court case in 1774 ended slavery within the country. From then until 1807, a determined movement sought abolition of the slave trade. It was led by William Wilberforce (1759-1833), aided by Hannah Moore and other Anglican Evangelicals, along with many Methodists and Quakers. Wilberforce repeatedly introduced bills into the House of Commons that would have eliminated the traffic in humans. His efforts were rewarded in 1807 when the trade was ended, although he and his allies had to continue to struggle for twenty-six more years, before they could achieve abolition in the British colonies. Religious humanitarians enforced other movements that originated in the Enlightenment. For example, the movements for legal reform and prison reform were both supported by religious groups before 1800. Education, extolled by rationalist thinkers, also aroused interest among the denominations. The Sunday School movement, particularly in England, was a forerunner of many private and quasi-public church schools. Finally, concern for the plight of slaves, coupled with rising missionary zeal, brought popular efforts to improve conditions for native peoples in European possessions overseas.

While it was not as openly political as other aspects of the Enlightenment, the new humanitarianism played a significant part in weakening absolutism. In general, it contributed to a spirit of restlessness and discontent and encouraged independent thought, particularly as it improved education. Its successful campaign against the slave trade also struck a direct blow at the old mercantilist economies, which depended heavily on plantation agriculture overseas. In time, the missionaries would also prove to be the most consistent enemies of colonialism.

The West By 1750

The three great currents of change - commercialization, cultural reorientation, and the rise of the nation-state - continued to operate in the West after 1700, along with the growing international influence of the West. Each strand, in fact, produced new ramifications that furthered the overall transformation of the West.

Political Patterns

On the whole, during the middle decades of the 18th century political changes seemed least significant. During much of the century English politics settled into a rather turgid parliamentary routine, in which key political groups competed for influence without major policy differences. Some popular concern for greater representation surfaced in the 1760s, as a movement for democracy surged briefly, but there was as yet no consistent reform current. Absolute monarchy in France changed little institutionally, but it became progressively less effective. It was unable to force changes in the tax structure that would give it more solid financial footing, because aristocrats refused to surrender their traditional exemptions. Political developments were far livelier in central Europe. In Prussia Frederick the Great, building on the military and bureaucratic organization of his predecessors, introduced greater freedom of religion while expanding the economic functions of the state. His government actively encouraged better agricultural methods, as in promoting use of the potato as a staple crop. It also codified its laws toward greater commercial coordination and greater equity; harsh traditional punishments were cut back. Later in the 18th century an Austrian emperor, Joseph II, tried a similar programme of state-sponsored improvements, including a major effort to roll back the power of the Catholic church. Rulers of this sort claimed to be enlightened despots, wielding great authority but for the good of society at large.

Enlightened or not, the policies of the major Western nation-states produced recurrent warfare. France and Britain squared off in the 1740s and again in the Seven Years' War (1756-1763); their conflicts focused on battles for colonial empire. Austria and Prussia also fought, with Prussia gaining new land. Wars in the 18th century were carefully modulated, without devastating effects, but they demonstrated the continued linkage between statecraft and war characteristic of the West.

Enlightenment Thought

In culture, the aftermath of the scientific revolution spilled over into a new movement known as the Enlightenment, centreed particularly in France but with adherents throughout the Western world. Enlightenment thinkers continued to support scientific advance. While there were no Newton-like breakthroughs, chemists gained new understanding of major elements and biologists developed a vital new classification system for the natural species.

The Enlightenment also pioneered in applying scientific methods to the study of human society, sketching the modern social sciences. The basic idea here was that rational laws could describe social as well as physical behaviour, and that knowledge could be used to improve policy.

Thus criminologists wrote about how brutal punishments failed to deter crime, whereas a decent society would be able to rehabilitate criminals through education. Political theorists wrote about the importance of carefully planned constitutions and controls over privilege, though they disagreed about what political form was best. A new school of economists developed. The Scottish philosopher Adam Smith set forth a number of invariable principles of economic behaviour, based on the belief that people act according to their self-interest but, through competition, work to promote general economic advance. Government should avoid regulation in favor of the operation of individual initiative and market forces. Here was an important specific statement of economic policy and an illustration of the growing belief that general models of human behaviour could be derived from rational thought.

More generally still, the Enlightenment produced a set of basic principles about human affairs. Human beings are naturally good and can be educated to be better. Reason was the key to truth, and religions that relied on blind faith or refused to tolerate diversity were wrong. Enlightenment thinkers attacked the Catholic church with particular vigour. Progress was possible, even inevitable, if people could be set free. Society's goals should centre on improvements in material and social life.

Enlightenment thinkers showed great interest in technological change, for greater prosperity was a valid and achievable goal. Coercion and cruelty could be corrected, for the Enlightenment encouraged a humanitarian outlook that was applied in condemnations of slavery and war.

Though not typical of the Enlightenment's main thrust, a few thinkers applied the general principles to other areas. A handful of socialists argued that economic equality and the abolition of private property must become important goals. A few feminist thinkers, such as Mary Wollstonecraft in England, argued that new political rights and freedoms should extend to women, against the general male-centreed views of most Enlightenment thinkers.

The Enlightenment, summing up and extending earlier intellectual changes, became an important force for political and social reform. It did not rule unchallenged. Important popular religious movements, such as Methodism in England, showed the continued power of spiritual faith. Many writers, particularly those experimenting with the novel as a new literary form in the West, rebelled against Enlightenment rationality to urge the importance of sentimentality and emotion. These approaches, too, encouraged rethinking of traditional styles.

The popularization of new ideas encouraged further changes in the habits and beliefs of many ordinary people. Reading clubs and coffeehouses allowed many urban artisans and businessmen to discuss the latest reform ideas. Leading writers and compilations of scientific and philosophical findings, such as the Encyclopaedia Britannica, won a wide audience and, in a few cases, a substantial fortune due to the sale of books. Groups and individuals formed to promote better agricultural or industrial methods, or bent on winning new political rights, referred directly to Enlightenment thinking. Some groups of artisans and peasants also turned against established churches and even withdrew from religious belief, as secular values gained ground.

Other changes in popular outlook paralleled the new intellectual currents, though they had deeper sources than philosophy alone. Attitudes toward children began to shift in many social groups. Older methods of physical discipline were criticized, in favor of more restrained behaviour that would respect the goodness and innocence of children. Swaddling began to decline, as parents were interested in freer movement and greater interaction for young children; no longer were infants tightly wrapped during their first months. Among wealthy families, educational toys and books for children reflected the idea that childhood should be a stage for learning and growth. At the most basic level, parents became increasingly likely to give young children names at birth and to select names different from those of older relatives - a sign of a new affection for children and new belief in their individuality. These changes were gradual, and they involved more adult control of children as well as a more humane outlook. The idea of shaping children and instilling guilt-stimulated consciences gained ground. Unquestionably, the net effect was to alter parent-child relations and also to produce novel personality ideals for adults themselves.

Family life generally was altered by a growing sense that old hierarchies needed to be rethought, toward somewhat greater equality in the treatment of women and children within the home. Love among family members gained new respect, and an emotional bond in marriage became more widely sought. Parents, for example, grew more reluctant to force a match on a son or daughter if the emotional vibrations were not right. Here was a link not only with Enlightenment ideas of proper family relations but with the novels that poured out a sentimental view of life.

Ongoing economic change, finally, paralleled the ferment in popular culture and intellectual life. Commerce continued its spread. Ordinary Westerners began to buy processed products, such as refined sugar and coffee or tea obtained from Indonesia and the West Indies, for daily use. Here was a sign of the growing importance of Europe's new colonies for ordinary life and of the beginnings of mass consumerism in Western society. Another sign of change was the growing use of paid, professional entertainment as part of popular leisure even in rural festivals. Not accidentally, circuses, first introduced in France in the 1670s, began to redefine leisure to include spectatorship and a taste for the bizarre. Agriculture began to change. Until the later 17th century Western Europe had continued to rely largely on the methods and techniques characteristic of the Middle Ages - a severe economic constraint in a still agricultural society. Now, first in the Netherlands and then elsewhere, new procedures for draining swamps added available land. Nitrogen-fixing crops were introduced to reduce the need to leave land fallow.

Stockbreeding improved, and new techniques like seed-drills or simply the use of scythes instead of sickles for harvesting heightened productivity. Some changes spread particularly fast on large estates, which was one reason that in England more and more land was enclosed, with ordinary farmers serving as tenants or labourers rather than owners. Other changes affected ordinary peasants as well. Particularly vital in this category was the spread of the potato from the late 17th century onward. A New World crop, the potato had long been shunned because it was not mentioned in the Bible and was held to be the cause of plagues. Enlightened government leaders and peasant desire to win greater economic security and better nutrition led to widespread adoption of this efficient crop. The West, in sum, improved its food supply and also its agricultural efficiency, leaving more labour available for other pursuits.

These changes, along with the steady growth of colonial trade and internal commerce, spurred increased manufacturing. The 18th century witnessed a rapid spread of household production of textiles and metal products, mostly by rural workers who alternated manufacturing with some agriculture. Hundreds of thousands of people were drawn into this domestic system in which capitalist merchants distributed supplies and orders and workers ran the production process for pay. While manufacturing tools were still hand operated, the spread of domestic manufacturing spurred important technical innovations designed to improve efficiency. In 1733 James Kay in England introduced the flying shuttle, which permitted automatic crossing of threads on looms; with this, an individual weaver could do the work of two. Improvements in spinning soon followed, as the Western economy began to escalate toward a full-fledged Industrial Revolution. Finally, agricultural changes, commercialism, and manufacturing combined, particularly after about 1730, to produce a rapidly growing population in the West. With better food supplies, more people survived - the potato was a crucial ingredient here. More commercial motives helped prompt landlords and some ambitious peasants to acquire more land and to push unneeded labour off, heightening proletarianization but also reducing the restraints some parents could impose over the sexual behaviour of their children: In essence, as some groups grew unsure of inheritance, they sought more immediate pleasures and also hoped to use the labour of the resultant children. Finally, new manufacturing jobs helped landless people support themselves, promoting in some cases earlier marriage and sexual liaisons. Growing population, in turn, promoted further economic change, heightening competition and producing a more manipulable labour force. The West's great population revolution, which would continue into the 19th century, both caused and reflected the civilization's dynamism, though it also produced great strain and confusion.

Western society was still essentially agricultural by the mid-18th century. Decisive new political forms had yet to be introduced, and in many ways government policies failed to keep pace with cultural and economic change after 1700. Established churches were forces to be reckoned with still. Even new developments, such as the spread of domestic manufacturing, functioned because they allowed so many traditional habits to persist. Thus while new market relationships described this growing system, the location and many of the methods of work as well as the association of family with production were not altered. Western society hovered between older values and institutions and the full flowering of change. Decades of outright political and economic revolution, which would build on these tensions and cause a fuller transformation, were yet to come.

Conclusion

The Enlightenment brought a new vision of the future, which forecast the end of absolute monarchy. Philosophers of the Enlightenment thought they had discovered a simple formula for perpetual human happiness. They sought to deliver individuals from restraints so that they could act freely in accordance with their natures. On the one hand, the formula promised that pursuit of self-interest would benefit society; on the other, it promised that a free human reason would produce sound moral judgments. In other words, individual freedom permitted the operation of natural laws. Believing they had learned these laws, eighteenth-century rationalists thought they had found the secret of never-ending progress. Rational philosophy undermined absolutism in all of its phases. Deism questioned the necessity of state churches and clergies. The physiocrats, Adam Smith, and other early economic liberals demonstrated the futility of mercantilism. Political theory in the Enlightenment substituted the social contract for divine right and emphasized natural human rights of political freedom and justice. Each of these ideas denied the absolute authority of monarchs.

Respect for rational philosophy was largely derived from the successes and popularity of science. The surprising discoveries of astronomers produced a new view of the individual's place in the universe; in his law of gravitation, Newton supplied mathematical evidence for their perspective. His laws, along with the other laws of science, suggested that human reason operated effectively only when it was interpreting sensory experience. Material reality was accepted as the only reality. Therefore, the natural laws affecting human society were also considered as basically materialistic. Toward the end of the eighteenth century, a reaction against reason countered this materialism without affecting the fundamental objectives of the Enlightenment. Idealistic philosophy and pietism both challenged the scientific view of the individual, emphasizing that intuition and faith are human qualities as essential as reason. These new movements merged with the humane concerns of rational philosophy to produce a new humanitarianism, which accented both reason and sentimentality but also continued the eighteenth-century concern for human freedom. Together with the rationalism of the Enlightenment, the reaction against reason before 1800 also challenged absolutism's domination of the human body, mind, and spirit.

Chapter 4

Plot Overview

Mr. Allworthy Makes a Discovery

In that part of the country which is commonly called Somersetshire there lately lived a gentleman whose name was Allworthy, and who might well be called the favourite of both nature and fortune. From the former of these he derived an agreeable person, a sound constitution, a solid understanding, and a benevolent heart; by the latter he was decreed to the inheritance of one of the largest estates in the country.

Mr. Allworthy lived, for the most part, retired in the country, with one sister, for whom he had a very tender affection. This lady, Miss Bridget Allworthy, now somewhat past the age of thirty, was of that species of women whom you commend rather for good qualities than beauty.

Mr. Allworthy had been absent a full quarter of a year in London on some very particular business, and having returned to his house very late in the evening, retired, much fatigued, to his chamber. Here, after he had spent some minutes on his knees-a custom which he never broke through on any account-he was preparing to step into bed, when, upon opening the clothes, to his great surprise, he beheld an infant wrapped up in some coarse linen, in a sweet and profound sleep, between his sheets. He stood for some time lost in astonishment at this sight; but soon began to be touched with sentiments of compassion for the little wretch before him. He then rang his bell, and ordered an elderly woman-servant to rise immediately and come to him.

The consternation of Mrs. Deborah Wilkins at the finding of the little infant was rather greater than her master's had been; nor could she refrain from crying out, with great horror, "My good sir, what's to be done?"

Mr. Allworthy answered she must take care of the child that evening, and in the morning he would give orders to provide it a nurse.

"Yes, sir," says she, "and I hope your worship will send out your warrant to take up the hussy its mother. Indeed, such wicked sluts cannot be too severely punished for laying their sins at honest men's doors; and though your worship knows your own innocence, yet the world is censorious, and if your worship should provide for the child it may make the people after to believe. If I might be so bold as to give my advice, I would have it put in a basket, and sent out and laid at the churchwarden's door. It is a good night, only a little rainy and windy, and if it was well wrapped up and put in a warm basket, it is two to one but it lives till it is found in the morning. But if it should not, we have discharged our duty in taking care of it; and it is, perhaps, better for such creatures to die in a state of innocence than to grow up and imitate their mothers."

But Mr. Allworthy had now got one of his fingers into the infant's hand, which, by its gentle pressure, seeming to implore his assistance, certainly out pleaded the eloquence of Mrs. Deborah. Mr. Allworthy gave positive orders for the child to be taken away and provided with pap and other things against it waked. He likewise ordered that proper clothes should be procured for it early in the morning, and that it should be brought to himself as soon as he was stirring.

Such was the respect Mrs. Wilkins bore her master, under whom she enjoyed a most excellent place, that her scruples gave way to his peremptory commands, and, declaring the child was a sweet little infant, she walked off with it to her own chamber.

Allworthy betook himself to those pleasing slumbers which a heart that hungers after goodness is apt to enjoy when thoroughly satisfied.

In the morning Mr. Allworthy told his sister he had a present for her, and, when Mrs. Wilkins produced the little infant, told her the whole story of its appearance.

Miss Bridget took the good-natured side of the question, intimated some compassion for the helpless little creature, and commended her brother's charity in what he had done. The good lady subsequently gave orders for providing all necessaries for the child, and her orders were indeed so liberal that had it been a child of her own she could not have exceeded them.

The Foundling Achieves Manhood

Miss Bridget having been asked in marriage by one Captain Blifil, a half-pay officer, and the nuptials duly celebrated, Mrs. Blifil was in course of time delivered of a fine boy.

Though the birth of an heir to his beloved sister was a circumstance of great joy to Mr. Allworthy, yet it did not alienate his affections from the little foundling to whom he had been godfather, and had given his own name of Thomas; the surname of Jones being added because it was believed that was the mother's name.

He told his sister, if she pleased, the newborn infant should be bred up together with little Tommy, to which she consented, for she had truly a great complaisance for her brother.

The captain, however, could not so easily bring himself to bear what he condemned as a fault in Mr. Allworthy; for his meditations being chiefly employed on Mr. Allworthy's fortune, and on his hopes of succession, he looked on all the instances of his brother-in-law's generosity as diminutions of his own wealth.

But one day, while the captain was exulting in the happiness which would accrue to him by Mr. Allworthy's death, he himself died of apoplexy.

So the two boys grew up together under the care of Mr. Allworthy and Mrs. Blifil, and by the time he was fourteen Tom Jones-who, according to universal opinion, was certainly born to be hanged-had been already convicted of three robberies-via., of robbing an orchard, of stealing a duck out of a farmer's yard, and of picking Master Blifil's pocket of a ball.

The vices of this young man were, moreover, heightened by the disadvantageous light in which they appeared when opposed to the virtues of Master Blifil, his companion. He was, indeed, a lad of remarkable disposition-sobre, discreet, and pious beyond his age; and many expressed their wonder that Mr. Allworthy should suffer such a lad as Tom Jones to be educated with his nephew lest the morals of the latter should be corrupted by his example.

To say the truth, the whole duck, and great part of the apples, were converted to the use of Tom's friend, the gamekeeper, and his family; though, as Jones alone was discovered, the poor lad bore not only the whole smart, but the whole blame.

Mr. Allworthy had committed the instruction of the two boys to a learned divine, the Reverend Mr. Thwackum, who resided in the house; but though Mr. Allworthy had given him frequent orders to make no difference between the lads, yet was Thwackum altogether as kind and gentle to Master Blifil as he was harsh, nay, even barbarous, to the other. In truth, Blifil had greatly gained his master's affections; partly by the profound respect he always showed his person, but much more by the decent reverence with which he received his doctrine, for he had got by heart, and frequently repeated, his phrases, and maintained all his master's religious principles, with a zeal which was surprising in one so young.

Tom Jones, on the other hand, was not only deficient in outward tokens of respect, often forgetting to pull off his cap at his master's approach, but was altogether unmindful both of his master's precepts and example.

At the, age of twenty, however, Tom, for his love of hunting, had become a great favourite with Mr. Allworthy's neighbour, Squire Western; and Sophia, Mr. Western's only child, lost her heart irretrievably to him before she suspected it was in danger. On his side, Tom was truly sensible of the great worth of Sophia. He liked her person extremely, no less admired her accomplishments, and tenderly loved her goodness. In reality, as he had never once entertained any thoughts of possessing her, nor had ever given the least voluntary indulgence to his inclinations, he had a much stronger passion for her than he himself was acquainted with.

An accident occurred on the hunting-field in saving Sophia from her too mettlesome horse kept Jones a prisoner for some time in Mr. Western's house, and during those weeks he not only found that he loved Sophia with an unbounded passion, but he plainly saw the tender sentiments she had for him; yet could not this assurance lessen his despair of obtaining the consent of her father, nor the horrors which attended his pursuit of her by any base or treacherous method.

Hence, at the approach of the young lady, he grew pale; and, if this was sudden, started. If his eyes accidentally met hers, the blood rushed into his cheeks, and his countenance became all over scarlet. If he touched her, his hand, nay, his whole frame, trembled.

All these symptoms escaped the notice of the squire, but not so of Sophia. She soon perceived these agitations of mind in Jones, and was at no loss to discover the cause; for, indeed, she recognized it in her own breast. In a word, she was in love with him to distraction. It was not long before Jones was able to attend her to the harpsichord, where she would kindly condescend for hours together to charm him with the most delicious music.

The news that Mr. Allworthy was dangerously ill (for a servant had brought word that he was dying) broke off Tom's stay at Mr. Western's, and drove all the thoughts of love out of his head. He hurried instantly into the chariot which was sent for him, and ordered the coachman to drive with all imaginable haste; nor did the idea of Sophia once occur to him on the way.

Tom Jones Falls into Disgrace

On the night when the physician announced that Mr. Allworthy was out of danger Jones was thrown into such immoderate excess of rapture by the news that he might be truly said to be drunk with joy-an intoxication which greatly forwards the effects of wine; and as he was very free, too, with the bottle, on this occasion he became very soon literally drunk.

Jones had naturally violent animal spirits, and Thwackum, resenting his speeches, only the doctor's interposition prevented wrath kindling. After which, Jones gave loose to mirth, sang two or three amorous songs, and fell into every frantic disorder which unbridled joy is apt to inspire; but so far was he from any disposition to quarrel that he was ten times better-humoured, if possible, than when he was sobre.

Blifil, whose mother had died during her brother's illness, was highly offended at a behaviour which was so inconsistent with the sobre and prudent reserve of his own temper. The recent death of his mother, he declared, made such conduct very indecent.

"It would become them better," he said, "to express the exultations of their hearts at Mr. Allworthy's recovery in thanksgiving, than in drunkenness and riot."

Wine had not so totally overpowered Jones as to prevent him recollecting Blifil's loss the moment it was mentioned. He at once offered to shake Mr. Blifil by the hand, and begged his pardon, saying his excessive joy for Mr. Allworthy's recovery had driven every other thought out of his mind.

Blifil scornfully rejected his hand, and with an insulting illusion to the misfortune of Jones's birth provoked the latter to blows. The scuffle which ensued might have produced mischief had it not been for the interference of Thwackum and the physician.

Blifil, however, only waited for an opportunity to be revenged on Jones, and the occasion was soon forthcoming when Mr. Allworthy was fully recovered from his illness.

Mr. Western had found out that his daughter was in love with Tom Jones, and at once decided that she should marry Blifil, to whom Sophia professed great abhorrence.

As for Blifil, the success of Jones was much more grievous to him than the loss of Sophia, whose estate, indeed, was dearer to him than her person.

Mr. Western swore that his daughter shouldn't have a happens, nor the twentieth part of a brass farthing, if she married Jones; and Blifil, with many sighs, professed to his uncle that he could not bear the thought of Sophia being ruined by her preference for Jones.

"This lady, I am sure, will be undone in every sense; for, besides the loss of most part of her own fortune, she will be married to a beggar. Nay, that is a trifle; for I know him to be one of the worst men in the world."

"How?" said Mr. All worthy. "I command you to tell me what you mean."

"You know, sir," said Blifil, "I never disobeyed you. In the very day of your utmost danger, when myself and all the family were in tears, he filled the house with riot and debauchery. He drank, and sang, and roared; and when I gave him a gentle hint of the indecency of his actions, he fell into a violent passion, swore many oaths, called me rascal, and struck me. I am sure I have forgiven him that long ago. I wish I could so easily forget his ingratitude to the best of benefactors."

Thwackum was now sent for, and corroborated every circumstance which the other had deposed.

Poor Jones was too full of grief at the thought that Western had discovered the whole affair between him and Sophia to make any adequate defence. He could not deny the charge of drunkenness, and out of modesty sunk everything that related particularly to himself.

Mr. Allworthy answered that he was now resolved to banish him from his sight for ever. "Your audacious attempt to steal away a young lady calls upon me to justify my own character in punishing you. And there is no part of your character which I resent more than your ill-treatment of that good young man (meaning Blifil), who hath behaved with so much tenderness and Honour towards you."

A flood of tears now gushed from the eyes of Jones, and every faculty of speech and motion seemed to have deserted him. It was some time before he was able to obey Allworthy's peremptory commands of departing, which he at length did, having first kissed his hands with a passion difficult to be affected, and as difficult to be described.

Mr. Allworthy, however, did not permit him to leave the house penniless, but presented him with a note for £500. He then commanded him to go immediately, and told Jones that his clothes, and everything else, should be sent to him whithersoever he should order them.

Jones had hardly set out, which he did with feelings of agony and despair, before Sophia Western decided that only in flight could she be saved from marriage with the detested Blifil.

Mr. Western, in spite of tremendous love for his daughter, thought her inclinations of as little consequence as Blifil himself conceived them to be; and Mr. Allworthy, who said "he would on no account be accessory to forcing a young lady into a marriage contrary to her own will," was satisfied by his nephew's disingenuous statement that the young lady's behaviour to him was full as forward as he wished it.

Sophia, having appointed her maid to meet her at a certain place not far from the house, exactly at the ghostly and dreadful hour of twelve, began to prepare for her own departure.

But first she was obliged to give a painful audience to her father, and he treated her in so violent and outrageous a manner that he frightened her into an affected compliance with his will, which so highly pleased the good squire that he at once changed his frowns into smiles, and his menaces into promises.

He vowed his whole soul was wrapped in hers, that her consent had made him the happiest of mankind.

He then gave her a large bank-bill to dispose of in any trinkets she pleased, and kissed and embraced her in the fondest manner.

Sophia reverenced her father piously and loved him passionately, but the thoughts of her beloved Jones quickly destroyed all the regretful promptings of filial love.

Tom Jones's Restoration

After many adventures on the road Mr. Jones reached London; and as he had often heard Mr. Allworthy mention the gentlewoman at whose house in Bond Street he used to lodge when he was in town, he sought the house, and was soon provided with a room there on the second floor. Mrs. Miller, the person who let these lodgings, was the widow of a clergyman, and Mr. Allworthy had settled an annuity of £50 a year on her, "in consideration of always having her first floor when he was in town."

Tom Jones's fortunes were now very soon at the lowest. Having been forced into a quarrel in the streets with an acquaintance named Fitzpatrick, and having wounded him with his sword, a number of fellows rushed in and carried Jones off to the civil magistrate, who, being informed that the wound appeared to be mortal, straightway committed the prisoner to the Gatehouse.

Sophia Western was also in London at the house of her aunt; and soon afterwards Mr. Western, Mr. Allworthy, and Blifil all reached the city.

It was just at this time that Mr. Allworthy, consenting to his nephew once more offering himself to Sophia, came with Blifil to his accustomed lodgings in Bond Street. Mrs. Miller, to whom Jones had showed many kindnesses, at once put in a good word for the unfortunate young man; and, on Blifil exulting over the manslaughter Jones was alleged to have committed, declared that the wounded man, whoever he was, was in fault. This, indeed, was shortly afterwards corroborated by Fitzpatrick himself, who acknowledged his mistake.

But it was not till Mr. Allworthy discovered that Blifil had been arranging with a lawyer to get the men who had arrested Jones to bear false witness, and learnt further that Tom Jones was his sister Bridget's child, and that on her death-bed Mrs. Blifil's message to her brother confessing the fact had been suppressed by her son, that his old feelings of affection for Tom Jones returned. Before setting out to visit Jones in the prison Mr. Allworthy called on Sophia to inform her that he regretted Blifil had ever been encouraged to give her annoyance, and that Mr. Jones was his nephew and his heir.

Men over-violent in their dispositions are, for the most part, as changeable in them. No sooner was Western informed of Mr. Allworthy's intention to make Jones his heir than he joined heartily with the uncle in every commendation of the nephew, and became as eager for his daughter's marriage with Jones as he had before been to couple her to Blifil.

Fitzpatrick being recovered of his wound, and admitting the aggression, Jones was released from custody and returned to his lodgings to meet Mr. Allworthy.

It is impossible to conceive a more tender or moving scene than this meeting between the uncle and nephew. Allworthy received Jones into his arms. "O my child!" he cried, "how have I been to blame! How have I injured you! What amends can I ever make you for those unkind suspicions which I have entertained, and for all the sufferings they have occasioned you?"

"Am I not now made amends?" cried Jones. "Would not my sufferings, had they been ten times greater, have been now richly repaid?"

Here the conversation was interrupted by the arrival of Western, who could no longer be kept away even by the authority of Allworthy himself. Western immediately went up to Jones, crying out, "My old friend Tom, I am glad to see thee, with all my heart. All past must be forgotten. Come along with me; I'll carry thee to thy mistress this moment."

Here Allworthy interposed; and the squire was obliged to consent to delay introducing Jones to Sophia till the afternoon.

Blifil, now thoroughly exposed in his treachery, was at first sullen and silent, balancing in his mind whether he should yet deny all; but finding at last the evidence too strong against him, betook himself to confession, and was now as remarkably mean as he had been before remarkably wicked. Mr. Allworthy subsequently settled £200 a year upon him, to which Jones hath privately added a third. Upon this income Blifil lives in one of the northern counties. He is also lately turned Methodist, in hopes of marrying a very rich widow of that sect. Sophia would not at first permit any promise of an immediate engagement with Jones because of certain stories of his inconstancy, but Mr. Western refused to hear of any delay.

"To-morrow or next day?" says Western, bursting into the room where Sophia and Jones were alone.

"Indeed, sir," says she, "I have no such intention."

"But I can tell thee," replied he, "why hast not; only because thou dost love to be disobedient, and to plague and vex thy father. When I forbid her, then it was all nothing but sighing and whining, and languishing and writing; now I am for thee-(this to Jones)-she is against thee. All the spirit of contrary, that's all. She is above being guided and governed by her father, that is the whole truth don't. It is only to disoblige and contradict me."

"What would my papa have me do?" cries Sophia.

"What would I ha' thee do?" says he, "why gee un thy hand this moment."

"Well, sir," said Sophia, "I will obey you. There is my hand, Mr. Jones."

"Well, and will you consent to ha' un to-morrow morning?" says Western.

"I will be obedient to you, sir," cries she.

"Why, then, to-morrow morning be the day," cries he.

"Why, then, to-morrow morning shall be the day, papa, since you will have it so," said Sophia. Jones then fell upon his knees and kissed her hand in an agony of joy, while Western began to caper and dance about the room, presently crying out, "Where the devil is Allworthy?" He then sallied out in quest of him, and very opportunely left the lovers to enjoy a few tender minutes alone.

But he soon returned with Allworthy, saying, "If you won't believe me, you may ask her yourself. Hast not gin thy consent, Sophy, to be married to-morrow?"

"Such are your commands, sir," cries Sophia, "and I dare not be guilty of disobedience."

"I hope there is not the least constraint," cries Allworthy.

"Why, there," cried Western, "you may bid her unsay all again if you will. Dost repent heartily of thy promise, dost not, Sophie"

"Indeed, papa," cried she. "I do not repent, nor do I believe I ever shall, of any promise in favor of Mr. Jones."

"Then, nephew," cries Allworthy, "I felicitate you most heartily, for I think you are the happiest of men."

Mr. Allworthy, Mr. Western, and Mrs. Miller were the only persons present at the wedding, and within two days of that event Mr. Jones and Sophia attended Mr. Western and Mr. Allworthy into the country.

There is not a neighbour or a servant, who doth not most gratefully bless the day when Mr. Jones was married to Sophia.

Chapter 5

Major Characters

Tom Jones

Tom Jones, a "bastard" raised by the philanthropic Allworthy, is the novel's eponymous hero and protagonist. Although Tom's faults (namely, his imprudence and his lack of chastity) prevent him from being a perfect hero, his good heart and generosity make him Fielding's avatar of Virtue, along with Allworthy. Tom's handsome face and gallantry win him the love and affection of women throughout the countryside. His dignified, though natural air induces characters to assume that he is a gentleman—which ultimately turns out to be true.

Sophia Western

Sophia Western is Fielding's beautiful, generous heroine and the daughter of the violent Squire Western. Like Tom, Sophia lavishes gifts on the poor, and she treats people of all classes with such respect that one landlady cannot believe she is a "gentlewoman." Sophia manages to reconcile her love for Tom, her filial duty to her father, and her hatred for Blifil through her courage and patience. Sophia's natural courtesy can be contrasted with her Aunt Western's artificial manners.

Mr. Allworthy

Mr. Allworthy is just what his name implies - all worthy. Allworthy has a reputation throughout England because of his benevolent, altruistic behaviour. The moral yardstick of the novel, Allworthy's only fault (which ironically propels much of the plot) is that—due to his goodness—he cannot perceive the evil in others.

Master Blifil

Blifil is antagonist to Tom Jones and the son of Bridget Allworthy and Captain Blifil. Although he appears at first to be a virtuous character, his hypocrisy soon exposes itself—Blifil pretends to be pious and principled, but greed governs him. The fact that Blifil has few redeeming qualities makes Tom compassion for him at the end of the novel—after the revelation that Blifil kept the secret of Tom's birth to himself—even more commendable. Blifil's dearth of natural human appetites—he at first does not desire Sophia—does not distinguish him as a virtuous character, but rather provides a depressing picture of what humanity would be like if devoid of passion.

Squire Western

Squire Western is a caricature of the rough-and-ready, conservative country gentleman. Affectionate at heart, the Squire nevertheless acts with extreme violence towards his daughter Sophia, by constantly incarcerating her, and even verbally and physically abusing her. However, since the Squire is a caricature, Fielding does not intend for us to judge these actions too harshly. Similarly, the Squire's insistence on Sophia marrying Blifil has less to do with greed than with his stubbornness and adherence to tradition. Squire Western's speaks in West Country dialect, and peppers his speech with curses.

Mrs. Western

Mrs. Western, the foil of her brother Squire Western, is a caricature of the artificial city lady who always acts out of expediency. Mrs. Western prides herself on being adept at all intellectual pursuits—from politics to philosophy to feminism to amour—yet her ignorance reveals itself on numerous occasions (she thinks that Socrates lectured to students instead of engaging in conversational debate). Mrs. Western's sole aim in the novel is to improve the Western name by marrying off Sophia to the richest, most prosperous man she can find.

Partridge

Partridge is the teacher whom Allworthy accuses of being Tom's father. He is a kind of comedic Harlequin character (Fielding even compares him to Harlequin). Although pathetic, bumbling, and cowardly, Partridge remains a loyal servant to Jones and deserves his reward at the end of the novel. Partridge has a passion for speaking in Latin non sequiturs. Although Partridge creates problems for Tom and Sophia by boosting Tom's reputation and defiling Sophia's to all and sundry, Tom cannot help forgiving Partridge, who always has the best of intentions.

Jenny Jones

Jenny Jones (Mrs. Waters) is the student of Partridge whom Allworthy banishes for being Tom's mother—at the end of the novel we learn that Jenny is not Tom's mother. Jenny reappears as "Mrs. Waters" at Upton, where Tom saves her from a robbery. Although Jenny does not possess the beauty of a Sophia, her very white breasts attract Tom to her. Although she protests to Mr. Allworthy at the end of the novel that she has led a virtuous life, her seduction of Tom in Upton suggests otherwise. She eventually marries Parson Supple, a friend of Western.

Bridget Allworthy

Bridget Allworthy is the mother of Blifil and Tom. An unattractive lady who resents beautiful women, Bridget marries Captain Blifil because he flatters her religious views. Although Bridget's affection wavers between Blifil and Tom as the boys mature, she becomes devoted to Tom before her death—largely due to his good looks and gallantry.

Lady Bellaston

Lady Bellaston is a London lady, and a relative of Sophia, whose passionate, lusty personality leads her to dabble in intrigues. The stem of her last name "Bella-", meaning "war" in Latin, points to her malicious nature—she thinks of no one but herself. Lady Bellaston carries out a vengeful battle against Tom and Sophia with the utmost glee.

Harriet Fitzpatrick

Harriet Fitzpatrick is Sophia's cousin and the wife of Mr. Fitzpatrick. Pretty and charming, she is nevertheless selfish and contrives against Sophia in order to improve her relationship with Squire Western and Mrs. Western.

Mr. Fitzpatrick

Mr. Fitzpatrick is a rash Irishman whom Harriet Fitzpatrick casts in the light of an ogre chasing her across the countryside. Fitzpatrick becomes admirable, however, when he admits to initiating the duel with Tom at the end of the novel.

Mr. Dowling

Mr. Dowling is a shrewd, shifty lawyer who becomes a friend of Blifil. Always operating out of expediency, when Dowling realises that Blifil will not be able to reward him for his efforts, he defects to Tom and Allworthy's side.

Mrs. Miller

Mrs. Miller is a faithful friend to Tom and the most caring and concerned of mothers to Nancy and Betty. Feisty and active, Mrs. Miller carries through on her promises and becomes Tom's biggest advocate to Allworthy. She is trusting and loyal.

Nightingale

Nightingale, although a foppish city gentleman, possesses the laudable traits of loyalty and compassion—although not always in affairs of love. It takes a little time for Tom to convince Nightingale not to abandon Nancy, since Nightingale is caught up in his image in London. To his credit, Nightingale transforms and follows Tom's principles of Honour—that is, fulfilling verbal commitments.

Lord Fellamar

Lord Fellamar is a suitor of Sophia who, though he has a conscience, easily allows him to be manipulated by Lady Bellaston.

Square

Square is a philosopher who lives with Allworthy. He justifies his questionable behaviour (such as making love to Molly Seagrim) by contorting his philosophical notions. Square, although a foil to Thwackum is less sinister than the latter. Indeed, Square's virtuous transformation at the end of the novel allows Allworthy to forgive Tom.

Thwackum

Thwackum is the vicious tutor of Blifil and Tom who constantly beats Tom and praises Blifil. Thwackum, who claims to value Religion above all else, seeks only his own good.

Molly Seagrim

Molly Seagrim is the rugged, unfeminine daughter of Black George who seduces Tom. Feisty and aggressive, Molly enjoys the company of men, and fights fiercely for her rights.

Black George

Black George is the servant who is favored by Tom. Although of dubious moral tincture (Black George steals and lies), Black George's loyalty to and love of Tom nevertheless emerges.

Nancy Miller

Nancy Miller is the daughter of Mrs. Miller who becomes Nightingale's wife.

Narrator

The ironic, intrusive narrator can be assumed

Chapter 6

Chapter Wise Summary and Analysis

BOOK 1

Chapter I

The narrator sets up a contract with the Reader, casting himself as a Restaurateur, his work as a "Feast," and the Reader as his patron. Since the Reader must pay for what he eats—the book—the narrator invites the Reader to mull over the menu, which he promises to provide in the way of an introductory clause at the opening of each Book and each Chapter. The type of cuisine is none other than "human nature," a topic which has been written about in the cheaper kind of literature, —thought it has been grossly bandied about in stall-bound "Romances, Novels, Plays and Poems"—may have refinement depending on the "Cookery of the Author." The narrator intends to mimic the cookery of Heliogabalus, a Roman emperor who initiated his guests with simple fare, slowly building to more sophisticated delicacies. After serving up his simple fare of country characters, the narrator will present the Reader with the "high French and Italian Seasoning of Affectation and Vice which Courts and Cities afford."

Chapter II

In the western domain of England lives a retired gentleman, Mr. Allworthy, blessed by Nature with good looks, robust health, understanding, an altruistic disposition, and one of the most prosperous estates in the county of Somersetshire. Five years before the story begins, Allworthy's beautiful and virtuous wife passed away, following their three children, who died as infants. Allworthy, however, still considers himself married—a sentiment that inspires the praise of his neighbours. Allworthy lives with his only sibling, his beloved sister, Miss Bridget Allworthy, who is called an "old Maid" because she is thirty years old and unmarried. Miss Bridget is one of those "very good sort of Women," which is the description women give to other women who are deprived of beauty.

Chapter III

The reader may assume, based on the previous chapter's description, that Allworthy does nothing other than perform benevolent deeds. But if this were the case, the narrator says, he would not have wasted his time producing a work of such epic length. If the Reader would rather read such matter, he can peruse instead one of those boring books called The History of England.

An exhausted Allworthy, returning from business in London, retires to bed. On pulling back the sheets he discovers a baby boy, swaddled in linen, sleeping sweetly. Although greatly surprised, Allworthy cannot help but feel empathy for the little being, and awe at its beauty. Allworthy rings his bell to summon his old-time servant, Mrs. Deborah Wilkins. Mrs. Deborah takes some time to preen herself, in spite of the urgency of Allworthy's summons, and it should therefore come as no surprise, the narrator says, that she is shocked to find Allworthy, who in his haste has forgotten to dress, wearing only his nightshirt. After delivering a long monologue on the indecency of unchaste women—whom she calls "wicked Sluts", Mrs. Deborah advises Allworthy to discard the baby at the parish door. But, during Mrs. Deborah's speech, the baby has clasped Allworthy's finger in his tiny hand, winning the man's heart. Allworthy orders Mrs. Deborah to carry the boy to her bed, prepare food for him, and to seek out appropriate clothes the next day. Mrs. Deborah, always loyal to her master, now calls the boy a "sweet little Infant" and whisks the child away in her arms.

Chapter IV

Allworthy's Gothic-style house, which resides on a hill beneath a grove of old oaks, is on a property that stretches out beyond lawns, meadows, and woods, and out to the sea. Allworthy takes in this view during a mid-May morning walk, in which his mind stews over the noble question of how he "might render himself most acceptable to his Creator, by doing most Good to his Creatures." At breakfast, Allworthy tells Miss Bridget he has a gift for her, which she suspects will be a gown, or jewelry. She is therefore speechless with surprise on first being presented with the baby boy Allworthy found in his bed the night before. Miss Bridget calls the unknown mother every vile name she knows, but she nevertheless shows some compassion for the child. All the female servants in the house are suspected, but all are "acquitted" by Mrs. Wilkins, to whom the task of inspecting all the women in the parish is given. Miss Bridget agrees to take care of the child, at her brother's request.

Chapter V

Once Allworthy departs, Mrs. Deborah waits for contradictory orders from Miss Bridget, since she knows that the brother and sister's opinions begin to differ as soon as they are apart. Miss Bridget, after staring for a little while at the baby sleeping in Mrs. Deborah's lap, cannot refrain from kissing it and praising its beauty. She then sets about ordering "Necessaries" for the child, and appoints one of the best rooms in the house to be its nursery. This is not without a sly and contradictory quip at her brother, however, whom she scorns for desiring to support Vice by adopting "the little Brat."

Chapter VI

Mrs. Deborah hurries to the parish in pursuit of the mother of the baby. Due to her habit of treating the parish inhabitants with disdain and ill will, none of the matrons there look forward to Mrs. Deborah's visit, but one old woman, who is equal to Mrs. Deborah in age and ugliness, likes her better than the others. The two women discuss the characters of various young women, and decide that a certain Jenny Jones must have committed the crime.

Though Jenny is not beautiful, she has been endowed with "Understanding." She has developed this quality through study, as she is the servant of a schoolmaster who has undertaken to teach Latin to Jenny. The narrator grants that Jenny is "perhaps, as good a Scholar as most of the young Men of Quality of the Age," but, because of her superior intellect and accompanying pride, Jenny has become the envy of her neighbours. This is why the elderly woman suspects Jenny to be the mother of the foundling. Mrs. Wilkins, has additional reason to suspect Jenny, because Jenny has recently spent time at Allworthy's house nursing Miss Bridget out of an illness.

Summoned to face Mrs. Deborah, who dubs her an "audacious Strumpet," Jenny confesses to being the mother of the child. Even though Jenny shows remorse, Mrs. Deborah upbraids her even more, backed up by a chorus of female on-lookers who have gathered around. Mrs. Deborah conveys the news to Mr. Allworthy, who is greatly surprised, since he intended to reward Jenny's diligence self- improvement by arranging for her a decent living and a marriage with a neighbouring Curate. Mrs. Bridget is sent to summon Jenny to a conference with Allworthy.

Chapter VII

Jenny meets Allworthy in his study, where he delivers an effusive monologue on the crime of a woman's spoiling her Chastity. Allworthy reminds Jenny that fleeting pleasure can overwhelm reason, which should remind one of the dire consequences of passion. He argues that a woman cannot invoke love as an excuse for her behaviour, since no man who truly loved a woman would use her in so base a way.

On a more positive note, Allworthy expresses admiration for Jenny's decision not to abandon the child, as some callous mothers might have. He appreciates her judgment in leaving the child to his care. When Allworthy asks the name of the child's father, Jenny pleads with him, claiming she is "under the most solemn Ties and Engagements of Honour, as well as the most religious Vows and Protestations" not to reveal the father's name. Allworthy asserts that he does not desire to know the man's name out of curiosity, but so that he may at least know who to avoid doing favors for in the future. Jenny assures Allworthy that the man is "entirely out of his Reach." Allworthy therefore respects Jenny's wish that the man's name remain private and bids her to seek forgiveness from God.

Commentary

The narrative begins with the voice of the author predominating. He tells his readers what the theme will be and what they can expect from the history. Human Nature is a predominant theme and we learn that we will see it in it's many forms. Fielding is excellent at unique similes, metaphors and comparisons and we get a sample of this in the first chapter itself. This is when he equates the narrative to a meal that will be served and which will satisfy every appetite.

We are then introduced to two main characters who are responsible for the growth of this narrative. They are Squire Allworthy and his sister, Miss Bridget Allworthy. Each introduction of a character is accompanied by a description of the person. We learn immediately that the Squire will be presented in a positive light throughout. He is blessed with both Fortune and Nature's blessings. Miss Bridget seems to be a prude and a hypocrite though.

Fielding does not delay in jumping right into the narrative. When Squire Allworthy comes back home and is about to go to sleep, he finds a little baby in his bed. This finding is the main fount of the narrative. We see that the Squire is a kind man who does not remove the baby, just because it is a bastard. He asks his elderly maidservant to look after it. It is not for no reason that the Squire enjoys a reputation of being benevolent. But, his character is one of the few large hearted characters in the story. There is also a bevy of small-minded people such as Mrs. Deborah Wilkins, who is a maidservant in the Squire's house. She condemns the infant for being a bastard and is only reconciled to look after it, because of her master's orders. Chapters 2-7 revolve around the circumstance of this baby's being found in the Squire's bed.

The Squire decides to adopt it and look after it. He presents the child to his sister and we are surprised to see that she does not refuse to keep the child. In keeping with her prudence and 'put- on' holiness, we would have thought that she would refuse to entertain a bastardly child. Most believe that the sister is compliant, simply in order to humour her brother. She knows that she is under his protection and tends to agree with him as far as possible. But, it is only towards the end of the narrative that we learn why she had agreed readily to look after the child in their house. It is because the child was her own and it's father was one Mr. Summers, with whom Miss Bridget had had an affair. But, for a long while this secret remains hidden and the readers are made to understand that Tom is a bastard.

The Squire wishes to find out who the mother is and his servant - Mrs. Deborah Wilkins is given this task. She loves scrounging around matters such as this and easily lifts the blame off any of the maidservants at the house. She has a selfish motive behind this and that is that she has hired these women and she wouldn't have liked to accept the fact that any of them are guilty. So, she resolves to go to the parish to find out the culprit. Once again, Fielding uses an excellent simile to describe how Mrs. Deborah descends on the parish. She is equated with a kite and the equation is not a very flattering one. She consults with an old matron and their suspicion falls on Jenny Jones.

Jenny Jones seems to be an interesting and a contradictory character. She is plain looking and yet attractive. She is intelligent and diligent. She is educated by a schoolmaster Partridge and grows to learn more than him. We are surprised to see that she confesses without any trouble and gives no defence. It is much later that we learn why she behaves like this. But, for now we are surprised at her self-control and her refined manners. She is indeed quite unlike an ordinary maid. She meets the Squire and he gives her a long talk about morals. She seems to have great respect for him and cries in his presence. She refuses to reveal the name of the father though and says that he is beyond Mr. Allworthy's governance and that is quite true, since we later learn that it is a Mr. Summers that she is talking about and that he had died by the time his son was born.

We see how the Squire is a man with a large heart and a sense of justice. He feels sympathetic for Jenny and decides to have her removed far away from her village, so that she might not continue to be insulted. The generosity of the Squire is revealed at many other occasions in the novel. But, despite his large heart, he at times is not discerning enough to see the truth. We also note how he misreads the character of his foundling Tom and wrongly throws him out of the house. At the same time, he doesn't realise the viciousness of Blifil, till very late.

In the first seven chapters, the base of the story is founded, and we meet the little infant who is the main hero of the story. The background of his birth is important as it effects the future course of events. We also meet the lady who plays a crucial part in this background and that is none other than Miss Bridget. She, as well as Mrs. Wilkins seem to be well versed with the hypocrisies practiced by the human race, especially by women. Both can be diplomatic and can reveal their true intentions and opinions artfully. They go more by what would benefit them and then behave accordingly.

Chapter VIII

Miss Bridget and Mrs. Deborah, who have used the keyhole of the adjoining room as a conduit to eavesdrop on Allworthy and Jenny's conversation, debate the proceedings. Mrs. Deborah speaks out first, shrilly proclaiming that Mr. Allworthy should have been harsher in his treatment of Jenny.

She swears that if she had been in his position, she would certainly have extracted the name of the father. At this Miss Bridget smiles, a rare occurrence. Miss Bridget contradicts Mrs. Deborah's outburst by praising Jenny for confessing to her crime and hypocritically chastises Miss Bridget for prying into other people's business. Mrs. Deborah, who normally reserves her judgment until her mistress has spoken, now retracts all she said earlier. The women essentially take Jenny's side because, like them, she is not beautiful, and the conversation ends with "a general and bitter Invective against Beauty, and with many compassionate Considerations for all honest, plain Girls, who are deluded by the wicked Arts of deceitful Men."

Chapter IX

When the neighbours learn that instead of sending Jenny to a House of Correction, Allworthy has simply banished her from the parish, they unleash invectives against her. Jenny's distance prevents her from being the recipient of their animosity, so the neighbours begin directing their maliciousness toward Mr. Allworthy himself and spread rumors that he is the father himself. The narrator assures the Reader that "Mr. Allworthy was, and will hereafter appear to be, absolutely innocent of any criminal Intention whatever."

Chapter X

Although he favors "Men of Merit" and "Men of Genius and Learning," Allworthy opens his house and heart to anyone. Men flock to Allworthy's company not only because they are certain of being showered with hospitality, but because Allworthy allows every guest to spend his time according to that guest's inclination. The gentleman Dr. Blifil, one such visitor, has won Allworthy's pity. This is due to the fact that Dr. Blifil's father forced him to study medicine or "Physic" against his will and Allworthy pities anyone who has found misfortune because of the "Folly or Villainy of others." Since he detests his profession, Dr. Blifil hardly practices and, thus, has accumulated very little fortune. Dr. Blifil's one shining quality, which is his "great Appearance of Religion," attracts Miss Bridget to him. A romance springs up between the two based on their particular "sympathy" of religious views. The narrator expresses no surprise at this event, since he wryly observes that "Sympathies of all Kinds are apt to beget Love; so Experience teaches us that none have a more direct Tendency this Way than those of a religious Kind between Persons of different Sexes."

One obstacle stands in Miss Bridget and Dr. Blifil's way: Dr. Blifil is married. There is nothing for Dr. Blifil to do but try to conjure a match between Miss Bridget and his brother. The narrator muses as to the reason for such a decision, especially since Dr. Blifil "had no great Friendship for his Brother." The narrator speculates that Dr. Blifil might just have an evil nature, or that he wishes to be an accomplice in the "Theft" of a wealthy lady, or that he hopes his status will vicariously be raised through his brother's marriage.

Captain Blifil, Dr. Blifil's brother, arrives at Allworthy's house almost immediately after receiving the summons from his brother. The thirty-five-year- old Captain is well built and has a scar on his forehead. His demeanor and voice are rough, yet he is "not ungentle, nor entirely void of Wit." The Captain's father wanted his son to become a priest, but died before the ordination, and the Captain became an army man instead. After an argument with his Colonel, however, the Captain was forced to resign his commission and has since been devoting himself to Biblical study in the countryside. Only a week after his arrival at Allworthy's estate, Captain Blifil begins to make an impression on the "Saint-like" character of Miss Bridget, thus fulfilling his brother's hopes for him.

Chapter XI

Miss Bridget falls for Captain Blifil, even though the Captain is not good- looking, which the narrator ascribes to Bridget's search for something profound and meaningful. Bridget is not beautiful either, making it unnecessary for the narrator to "draw her Picture." Moreover, the narrator relates, a better artist—the famous Mr. Hogarth—has already undertaken that task. Once the Captain catches scent of Bridget's passion for him, he returns it. The Captain, however, has actually fallen in love with Mr. Allworthy's estate. He harbors a fear that Allworthy will not approve of a match between his sister and a man who is so much poorer than her, so he attempts to conceal his brief courtship from Allworthy. The Captain proposes and is rejected twice before Miss Bridget finally submits.

Chapter XII

Dr. Blifil takes the task of breaking the news of Dr. Blifil and Miss Bridget's marriage to Allworthy upon himself. Finding Allworthy strolling in the garden, Dr. Blifil greets him with a bitter speech about men's self- interestedness and women's debauchery. Mr. Allworthy, however, already knows about his sister's marriage and wholeheartedly supports it in spite of Captain Blifil's lack of finances. Allworthy stops Dr. Blifil mid-sentence with his angelic philosophies about marriage being based on love. Allworthy does not believe that physical attraction and financial concerns should be renounced entirely, but he also believes that they should not be the sole basis for matrimony.

Chapter XIII

Dr. Blifil tells his brother about how he pretended to be angry when he met Allworthy in the garden, saying that he wanted to dismiss any suspicions Allworthy might have that Dr. Blifil set up the marriage. The narrator says that the Captain will later make use of this disclosure. Now that the Captain possesses Miss Bridget and her money, he treats his brother with the utmost disdain. No one can help noticing this behaviour, not even Allworthy, to whom the Captain confides that he can never forgive his brother for a past injury. Allworthy protests so loudly against not forgiving that the Captain affects a pretense of goodwill toward his brother when they are in company, but in private his contempt continues. Dr. Blifil appeals to his brother, but the Captain rudely tells him to quit the house if he is not content. The narrator hints that Dr. Blifil is indeed guilty of some former crime, and submits to his brother's behaviour because he does not want the Captain to reveal this secret to Allworthy. Moreover, the Captain, who is proud and fierce, has long resented his brother's intellectual capacities. The narrator concludes that envy mangled with contempt and obligation tends to breed indignation rather than gratitude. Dr. Blifil can no longer bear his brother's cruelty and departs for London, where he dies of a broken heart.

Commentary

From the eighth chapter to the thirteenth, the narrative mainly revolves around the developments in Squire Allworthy's household. In the eighth chapter, Mrs. Deborah, the elderly maidservant overhears the conversation between the Squire and Jenny Jones. She has a nasty habit of overhearing at doors. This is one trait that is characteristic of women servants. We are told that Allworthy's sister, Miss Bridget has this habit too. It is a custom borne out of a driving curiosity. We do not notice a crucial behaviour pattern now, but recall it later. This is that Ms. Bridget behaves quite unlike herself. She reprimands Mrs. Deborah for her curiosity and praises Jenny. In keeping with her frigidity, one might have thought that she would have condemned the hussy rather than praise her courage. At the end of the book, when we learn that Bridget herself is Tom's mother and that she had bribed Jenny to help her, we are able to understand her present behaviour.

Mrs. Deborah Wilkins's character is not outlined positively. She is a woman who is not very well positioned in society herself but she looks down on anyone inferior to her in rank. She is proud and mean and highly curious about the identity of Jenny's husband. But, she is worldly enough to know that she should agree with Miss Bridget's sentiments in order to be agreeable to her. So, she outwardly agrees with Miss Bridget though her heart condemns Jenny. The two then get together in typical old maid fashion to deride beauty. They go on to criticize the men who mislead women. In this case they feel that some villainous man has misled Jenny. It is much later that we learn that no one has been misled. Miss Bridget herself gives into her passion by having an affair with Mr. Summers and the little infant is a product of that. She is a brilliant actress to be able to put up the farce of condemning Jenny's acts.

We see how village gossip can be quite vicious. When Jenny appears to be pleased after her meeting with Squire Allworthy, she is taunted at being a favourite of the nobleman. When the Squire removes her from the village, awful rumors abound of her being the mistress of the Squire himself. Many have the gall to say that the Squire himself might have fathered the baby. Fielding paints the picture of a typical, small-minded gossipy village. At the same time, the narrator intervenes to defend the Squire and to point out that his character cannot be condemned.

In this chapter, the topic moves away from Jenny and her baby finally. We read about the other guests that frequent the Squire's house. The Squire is known to be especially kind to men of intellect, especially if they are having financial problems. We meet Dr. Blifil, who is quite a decent fellow. He might have been a brilliant intellectual but was forced by his parents to study medicine, the result being that he does not do too well in this profession and lacks bread to eat at the age of forty. He eyes the benefits that he might achieve by marrying Bridget. But, there is a hurdle to the attainment of this happiness and that is his wife. So, he decides to introduce his brother to Bridget instead. We note that though he is not very close to his sibling, he still thinks of helping his brother. But, as we see, this entire affair does not have a happy conclusion.

The Captain is a shrewd man and knows the arts of love. It is not long before he is able to make Miss Bridget fall in love with him. She is smitten by his glib style of talking, little does she know that it is just an act to attain her person and moreover, her fortune. She extends the courtship with the Captain for over a month. All this while, both the lovers are so discreet that the Squire is not able to guess the going ones.

Indeed, the brother is much simpler than his artful sister Bridget.

The Captain and Miss Bridget marry secretly. Secrecy seems to be the leitmotif of Miss Bridget's life. The Squire takes this news as a gentleman. He is a large hearted and sensible man and says that his sister has full right to choose her own means to happiness. Doctor Blifil on the other hand pretends to be annoyed at his brother for marrying the Squire's sister secretly. This annoyance is merely an act put on so that the Squire may not become suspicious of the real motive behind the marriage: that of greed.

The last chapter of this Book reveals a sad incident. The other brother - Captain Blifil is a treacherous man, who distances himself from his brother after having received a massive favor from him. He knows that without Doctor Blifil's invitation, he would have never reached the Squire's house and would never have had the opportunity of winning Bridget's heart. But, instead of being obliged to his brother, he decides to get rid of him and starts being very cold to him. The Doctor is very hurt and even the Squire notices this behaviour. The Squire also asks the Captain to be nice to his brother, but while he pretends to be agreeable, the rancor still dominates his heart. Finally, the Doctor cannot take more of this attitude and leaves for London. The poor man dies there of a broken heart. We feel deep pity for such a creature and contempt for a cruel brother such as his.

Through this incident, Fielding reveals how Human Nature can be cruel to its own relatives and siblings. We all must have seen such cases in real life too and so do not disbelieve what Fielding writes about the two brothers.

BOOK II

Chapter I

This is to be a different kind of History, the narrator informs us, one that chooses carefully where to devote its "Pains" and "Paper." The narrator invokes the simile of a lottery, declaring that he will focus on the prizes drawn, not on the blanks. The narrator dubs himself "the Founder of a new Province of Writing" and states that this entitles him to operate by his own laws, which readers will have to respect. The narrator hopes that the Reader will recognize his authority, but he promises not be a tyrant nor to make the readers his slaves.

Chapter II

Eight months after Miss Bridget and Captain Blifil's wedding, Miss Bridget gives birth to a boy. Even though Mr. Allworthy relishes the fact that his sister has given birth to an heir, it does not diminish his love for the foundling, whom he has named Thomas after himself, and for whom he has taken on the role of godfather. Allworthy visits the baby Tom in his nursery at least once a day. Allworthy tells Bridget that her son will be brought up with Tom, and after some resistance, she finally agrees. The Captain voices more opposition than his wife by quoting scripture about the unworthy status of children born out of wedlock. Allworthy counters with his own set of quotations, arguing that children are born innocent and should not have to bear their parents' guilt. The truth is that the Captain envies Allworthy's attentions to Tom. Miss Bridget, while verbally abusing Allworthy and Tom behind their backs, has a tongue of honey in public. Mrs. Deborah, the narrator concludes, has discovered Tom's rascal of a father.

Chapter III

The narrator explains the history of Tom's mother, Jenny Jones, and the schoolmaster, Mr. Partridge. Although Partridge and his shrew of a wife have been married for nine years, they have no children. The narrator confides that the reason for this is that "Children are rightly called the Pledges of Love; and [Partridge] ... had given [his wife] no such Pledges..." Terrified that her husband will be less abstinent with other women, Mrs. Partridge handpicks her maidservants, choosing the least attractive women. Jenny Jones is one such maidservants.

Jenny, however, is allowed to set aside her housework in order to pursue her studies with Mr. Partridge. One day, about four years after Jenny has arrived, Mrs. Partridge strolls past her husband's study and notices Jenny suddenly rise up from her reading. Mrs. Partridge interprets this as evidence that Jenny and her husband are having an affair. She believes that their guilt is proven beyond reasonable doubt when, at dinner, she witnesses Jenny smiling when Partridge asks her to "give him some drink" in Latin. Mrs. Partridge glares at Jenny, who blushes. Taking this blush as even further corroboration, Mrs. Partridge grabs a knife and threatens Jenny and her husband. Jenny escapes by running from the room, while Partridge simply sits and trembles. That night Mrs. Partridge orders Jenny to leave her house. Jenny protests her innocence, but Partridge does not defend her. Instead, he wins back his wife's favor by making love to her. Partridge is secretly happy that Jenny has been dismissed, since the girl was beginning to exceed his intellectual heights.

Chapter IV

Mrs. Partridge, once frigid, now lavishes her husband with affection. However, the narrator warns, this is the calm before the storm, for the women in the parish now report that Jenny has given birth to a second bastard. Since it is less than nine months since Mrs. Partridge ousted Jenny, Mrs. Partridge assumes that Mr. Partridge must also be the father of this child. Tearing home, Mrs. Partridge attacks her husband, scratching him into a bloody mess. He attempts to restrain her, but she fights so furiously that her cap falls off, and the "stays" at the front of her dress split open, leaving her breasts exposed. Mad with terror, Mr. Partridge runs into the street imploring his neighbours to help his wife. A gaggle of women attend to him. Mrs. Partridge slanders her husband, accusing him of wrenching off her cap and stays, pulling hair from her head, and beating her. Mr. Partridge, his face scarred from his wife's nails, stands stunned and speechless. The parish women, interpreting this silence as guilt, scream at his insolence.

Chapter V

Rumors begin to fly around the Little Baddington parish that Partridge has beaten his wife. Different reasons are given for Partridge's behaviour: some report that he was having an affair, while others believe that Mrs. Partridge is the guilty party. Mrs. Wilkins scavenges for information that might reduce Allworthy's affection for Tom in an effort to please the Captain. When she hears that Partridge is Tom's father, she passes the news on to Captain Blifil. Instead of rewarding Mrs. Wilkins, however, the Captain, who does not want to ally himself with a servant for fear of being blackmailed, dismisses Mrs. Wilkins.

Mrs. Wilkins says nothing to Mr. Allworthy, nor does she mention her secret to Mrs. Blifil, with whom her friendship has faded due to their differing opinions of Tom. Captain Blifil debates the meaning of "Charity" with Allworthy. The Captain believes that "Charity" does not stipulate the actual distribution of money, whereas Mr. Allworthy believes that it does. At the conclusion of the conversation, the Captain subtly drops the news that Partridge is Tom's father. Allworthy summons Mrs. Wilkins to corrugate the story, which she does. The Captain advises Allworthy to treat Partridge with mercy.

Commentary

The narrator often appears in the middle of the narration to make comments on the story or to add his notes on life in general. Thus, he assumes the role of an omniscient narrator who sees all and who wields power over his narrative. His appearance here is also to make a point and that is that his history will not always follow the same tone. It will heave up and down, sometimes at a fast pace and a slower one at other times. By writing this, the narrator seeks to prepare the reader mentally.

We now see how the second generation in the Squire's family comes about. Mrs. Blifil gives birth to a little boy. But, while the Squire is happy for his sister, he continues to be fond of the little foundling too. The foundling is named Tommy.

We see that the Squire is broad minded enough not to hold Tommy's birth against him. He is fond of the little kid. But, Captain Blifil does not approve of this affection and naturally so. He does not want the foundling to retain the Squire's affection, which might mean that he would inherit the property too. Captain Blifil is selfish and concerned about his interests alone.

The Captain often tells the Squire how it is sinful to keep a bastard at home. But, the Squire's religion is not as narrow as the Captain's and he refuses to remove the child from his home. In the meanwhile, Mrs. Deborah's curiosity has not abated and she is still as keen to know the father of the bastard child. Now, is related the background of Jenny and how the suspicion of Tom's birth falls on a school master Partridge. Partridge is described in a positive manner and we will later see how he will play a more major role in the upcoming narration. The accusation of being Tom's father is mainly a product of his wife's jealous mind. Partridge in turn is unable to defend himself before an Amazonian woman.

We see the perils of having a bad tempered wife. Mrs. Partridge is not only unfairly suspicious of her husband, she even resorts to violence with him. Moreover, after attacking him herself, she later blames him for having laid violent hands on her. We see that society tends to believe the violence of a man against a woman more than that of a woman against a man.

Village gossip once again plays a role. When the villagers starts gossiping about the Partridges, news eventually reaches Mrs. Wilkins and when she hears that Partridge might be the father of Tom, she informs Captain Blifil. We see Mrs. Deborah's vicious mind working again. She only informs the captain so that she may be in his good books, for he might be her master one day. Indeed, she is a selfish, self - seeking maidservant. Captain Blifil is no less vicious and waits patiently to reveal the news of Tom's father to the Squire. Eventually, he tells the Squire about Partridge. The Squire immediately summons Mrs. Deborah, who seems to have become the arbitrator in all such matters. A man like Partridge is condemned already if a vicious character such as Mrs. Wilkins is given the mantle of assessing him.

Fielding has mastered the art of handling many events and characters together. We see this is the way he narrates the various diverse incidents within these chapters. Partridge is a crucial character who is introduced here. While we do not see much of him here, we fall in love with his quirky ways later.

Chapter VI

The news of Partridge's guilt comes as a shock to Allworthy, who is the only person in the county who has not already heard the rumors. Mrs. Wilkins, having been sent to unearth more evidence of the scandal, returns to Allworthy with "confirmation," which is actually the word of a neighbour. The Partridge couple appears before Allworthy to make their "Defence." Allworthy, in the Chair of Justice, first listens to Mrs. Partridge's story. Mr. Partridge then proclaims his innocence, at which point Mrs. Partridge bursts into tears and launches into further accusations, now attesting that Mr. Partridge has had affairs with numerous women. The narrator takes this opportunity to refer to the common law, which states that a wife cannot provide evidence either for or against her husband. Mr. Partridge pleads that Jenny be allowed to testify to his innocence, but a messenger who is sent to find her brings the news that Jenny has run away with a recruiting officer. Allworthy decides that the testimony of "such a Slut" could not be trusted, and that Mrs. Partridge has won the case. Mr. Partridge loses his annuity and falls into slothful poverty. Mrs. Partridge dies of smallpox shortly after. Mr. Partridge leaves the county.

Chapter VII

In spite of what Captain Blifil hopes, Allworthy's affections for Tom are steadily increasing, and the narrator observes that it is as though Allworthy feels a need to atone for his severity to Partridge through extra affection for Tom. This disgruntles the Captain, who fears that Tom's existence will lessen his own inheritance. Captain Blifil and Bridget's marriage has rapidly descended from infatuation to hatred. Their religious views are diametrically opposed, and the narrator reveals that during their courtship, the Captain made a point of conceding to Bridget even when he did not agree. Now that the Captain has no reason to comply with Bridget, he belittles her arguments. They remain together, however, because, the narrator philosophizes, married couples sometimes find more enjoyment in tormenting one another than in being separated. Although Allworthy notices the tension, he does not realise the magnitude of the discord, and the Captain and Bridget try to conceal it before him. In spite of his noble character, Allworthy "might" notice some flaws in the Captain, but the narrator condones this, since he believes that a good friend will recognize the faults of others and not try to cure them.

Chapter VIII

Captain Blifil meditates on how much he will inherit, and what improvements he will make to Allworthy's house and gardens once Allworthy has died. Captain Blifil's greed prompts him to lay his hands on every book available about life expectancy, from which he calculates how long he will have to wait for Allworthy's death. One night, as he takes his solitary evening walk to ponder such questions, Captain Blifil dies of Apoplexy.

Chapter IX

Mr. Allworthy, concerned about the Captain's absence from the dinner table, orders the outside bell to be rung. Allworthy himself heads for the gardens while a friend who has joined them for dinner attempts to calm Bridget down with words and wine. When Allworthy returns, silent and upset, Bridget wails and laments that someone must have murdered her husband. Suddenly a servant bursts in, crying that the Captain has been found. Two servants carry in his dead body, and Allworthy weeps at the sight, while Bridget screams and faints. Two doctors Dr. Y. and Dr. Z., arrive and debate the cause of death. Each doctor has a favourite disease that he invokes for every autopsy. Although Captain Blifil is now confirmed to be dead, Dr. Y and Dr. Z need to invent an excuse to stay longer so they will receive more money. Bridget remains bed-ridden for a month and Allworthy generously commissions an epitaph for the Captain's grave.

Commentary

Mrs. Wilkins is convinced of Partridge's guilt and that is because she easily believes the petty gossip of others. Moreover, Partridge has to face a major disadvantage when his own wife condemns himself so openly and easily. Most people tend to believe the evidence of a wife against her husband, especially if the condemnation has to do with a sexual affair.

Mr. and Mrs. Partridge meet the Squire. He questions them about what he has heard. Mrs. Partridge gives evidence against her husband while the latter pleads for mercy. He insists that he has not committed adultery and has had nothing to do with Jenny. But, the Squire does not tend to believe him. We feel quite bad for the poor Partridge but we see that luck is just not on his side. He asks the Squire to get Jenny to give her evidence. But, we read that Jenny is not in the place that the Squire had sent her to. She has left the place with an officer. The Squire condemns her action, saying that the evidence of such a woman was anyway not reliable.

Later, even Mrs. Partridge regrets giving this evidence against her husband. This is because; Mrs. Wilkins had convinced her that the annuity received by the couple would not be discontinued even if Mr. Partridge is held guilty. But, this annuity is stopped when the Squire feels convinced about Mr. Partridge's guilt. The couple is now in abject poverty and all this is a result of Mrs. Partridge's unfounded suspicions. Mrs. Wilkins is no less to be blamed for the false promises she makes to Mrs. Partridge.

We now learn more about the Blifil-Bridget marriage. The farce of agreeableness in Captain Blifil's character is removed and Bridget realises how chauvinistic he can be. He does not have a high opinion of women and no longer listens to Bridget patiently. He had only been patient with her opinions before marriage when he had wanted to attain her person. Thus, their marriage is a strained one. While they try not to show this strain to others, the Squire can make out a part of it and he is not too happy with the result. He too can notice some faults in Captain Blifil's demeanor but as he is always looking at the positive aspect of a situation, he tries not to take the negatives too seriously.

Meanwhile, we get to see what is going on in Captain Blifil's mind. All that makes him happy is the contemplation of the value of the Squire's estate and over this calculation, he spends many happy hours. Here we get to see the extent of his mean mindedness and materialistic outlook. We later see how his son is just as mean and vicious. But, Fielding springs another surprise on us in the form of Captain Blifil's death by apoplexy. It was of importance that this character be removed, for the narrative to move forward at a faster pace.

One of the Themes of this novel is to depict the hypocrisy of society. We see how Mrs. Blifil falls ill after Mr. Blifil's death. We are given sufficient hints to guess that this illness is more of pretence. Mrs. Blifil is shown as mourning to just the right degree. Indeed, Fielding seems to be poking fun at the hypocrisy which makes a spouse mourn for the other, even if he/she had not loved the other. In this case, we had seen how Bridget had started disliking her spouse and yet she mourns him plentifully after his death. With the death of the Captain, there is more space to introduce other characters as will be done in the next Book.

BOOK III

Chapter I

The narrator reminds us of his earlier warning that his History will not document every second of time, and that the reader must therefore flesh out the time by arriving at his own opinions of the characters. Through a series of rhetorical questions, the narrator suggests that he does not need to describe the grief Allworthy experienced at the death of Captain Blifil, nor does he need to elaborate on the character of Mrs. Bridget Blifil. The narrator says that such analysis would be for a lower class of reader, and he expects much more from "the upper Graduates in Criticism." Since the narrator knows that most of his readers are of superior intellect, he has granted them twelve years in which to exercise their skills of penetration. Now he is impatient to introduce the novel's hero at fourteen years of age.

Chapter II

Tom Jones is introduced with an unfortunate anecdote. Tom possesses many faults, chief among them being his passion for stealing. Tom has recently stolen fruit from an orchard. a farmer's duck, and a ball from the pocket of Master Blifil, the son of the late Captain Blifil. Master Blifil abounds in "Virtues" and is praised by the neighbourhood whereas Tom is despised. Blifil's virtues, in a nutshell, are sobriety, discretion, and piety.

The narrator presents us with a vignette to reveal these boys' opposing characters. Tom's only friend is one of the servants of the household, a gamekeeper, and Tom's give the things he steals to this man's family. One day, Tom goes hunting with the game-keeper, and, at Tom's bidding, they follow some partridges into the estate of Allworthy's neighbour, which Allworthy has warned the game-keeper not to do. The neighbour hears the sound of the game- keeper shooting one of the partridges and, arriving at the scene of the crime, finds Tom with the dead bird, since the game-keeper has leapt into a bush to hide him. The neighbour goes straight to Allworthy and tells Allworthy there must have been two people involved because he found two guns. Yet when Allworthy asks Tom who his accomplice was, but the boy maintains that he was alone. The game-keeper also pleads innocent. Tom receives a flogging from Mr. Thwackum, the Reverend whom Allworthy has hired to educate Tom and

Master Blifil. Later, Allworthy relents and tries to remedy the situation by giving Tom a little horse as a present. The narrator predicts that a dinner between Allworthy, Thwackum, and a third unnamed gentleman will soon ensue.

Chapter III

Mr. Square, who has been living some time with Allworthy, is introduced. Although not naturally intelligent, Square has improved himself through education, and is well-read in the ancient philosophers. Square believes that a man should always be a speculator and sees virtue as a "Matter of Theory." Square and Thwackum are always arguing, and their only similarity is that neither will ever refer to the concept of "Goodness" in arguments. Square maintains that human nature is inherently virtuous, while Thwackum believes in original sin. Over dinner at Allworthy's table, Square and Thwackum debate whether honour can exist independent of religion. Their voices rise in volume and anger until something interrupts their debate. The narrator tells us we will have to wait until the next chapter to find out the nature of the interruption.

Chapter IV

Before continuing his story, the narrator takes it upon himself to rebut the arguments of both Square and Thwackum, arguing that neither of them should ignore the "natural Goodness of Heart."

The dinner is interrupted by Master Blifil who has a bloody nose from a fight with Tom. Tom is smaller, but is by far the better boxer, and Blifil has "Tears galloping... from his Eyes." Tom explains that he punched Blifil after the latter called him a "Beggarly Bastard." Blifil denies this and accuses Tom of lying. Blifil reveals that Tom's accomplice in the partridge incident was Black George, the game-keeper. Tom pleads with Allworthy to have mercy on Black George and his family, and takes full blame for the incident, saying it was his idea to trespass. Allworthy dismisses the boys, asking them to treat one another more amicably in future.

Chapter V

As usual, Square and Thwackum take Blifil's side, praising him and denouncing Tom. Allworthy refuses to let Thwackum beat Tom, but he summons Black George and dismisses him from the Estate, albeit with a generous severance package. Allworthy's harsh punishment stems from his belief that it is worse to lie to save yourself than it is to save another. When the story begins to circulate, many people applaud Allworthy's judgment, commend Tom as "a brave Lad," and indict Blifil as a "sneaking Rascal."

Blifil has won over Square and Thwackum by always agreeing with their doctrines, which means that he has to keep silent when they are together, since their teachings always clash. Blifil, young as he is, has also learnt the art of "second-hand flattery"—praising Square and Thwackum to Allworthy, who goodheartedly conveys all of Blifil's compliments back to the men. Thwackum was recommended to Allworthy by a friend, and although Allworthy perceives Thwackum's faults, he has faith that Square will balance them out. Square and Thwackum despise Tom, who, the narrator admits, is "a thoughtless, giddy Youth, with little Sobriety in his Manners." Allworthy, however, allows Tom to call him "father."

Commentary

In the first chapter, we are told that a period of twelve years has elapsed. This is a common narrative device when the author skips a certain part of history in order to hurry on the story or simply when nothing very important develops during the skipped time.

In the previous books, the narrative had moved forward but not much attention was paid to little incidents. In this book, we see this trend changing. We are introduced to young Tom, who is the hero of this story. We also meet the boy who is closest to being an antagonist in this narrative and that is Blifil, Captain Blifil's son. Young Tom is naughty and wild, but at the same time he is decent and large-hearted. Blifil might be sobre and pious, but hidden beneath this is a vicious and selfish heart.

An incident involving Black George is recounted. Tom and the gamekeeper trespass into the neighbour's territory while chasing a covey of partridges. Tom is caught while the gamekeeper manages to hide in some bushes. We can see the largeness of Tom's heart in his reluctance to reveal the fact that the gamekeeper too was involved. They both know that this could cost the gamekeeper his job and living. It is through small incidents such as this that the narrator is able to build the traits of the characters.

We meet Thwackum, one of Tom's tutors and do not like him too much. He is conceited and unnecessarily cruel to Tom. He loses no opportunity to give Tom a good thrashing, even though it is undeserved most of the times.

Square and Thwackum are outlined for us and we are told right in the beginning that they are objects of derision more than anything else. Neither has the generosity of spirit and both are hypocritical and false. We see that very few characters in Fielding's story are good and noteworthy. Many are petty and evil.

Tom and Blifil have a fight that ends their tutors' argument. Blifil is a cold-blooded liar and this has us enraged. He does curse Tom Jones but denies it completely to his elders. Blifil is not to be trusted with a secret and this becomes obvious when he divulges that Tom had told him that the gamekeeper was along with him when the neighbour caught them. Thus, Tom and the gamekeeper's secret is out.

Blifil and Tom are further contrasted in their contradictory behaviour. While Blifil uses manipulative arts to win over people, Tom is very straightforward in his approach and cannot be false. This is seen in their respective behaviour to their tutors. Blifil wins them over with flattery; Tom does not show them respect when he does not feel it. We later learn more reasons that explain why the tutors are more partial to Blifil, over Tom.

The characters of the children as seen here continue in the same note, as they grow older. It is a pity that the Squire is late in realizing Blifil's true nature, but if this wasn't the case the story would have not have developed and reached the interesting and climactic heights it does. Fielding is indeed a good painter of diverse characters that together create the variety that is Human Nature. All this while, he has remained true to his theme and we see that he will continue in the same vein.

Chapter VI

Both Square and Thwackum are interested in Bridget. The narrator says that one may wonder why so many male visitors to Allworthy's house have been attracted to Bridget, who is neither beautiful nor young. He then elaborates that men "have a Kind of natural Propensity to particular Females at the House of a Friend ... when they are rich." Both of the men have discovered that the easiest way to curry favor with Bridget is to show kindness to Blifil and contempt for Tom. Although Bridget flirts with both Square and Thwackum, all she truly desires is "Flattery and Courtship," for she does not wish to remarry. Square notices, however, that Bridget has hardly anything to do with the upbringing of her son, and harbors animosity towards Blifil because of the bitter memory of his father. On the other hand, she thrives on carrying out Allworthy's plans for Tom's well-being. The neighbours attribute Bridget's devotion to Tom to her obedience to her brother, but the narrator suggests that the maturing Tom has become attractive to women. Once the neighbours realise that Bridget is smitten with Tom, they call him a "rival" to Square and Thwackum. Bridget now revels in Tom's company.

Chapter VII

As soon as Allworthy realises that Bridget now neglects Blifil in favor of Tom, his relentless compassion for the underdog induces him to protect Blifil. The narrator preaches prudence and circumspection, arguing that it is not enough to be virtuous inside, and that one must take care to ensure that one's virtue shines through to the outside as well. The narrator hails himself as a kind of "Chorus."

Chapter VIII

Half a year has passed since Tom sold the horse Allworthy gave him at a fair. When Tom will not tell Thwackum what he has done with the money from the sale, Thwackum prepares to beat him. Allworthy walks in and questions Tom in private. Tom calls Thwackum a "tyrannical Rascal," and Allworthy cautions him against using such language. Tom tells Allworthy he gave all the money from the horse to Black George and his family, who have been living in poverty since Allworthy dismissed them. Allworthy sheds some tears in appreciation of Tom's compassion.

Chapter IX

Some time before, Tom sold a Bible given to him by Allworthy to Blifil. Blifil has been wielding the book about the house, reading from it more than he ever did from his own. Because Blifil flaunts the book so much, Thwackum eventually notices Tom's name on the Bible, "obliging" Blifil to divulge how he obtained the book. Thwackum condemns Tom's action as sacrilege, but Square and Bridget Blifil do not agree.

Squire Western, Allworthy's neighbour, arrives with further accusations against Black George head. On an evening walk, however, Tom leads Allworthy and Blifil to Black George's abode, where the family's poverty excites Allworthy's empathy. Allworthy gives money to Black George's wife for clothes for the children. At home, Tom further on the family's behalf, and Allworthy promises to support them. Tom runs through the rain to tell them the good news. The narrator warns, however, that Black George's fortune is about to take a down turn.

Chapter X

Although Blifil remains mute in Tom's presence, when Tom leaves he recalls an incident that occurred about a year after Allworthy dismissed Black George: with his family on the brink of starvation, Black George killed and sold a hare to a middleman. The middleman was suspected of poaching and, obliged to provide a scapegoat named Black George to Squire Western. In telling the story, Blifil contorts the facts and says that Black George poached dozens of hares. Disgusted, Allworthy promises Tom he will continue to support Black George's family, but he does not want to hear Tom mention the game-keeper's name again.

Tom attempts to clear Black George's name by appealing directly to Squire Western, with whom he has become friendly through his sporting skills. Squire Western, vastly impressed with Tom, now shares his horses, dogs, and guns freely with Tom. Squire Western loves his seventeen-year-old daughter, and Tom therefore decides to take his appeal to her. However, since this girl is "the intended Heroine of this Work," the narrator does not deem it appropriate to introduce her at the end of a book. The narrator cautions us that he himself is in love with her, and expects many readers to fall in love with her by the end of the novel.

Commentary

It is surprising to see that the unattractive Mrs. Blifil is such an object of affection to the opposite sex; the attraction lies less in her person and much more so, in her brother's vast fortune. Both Square and Thawckum eye the large estate despite all their pretensions to great intellect and religiosity. Mrs. Blifil on the other hand enjoys flattery but is too disillusioned with marriage to attempt it again. Out of Thwackum and Square, she favors the latter's person. Gossip soon abounds about Square and Mrs. Blifil, but it is soon subdued by yet another interesting tit-bit: that of the attraction of Mrs. Blifil towards the charming and now youthful Tom. Square does not like the attention being transferred to Tom and this is another reason why he is so mean to the young man.

Both Square and Thwackum feel that they can make Mrs. Blifil happy by being nice to her son Blifil and by being bad to Tom. But this decoy does not work, and as we learn later, Tom too is Bridget's own son.

Squire Allworthy upholds justice at all times. On seeing that Mrs. Blifil is not fond of her own son, the Squire starts paying special attention to him. So, while Tom rises in the eyes of Miss Bridget, he falls comparatively in the Squire's favor. The great thing about Fielding is that all his characters are realistic and we can imagine such situations in real life too.

Tom's sweet disposition is shown once again. He considers the gamekeeper a friend and is sorry for him and his family's destitute condition. He sells his horse and later even his Bible in order to provide for the family. While the Squire recognizes the good intention behind such gestures, Square, Thwackum and even the young Blifil criticize Tom. Blifil shows his viciousness again in the manner in which he arranges that his tutors discover that the Bible being used by him is Tom's, not his. He ensures that Tom gets into trouble as far as possible. Surprisingly, Miss Bridget comes to Tom's defence and says that Blifil is equally to blame for buying the Bible from Tom, as Tom is for selling it.

There are many tiny turn around here. The Squire decides to help Black George's family but later hears an exaggerated story of the gamekeeper's bad habits, and changes his mind about giving aid. Blifil is once again responsible for poisoning the Squire's mind. Tom never quite realises why the Squire changes his mind about the gamekeeper.

But, we see Tom's perseverance in trying to help his friend Black George. He now thinks of applying to Squire Western to employ George. For this, he decides to approach Squire Western's daughter. This is the first mention of the heroine of the story and we are promised that we shall meet her in the next chapter.

By now, we well realise the kind of antagonism Tom has to face in the world. His honesty is pitted against the manipulative and evil ways of persons, such as the young Blifil, and the elders - Square and Thwackum. We admire Tom in the way he continues to help the gamekeeper and his family. And, while the Squire is a nobleman, we see how he is often misled by false stories and is not able to apply his discretion.

So, while, Tom may be wild, he seems to do more right through his crazy ways, than the Squire does, by trying to be very just and upright.

Fielding, indeed, is remarkable in his presentation of the strengths and weaknesses of Human Nature. But, no one is perfect and the hero Tom too has a lesson to learn. He will have to learn to be more discreet, prudent and more disciplined.

BOOK IV

Chapter I

The narrator claims that Truth is the vital ingredient setting his story apart. The narrator, however, does not want this history to be the kind that is so boring it cannot be digested without a bout of ale. Since the heroine is to be presented in the following chapter, the narrator traces literary examples of hero introductions. He praises the tragic poets, who knew best how to welcome their heroes (with a resounding of drums) and their lovers (with gentle melodies). He self-consciously states: "Our Intention, in short, is to introduce our Heroine with the utmost Solemnity in our Power, with an Elevation of Stile, and all other Circumstances proper to raise the Veneration of our Reader."

Chapter II

Miss Sophia Western, Squire Western's daughter, is ushered into the spotlight. At first the narrator does not provide exact details, hailing instead a string of female characters from high literature and high society, with whom he compares Sophia. Reinforcing his reluctance to paint Sophia's portrait, the narrator elusively says: "most of all, she resembled one whose Image never can depart from my Breast, and whom if thou dost remember, thou hast then, my Friend, an adequate Idea of Sophia." Finally we are graced with the information that Sophia is symmetrical, of medium height, of perfect proportions, with saber-coloured hair, black eyes, and "two Rows of Ivory" in her mouth. Moreover, her inside matches her exquisite exterior. If jealousy should look to find fault with her, the narrator supposes that Sophia's forehead could be a little higher. He incorporates the words of John Suckling, John Donne, and Horace in his description of Sophia. Although Sophia's manners lack that polished finish found in the "Polite Circle," such airs are not needed in a character with such "sense" and "natural Gentility." Sophia has been educated by her aunt.

Chapter III

Sophia, at eighteen years old, loves her father more than any other living being. This is why Tom chooses to direct his plea on Black George's behalf to Sophia. The narrator steps back in time to describe the relationship between the neighbouring households—they have lived pleasantly enough as neighbours, and Tom, Sophia, and Blifil were playmates as children. Tom's gregariousness appealed more to little Sophia than Blifil's cautious solemnity. In their early youth, Tom presented Sophia with a bird that he had stolen from a nest and trained to sing. Sophia christened the bird "little Tommy" and became so attached to it that feeding and playing with the bird was her greatest pastime.

One day in the garden Blifil persuades Sophia to let him hold little Tommy for a moment. On acquiring the bird, Blifil quickly removes the string from the bird's leg and releases it. Beckoned by Sophia's screams, Tom runs to them and climbs the tree where the bird has perched itself. The branch breaks and Tom tumbles into the canal below. When the adults arrive at the scene, Blifil confesses that it is his fault and explains that he cannot stand to see anything not have its liberty. Tom and Blifil are sent home, Sophia retires to her chamber, and the adults return to their alcohol.

Chapter IV

Square, Thwackum, Squire Western, Allworthy, and a lawyer friend of Western's argue about whether Blifil's actions were right or wrong. Square and Thwackum praise Blifil.

Western, annoyed with Blifil for depriving Sophia of her bird, simply urges his guests to continue drinking. Allworthy thinks that the action was wrong, but the motivation good, and therefore resolves not to punish the boy. The lawyer enigmatically declares that property rights are "nullius in bonis," confounding the rest of the participants. Soon after, Allworthy whisks Square and Thwackum away.

Chapter V

From the day of the bird's death, Sophia develops a "Kindness" for Tom and an "Aversion" to Blifil. Many events, unnecessary to relate, further these sentiments. Sophia realises that Tom has no enemy in the world but himself, while Blifil has few enemies but loves only himself. Some people keep good people to themselves, for fear of losing dominion over their goodness. But Sophia acts otherwise—publicly praises Tom, and publicly disparages Blifil. Sophia has returned to her father's house after more than three years of living and studying with her aunt. She hears the story of Black George and the partridge one night while dining with Squire Western, her aunt, and Allworthy. Later, when her maidservant is undressing her, Sophia vents her hatred for Blifil.

In Squire Western's house, Sophia now reigns supreme. Tom often dines with the father and daughter, since he shares Squire Western's passion for hunting. However, Tom has gallantry, which sets him apart from the "boisterous Brutality of mere Country Squires." Tom is now twenty, and has earned a reputation of being a "pretty Fellow" by all the ladies of the neighbourhood. Sophia's natural ebullience increases whenever she has the pleasure of Tom's company, but Tom is too young to notice, and Squire Western is too much absorbed in his animals and sports. Unsuspecting, Squire Western allows Tom and Sophia plenty of time alone together. Sophia's heart is "irretrievably lost" to Tom before she even suspects it is in Danger.

Tom asks Sophia one afternoon if she will do him a favor. Sophia blushes, but Tom soon puts her beating heart to rest with his plea for Black George. Tom says that if Squire Western takes action against Black George, it will be surely be the death of him and his family. Sophia, having recovered her composure, smiles and says that this is not a big favor to ask. Indeed, the previous day she herself sent a "small Matter" to Black George's wife. The narrator informs us that this "small Matter" was in fact one of Sophia's own gowns, linen, and ten shillings. Tom had heard of Sophia's generosity, which encouraged him to ask for her assistance. Tom begs Sophia to urge her father to find employment for Black George. Sophia promises to try her best if Tom will return a favor. After exclaiming "I would sacrifice my Life to oblige you," Tom kisses Sophia's hand. This is the first time Tom's lips have ever touched Sophia's body, and she now feels "a Sensation to which she had been before a Stranger." Once Sophia regains her voice, she begs Tom not to take her father on such dangerous hunts. Tom gives his word, and then leaves.

Squire Western likes to hear Sophia play on the harpsichord every afternoon. Sophia, although an accomplished musician, has learned her father's favourite songs—mainly lewd ballads—to make him happy. On this night, Sophia plays his favourites, which elates him. Sophia takes this moment to make her request on behalf of Tom, and her father whole-heartedly agrees. The next morning, Squire Western summons his lawyer to write out a Deputation. Tom's actions are now made public and while some sing his praises others, including Square and Thwackum, harshly criticize him. Allworthy, however, is an advocate for Tom's virtue, which he says lies in the "Perseverance and Integrity of his Friendship." The narrator hints that Fortune will not be as kind to Tom in the following chapters.

Chapter VI

While Tom appreciates Sophia's beauty and abilities, he has not fallen in love with her. The narrator speculates that this may stem from idiocy, or from bad taste, but the truth is that Tom is in love with another woman. The narrator imagines that the reader will be indignant that he has heard nothing of this girl, who is in fact the second eldest of the five children of Black George. Molly Seagrim, one of the country's best-looking girls, has transfixed Tom's attentions to the point where his inclinations are to try and force himself upon her. Tom's morals, however, prevent him from doing so.

Molly's beauty is of a rough, unfeminine hue, and her personality is not particularly feminine either—we learn that "Jones had more Regard for her Virtue than she herself." Tom tries to stay away so that Molly will keep her chastity, but she is insistent and eventually has her way. Tom convinces himself, however, that he seduced Molly. Tom is the kind of hero who cannot receive without returning, in love, and he has therefore not returned Sophia's affections because he cannot bear to leave Molly in poverty. Nor does Tom wish to deceive Sophia as long as he is still attached to Molly.

Chapter VII

Mrs. Seagrim is the first to notice that Molly is pregnant and she tries to hide it from the neighbours by dressing her daughter in Sophia's gown. The following Sunday, Molly arrives at church looking extremely glamorous in this gown and some adornments from Tom. The other women do not recognize Molly at first, but when they do, they sneer at her.

Commentary

The first two chapters are entirely devoted to Sophia and her description. Fielding seems to follow the tradition of putting in his comments in the first chapter of a new Book. Here, the first chapter is devoted to the style that he thinks should be used to introduce the heroine Sophia. Fielding can get a little tiring in his elaborate similes and accounts.

We notice that Sophia is the only character to be introduced with such pomp and show. Two whole chapters are devoted to her introduction, her external and internal self. She is undoubtedly the heroine of the story and our narrator seems to be excessively fond of her. It was believed that she was styled after one of Fielding's real life loves. Going by the attention Fielding gives her we tend to agree. The only thing that Sophia seems to be lacking is a certain sense of ease. She is very much in control and deeply principled, not that these values need be condemned.

We read a little incident of the past. It involves Blifil, Tom and Sophia when they are kids. This small event itself says a lot about the respective characters of all the three. Here in this chapter we see how Fielding is a master of the art of interpolation between past and present.

We take a peep into the past and are then back again to the present. Since the freeing of her little bird, Sophia had taken a dislike to Blifil. This hatred deepens with the progression of years and it remains in her mind as something that can never be erased. For Tom, on the other hand, she slowly develops a deep affection and abiding love.

In the fourth chapter, we see how the adults react differently to the little bird incident. Squire Western only thinks about his daughter and does not approve of Blifil's action. His is a good natured and simple disposition. He adores his daughter, so anything done to make her unhappy is wrong. Thwackum and Square are not that simple in their thinking. Both think that Blifil is right as he frees a bird and speaks eloquently about freedom. Squire Allworthy does not make any comment and only intervenes to take the two disputing scholars away, in order to end the fight.

The narrative now adopts a youthful turn. Sophia's state of mind regarding Tom is described. The youngsters are no longer kids and are old enough to be in 'love'. While Sophia starts falling in love with Tom, he doesn't have such a disposition. He respects and admires her self and her breeding but has no romantic pretensions to her. The author adds a comment to the effect that Tom is foolish not to notice the charms of Sophia. She, on the other hand, has her heart fluttering whenever he comes close to her!

Soon, we learn why Tom is not so charmed by Sophia. That is because, he is attracted to a young girl - Molly Seagrim, who seduces him, without his knowing that he is the one who has been seduced. Fielding does a convincing job of describing Tom's state of mind. Tom is a young man who has his hormones peaking and he is spontaneous enough to express his passion with an obliging young maid. But, his passion is not a lustful one alone. He mingles feelings of pity, sympathy, and gratitude to assume the shape of love.

In the seventh chapter, is presented a loud, brash village incident. Molly, Tom's love, is a young girl, possessing all the little vanities that such possess. She decides to attend Sunday Mass in a gown given to her family by Sophia. On discovering the well-dressed woman among them to be Molly, they begin to laugh and taunt her. This goes on to take the form of a full-fledged physical fight between the saunters on one side and Molly on the other. This fight is presented in the next chapter.

We see the change in the note of the description. Tom and Sophia. our main characters have grown up and now the real content of the story starts forming. We also note that Tom's passionate disposition is not evil, but is sometimes too impetuous for his own good. At the same time, he is no hypocrite and comes to Molly's aid, in front of all the villagers. He helps to extract her from the mud and protects her decency.

Sophia on the other hand lives in a sheltered and polite world. Tom is a man and is allowed to roam around and he gets his hands soiled in the process!

Chapter VIII

Sophia is at church and is touched by Molly's beauty. Sophia later calls on Black George to tell him she would like to hire Molly as her maid servant. Black George is secretly shocked that Sophia has not noticed that Molly is pregnant. He heads home for advice from his wife, but the family is in an uproar over what happened at church, when the women assaulted Molly with "Dirt and Rubbish." In retaliation, Molly knocked out the leader of the pack and cleared herself a path using a skull and thighbone from the graveyard as her weapons. The narrator tells the story in an ironic Virgilian style, listing the names of the men and women who fell victim to Molly. Goody Brown is the only woman to fight back. She attacks Molly and tears out her hair. The narrator observes that since women never fail to aim for each other's breasts when fighting, Goody Brown, who is flat-cheated, has the upper hand. Tom's arrival quells the fight.

Chapter IX

Tom covers Molly with his own clothes and gives orders for Molly to be transported home. Tom departs with Square and Blifil after stealing a quick kiss from Molly. Back in the Seagrim household, Molly is chastised by her sisters. Mrs. Seagrim calls Molly a whore, and Molly reminds her mother that she was also pregnant with her first child before she was married. Black George tells his family about Sophia's offer. Molly does not want to wash dishes for Sophia, and after Molly slips her mother some money, Mrs. Seagrim agrees that Molly is too good to be a maid. Mrs. Seagrim accuses her husband of being a villain who causes trouble for the family by fighting everyone, and it is decided that Mrs. Seagrim will take the job herself.

Chapter X

The following morning, Tom goes hunting with Squire Western and returns to dine with him, Sophia, and Parson Supple the parish curate. Sophia radiates with charm and beauty, finally conquering Tom. Parson Supple is known for his reticence while eating, but after dinner, he makes amusing conversation. He happens to drop the news that Molly Seagrim is pregnant and that her father is swearing to send her to Bridewell. Tom excuses himself from the table, which leads Western to exclaim that Tom must be the father of the child. Now he says he understands why Tom pleaded so heartily on Black George's behalf. Parson Supple takes Tom's side, and Western calls Allworthy a "whoremaster," and implies that he was a lover-boy while at university. Parson Supple retorts that Allworthy never attended university. Sophia, having noticed Tom blush during Parson Supply's story, begins to suspect that her father is right. After the guests have left, Western wants Sophia to play the harpsichord for him, but she complains of a raging headache.

Chapter XI

Tom returns home on foot to find Molly about to be whisked off to Bridewell. He embraces her in front of everyone and swears he will protect her. Tom speaks to Allworthy and confesses that he is the father of the child. Allworthy sends Molly home and gives Tom a lecture on chastity. The narrator says there is no point in his transcribing this, since we have already witnessed Allworthy's speech to Jenny Jones, and most of what applies to women applies likewise to men. Allworthy disapproves of Tom's behaviour but appreciates Tom's honesty. Blifil relates the story to Thwackum, who is enraged that Tom is too old for a whipping. Thwackum conceives of a plan to corrupt Allworthy's opinion of Tom. Square suggests to Allworthy that Tom has only been friendly to Black George in order to win over Molly. The seeds of suspicion are laid in Allworthy's mind.

Chapter XII

Sophia does not sleep well and her maid, Mrs. Honour, finds her awake and fully dressed the next morning. Mrs. Honour imparts to Sophia that Tom is indeed the father of Molly's child. Sophia does not want to hear about it, and sends Mrs. Honour to see whether Sophia has to attend to her father at breakfast. The narrator reminds us of Sophia's burgeoning love for Tom, which has now overwhelmed her. Sophia decides that the only cure for her lovesickness is to avoid Tom by making a visit to her aunt. However, an accident will prevent her from leaving.

Chapter XIII

Mr. Western insists that Sophia join him on a hunting expedition, even though she has no love for violent sports. On the second day, Sophia's horse throws her off and Tom gallops in and catches her, breaking his left arm in the process. Western is elated that his daughter has been rescued and Sophia secretly cherishes Tom's bravery. The narrator delves into examples of philosophers who believe men to outshine women in bravery, and women who love courage in men. Whatever the case, the accident brings Tom and Sophia closer together.

Chapter XIV

A surgeon bleeds Sophia and performs surgery on Tom's arm. Mrs. Honour prattles to Sophia about Tom's magnamity and good looks, and accuses Sophia of being in love with Tom. Mrs. Honour also tells Sophia that she saw Tom passionately kissing Sophia's muff, which he found lying on a chair. Moreover, when Sophia was playing the harpsichord one day, Tom observed that he could not speak while Sophia was playing. Sophia hushes Honour, protesting that she does not want to hear such talk, but when Honour tells Sophia that Tom once called her a "goddess" Sophia listens intently.

Commentary

In the eighth chapter, we learn of Sophia's generosity. On seeing pretty Molly in the church, and the jealous eyes upon her, Sophia decides to offer her a job as her maid. She informs Black George of this offer. But, instead of being happy, he is in a tizzy, as he has just learned of Molly's pregnancy. He is in a fix about how he will put the matter in front of Sophia. So, he returns home to inform his wife and to form a plan of action with her. But, he finds his house in an uproar - with all the women fighting. The cause of the argument is none other than Molly herself. And, now is recounted an unpleasant incident at the church. After the members of the upper class community had left, all the villagers had gathered around Molly to insult her. But, she is not a docile woman herself and she defended herself with her tongue as well as her body. There resulted quite a muddy battle, which did considerable violence to her dress and body.

Fortunately, Blifil, Square and Tom together pass the courtyard and seeing the disorder, Tom comes to Molly's rescue. It is quite notable that he does not shy from helping her in front of all the villagers. Tom is a true gentleman in this sense and is not a hypocrite. He does come forward to help the woman he loves.

At Molly's house, her mother and sisters once again insult her. We notice the coarse language that the Seagrim use. This can be contrasted with the speech of the higher ups such as that of Squire Allworthy's family. Fielding is realistic in his depiction of English life and it's various dialects.

Molly's mother Goody Seagrim is only consoled when Molly gives her a few guineas. Theirs is an extremely poor condition. Fielding paints a broad spectrum, encompassing the rich and the poor.

We see how Tom starts noticing Sophia's charms. At a dinner at Squire Western's house, Sophia shines forth. She does not probably realise it herself, but her intention is to charm and impress Tom and she starts succeeding. But, then the curate tells the Squire about Molly being pregnant. Tom looks very guilty at this occasion by colouring up and then leaving the table. The curate is sure that Tom is the father of the child. Sophia is shocked and it is now that she realises that she had been falling in love with Tom. She is portrayed as a sensitive woman, one who is likely to think a lot. This evening, she takes permission to not attend her father and leads a very disturbed night, thinking only about Tom.

Meanwhile, Tom goes on foot to his own house and sees Molly there. He takes her in and confesses his guilt to the Squire. While the Squire is very unhappy with Jones' conduct, he is also impressed by Tom's honesty. Indeed, Tom is a straightforward man who does not run away from his deeds. He faces them and accepts his faults, if any. He could have left Molly to her own Fate, but doesn't. His enemies make the most of his mistakes and use the opportunities to condemn him blasphemously. Square is the most poisonous, when he suggests to the Squire that Tom was friendly to Black George, for the sole purpose of having the opportunity to deflower the daughter. Square indeed has a wicked, dirty mind and it is a pity that the Squire listens to such talk.

While Tom is being defiled thus, Sophia is tormented by thoughts of Tom. She realises her feelings for him and resolves to keep a distance. We see throughout that Sophia often reigns in her passion and tries to be in control of herself always.

But, in the thirteenth chapter, an incident occurs that makes Sophia even more susceptible to the arrows of love. While she is on a horse, the beast starts behaving wildly and she is in danger. Tom comes to her rescue and manages to catch her in his arms as she is thrown off the horseback. He hurts himself too. When Sophia's father comes on to the scene, he is happy that Sophia is not hurt. For him, she is of paramount importance and the wounds of Tom can wait. This incident is a typically chivalrous and romantic one.

They return to the Squire's house and the doctor attends to both Sophia and Tom. Fielding pokes fun at the profession of medicine when he writes how the doctor gives a long lecture on broken bones. Tom is shown as a brave and magnanimous young man, while Sophia is the quintessential delicate darling. Tom impresses most women - young, old, poor or rich. Mrs. Honour too appreciates his beauty and charm. She praises Tom to Sophia and this does have an effect on the latter. Sophia is inwardly very happy when Mrs. Honour tells her that Tom had kissed her muff many a time, on being told that it was the young lady's own. Fielding here develops naturally the circumstances that make Tom and Sophia develop an abiding passion for each other.

A major development has taken place here: the slow maturing of Sophia's affection for Tom into a feeling of love. Another crucial development is that of Tom becoming aware of Sophia in a romantic sense. These two developments form the base of the narrative.

BOOK V

Chapter I

The narrator prides himself on being the founder of "prosai-comi-epic Writing." He explains that the chapters that preface every book are meant philosophical and historical treatises. He then turns his focus on "critics," to whom he believes have received such authority that they think they can create rules for authors. The rules that critics have attempted to instigate, however, only "curb and restrain Genius." Returning to his prefacing remarks, the narrator explains that the introductory chapters are also intended to provide contrast: in their seriousness, they should excite the reader to reach the comic parts.

Chapter II

While Tom is in confinement because of his broken arm, Mr. Allworthy visits him every day and tries to make him deliberate on his misconduct. Thwackum often visits Tom to deliver dictatorial speeches out of his "duty" to urge reprobates, such as Tom, to repent. Thwacker says that Tom's broken arm is God's punishment for his sins. Square lectures Tom in a similar manner, but argues instead that a broken arm is nothing in the grand universal scheme. Blifil rarely visits, saying that he is scared to sully his character by spending time with Tom. Squire Western leaves Tom's room only to drink or hunt, while Sophia struggles to make herself stay at bay.

One day, while Tom and Squire Western listen to Sophia playing the harpsichord, Tom tells Western that, since his broken arm saved Sophia, he thinks of it as "the happiest Accident" of his life. Western wants to give Tom one of his horses as a reward. Sophia begins to play very badly, in such a way that Tom notices that something is bothering Sophia, and begins to suspect that she might be attracted to him.

Chapter III

Tom's love for Sophia is "bittersweet," since he is not completely sure that he has won her affection. Moreover, knowing that fortune and status are of fundamental importance to parents, Tom anticipates that Squire Western prohibit a marriage between him and Sophia. He does not want to abuse Western's hospitality to him, nor does he desire to offend Allworthy. Tom also thinks of Molly, to whom he has made promises of "eternal Constancy." He cannot bear to reflect on the image of Molly dying, which she has sworn to do if Tom deserts her. Molly's poverty has not once represented an obstacle to Tom. After a sleepless night, Tom resolves to remain faithful to Molly.

Chapter IV

Mrs. Honour visits Tom on his sick-bed. She was deserted after being fooled by a nobleman's footman, and has never trusted another man with her heart, but she still loves men. Mrs. Honour tells Tom that Sophia has sent her to check on Molly, and Tom begs her for any information on Sophia. After a good deal of wheedling, Honour reveals that Sophia will not buy a new muff, but holds on to the one that Tom had kissed earlier. Squire Western cnters to summon Tom to the harpsichord, where Sophia sits, wearing her muff and looking lovelier than ever. While Sophia is performing one of her father's favourite songs, the muff falls onto her fingers and prevents her from playing properly. Enraged, Western throws the muff into the fire, but Sophia immediately retrieves it from the flames.

Chapter V

Tom cannot get Molly out of his mind, and his compassion for her makes him overlook the fact that Sophia eclipses Molly in both appearance and character. Tom hopes that maybe he can apologize to Molly by offering her money, since her desperation might be greater than her love for him. One day, with his broken arm in a sling, Tom goes to visit Molly. Tom finds the upstairs door locked, and Molly eventually appears and tells Tom she has been sleeping. Tom tells Molly that Allworthy would be furious if he knew they were together, and says he wants Molly to find a man with whom she can lead a reputable life. She bursts into tears and accuses him of ruining and deserting her.

Suddenly, a rug that Molly has hung up to cover her clothes closet falls down, revealing Square. The narrator then tells the story of how Square and Molly came to be together. Square could not help noticing her beauty at church, and when he heard that her "Fortress of Virtue had already been subdued" by Tom, he felt perfectly justified in usurping Tom's place. Indeed, Square relishes the fact that Molly's lack of chastity allows him to have his way with her.

Tom bursts into laughter and helps Square out of the cupboard. Square says that Tom cannot blame him for "corrupting Innocence," and Tom assures Square that he will keep the discovery a secret. Square agrees with Tom that sexual desire evolves out of a healthy natural appetite. Tom tells Molly that not only will he forgive her, but he will continue to assist her as much as he can. After Tom leaves, Molly chastises Square for being the reason she has lost Tom, but Square's caresses and his money restore Molly's devotion to him.

Chapter VI

Jones worries that he has set Molly off on a course of debauched behaviour, but Betty, Molly's eldest sister, assures Tom that a certain Will Barnes deserves that blame. Moreover, the child could just as easily belong to Will as Tom. Now Tom can turn his thoughts to Sophia, whom he loves. Tom cannot conceal his awkwardness in front of Sophia, and he has become unusually quiet and shy in her company. Western does not notice, but Sophia does, and she happily realises the reason. One day, the two of them chance to cross paths in the garden. They meet suddenly and stroll together. When they arrive at the tree that Jones climbed to catch Sophia the bird when they were children, Sophia reminds him of the incident. She suspects that the memory must be emotional for him since he risked his life. Tom says he wishes he had died that day so he would not have to deal with the heartache of loving Sophia. Sophia, trembling, says that she must leave, but she stays to hear all that Tom has to say. They "totter" back together, hand in hand, with Sophia admonishing Jones not to say anything more on the matter. The narrator warns us that Jones must now face some bad news.

Commentary

When Tom is in his bed, different people visit him for myriad purposes. Square and Thwackum use this opportunity to lecture him on morality. They are self-serving hypocrites and play the part of the 'disliked' persons quite well. Blifil is another diplomatic creature. He visits Tom rarely and when he does he is patronizing. He expresses hope that Tom shall reform himself. Squire Western is fond of Tom and his visits are more genuine than the others. Because of the accident Tom gets to see more of Sophia. We now note how the attraction between the two increases and Tom falls deeper in love. He cannot resist Sophia's charms in proximity to her. Sophia also cannot hide her affections and Tom is quick to note them.

Tom has to wrestle with a scorpion though and that is the scorpion of doubts in love. While he loves Sophia he realises that the match would not be approved by either Squire Allworthy, or by Squire Western. He is also worried about his promise to Molly of being true to her. He is scared to think that she might stand ruined because of him. Tom is a scrupulous man who does not lack heart. This is one of the qualities that makes him the 'hero' of the novel.

Meanwhile, Mrs. Honour plays cupid for Tom and Sophia. She encourages the two by telling each the affection that the other had shown for his/her person. Tom's doubts regarding Molly are laid to rest in chapter six. We learn that Molly is also having an affair with Square. For all his talk about morality, Square too is a man of regular passions. On seeing Molly's beauty and on learning that she has already been soiled, Square pursues and then attains her. Tom actually finds Square in Molly's room. We as readers, have a very low opinion of Square's actions. Molly's sister also tells Tom that he is not the first person to have slept with Molly. Molly's first lover had been a country lover. Tom must be happy to know that Molly is pregnant with Will's child not his own.

Tom now is constantly thinking about Sophia. But his feelings for her are soured by the social distance between them. Thus Tom and Sophia's romantic affair begins. One day, when the couple bumps into each other at the garden, Tom is very awkward. We wonder at the delicacy of the two that when they meet like this, they can hardly support themselves. This delicacy makes us wonder if their description has been exaggerated. But now there is no doubt that the feeling of 'love' has taken complete possession of both Tom and Sophia.

Chapter VII

Tom has stayed with Western for two weeks without visiting Allworthy once, and in this time, Allworthy has fallen dangerously ill. Quoting the words of the Latin poet Cato, the narrator praises Allworthy for being calm in the face of death. He has no fears since he has lived an honest life. Allworthy summons his family to him and Tom races home, forgetting all thoughts of love.

At the bed, Blifil starts to cry and Allworthy delivers a long speech about the inevitability of death. He outlines the contents of his will to ascertain whether all are satisfied with their lot. The estate is to go to Blifil, with a smaller estate of 500 pounds a year set aside for Tom. In addition, Tom is to receive a flat sum of 1000 pounds. Tom throws himself at Allworthy's feet, thanking him for his generosity but insisting that he cannot think of anything as long as Allworthy's health lies in danger. Thwackum and Square are each to receive 1000 pounds and Allworthy has also made provisions for his servants. An attorney from Salisbury arrives and Allworthy composes himself to die.

Chapter VIII

Mrs. Wilkins launches on a long tirade about how she should not be grouped with the other servants in her master's will, and Thwackum and Square are not pleased with their inheritance either. Blifil returns from speaking to the attorney, from whom he has discovered that his mother has died from gout. Thwackum tells Blifil to bear the news like a "Christian" while Square tells him to bear it like a "Man." Blifil assures his tutors that he would not be able to survive if he did not have their sound lessons to fall back on. They debate whether or not to tell Allworthy about the death of his sister or not. In the sick room, the doctor declares that a miracle has occurred, and that Allworthy has recovered completely. The narrator lets the reader know that the situation was not actually as bad as the doctor had represented it. Blifil tells Allworthy about Bridget's death and Allworthy commissions Blifil to arrange the funeral.

Chapter IX

Tom remains with Allworthy, consternated by his illness. The doctor assures the family that Allworthy's state has improved and that he will survive. Delighted at this report, Tom gets drunk, and the doctor has to quell a fight between Tom and Thwackum. Blifil, who detests Tom's unruly behaviour since it is so different from his own, retorts that Tom should not behave in such a way when his mother has just died. Tom begs Blifil's pardon, but Blifil sneers that Tom cannot understand the pain of a parent's death since he does not even know who his parents were. Thwackum and the doctor have to stop Tom and Blifil from fighting.

Chapter X

On a beautiful June evening, Tom walks into a grove where nightingales are singing and breezes are fluttering the leaves. Alone, he meditates aloud on the beauty and charms of Sophia and swears eternal constancy to her. Suddenly Molly emerges from the brush and, after a brief conversation, Tom and Molly disappear together into the densest section of the grove. Thwackum and Blifil walk into this same grove and pursue Tom and his woman.

Chapter XI

Tom is like a wild beast defending his mate. Thwackum swears he will track down the guilty woman, but Tom restrains him. The three men begin to fight, and are eventually joined by a "fourth Pair of Fists" that belong to Squire Western, who takes Tom's side. Tom and Western win the battle.

Chapter XII

Sophia and Mrs. Western arrive at the scene of combat. Everyone rushes to help Blifil, who appears dead, but Sophia's fainting distracts them. Tom grasps Sophia in his arms and revives her in a brook. Western is so pleased with Tom for saving Sophia's life that he offers to give anything—except, of course, Sophia or his estate. Sophia sighs on seeing Tom's bruises from the brawl, and these sighs send Tom into a state of rapture. The narrator philosophizes on war, and wishes that all people could resolve disputes with their fists instead of with unnatural weapons. Thwackum tells Western what initiated the fight and Western chuckles, calling Tom a "liquorish Dog." Sophia, on the cusp of fainting again, begs to be taken home.

Commentary

Several small and yet crucial incidents take place. Tom continues living in Squire Western's house for some time. It is obvious that he enjoyed his stay, because of Sophia's proximity. We see that Squire Western is very fond of Tom. But, later we learn that this liking is not strong enough for the Squire to consider Tom as husband material for his daughter, Sophia.

There is a sudden development and that is Squire Allworthy's illness. Tom rushes to the Squire's bedside Tom genuinely loves his benefactor and is very worried about his health. The Squire's health had deteriorated suddenly, owing to lack of care. He collects every member of the house around his bed in a very typical 'about to die' style. The Squire is a mature, balanced man who is not afraid of death. He is ready to face it bravely and is competent enough to draw a rational will. The Squire appears to be a fair-minded person, who caters for all members in his will. In the response to the Squire's will, we note the various kinds of persons and their characteristics. Mrs. Deborah Wilkins, Squire and Thwackum are selfish and materialistic. All three complain that they should have been granted more by the Squire. It is in their response that we note the hypocrisy of their characters. In contrast Tom is concerned about the Squire and not about how much he will gain from his will and his death. Tom is truly generous, whereas some others in the novel merely claim to be good, but are not so.

At this time a messenger arrives from Salisbury. He informs Blifil about his mother's death. When we read this little occurrence we do not give it much thought. The relevance of this particular incident is revealed in another book. The messengers, as we later learn is an attorney called Dowling. He had also given a letter to Blifil, for Squire Allwrothy. But it is only much later, that we learn that this letter never reaches the Squire. If Allworthy had read the letter, Tom's history would have been otherwise. The letter contained the vital information that Tom is in reality Squire Allworthy's nephew. Blifil on reading this must have decided to hide this secret from the Squire. The Squire learns about the undelivered letter from Dowling, towards the end of the novel. When the Squire does realise Blifil's malevolency, he feels even more sympathetic towards Tom.

We see Tom's natural 'animal spirits' in these chapters. When he learns that the Squire will be well, he is so happy that he drinks more. Also, he cannot stop himself from getting into an argument with Blifil. He goes for a walk to soothe his nerves. Here we read a surprising thing. Tom remembers Sophia and decides to carve her name on a tree. He is lovesick but the minute Molly appears before him, he gets talking to her and finally has a sexual altercation with her right there in the woods. This does not say much of our hero. He gives into his physical passions too quickly. And, the lesson that he learns through this experience is that he cannot let his instinctive passion carry him away.

He develops restraint eventually, in order to become capable of marrying Sophia. She, on the other hand, had always been prudent, and unlike Tom, has no other affairs. In this manner, Fielding's hero is believable. Tom is not a perfect paragon of virtue and has his faults. He has to overcome them to be successful in romance as well as otherwise.

Thwackum and Blifil have a physical fight with Tom. Tom is honourable and chivalrous enough to want to hide his lover Molly from the other men's accusing eyes.

Sophia faints on seeing blood and violence. She is an archetypal delicate female prototype. Tom's affection for Sophia is getting apparent now - he leaves Blifil to come to Sophia's aid. She doesn't realise his tender caresses because she is quite faint. Her tender constitution must have received on even larger blow by the information that Tom had been with a 'wench' in the woods. Squire Western makes fun of Tom's sexual exploits. He is a robust and loud man himself.

Tom once again joins the Westerns for dinner. He does this for Sophia's company more than anything else. We, as readers begin to question his emotional integrity when we see how easily he gets carried away with Molly.

BOOK VI

Chapter I

Since the previous book was about the "Passion of Love," this book will probe the notion of love even further. The narrator defines love by means of four points: first, there are minds that do not experience love; second, love cannot be ruled by lust; third, love does seek self-satisfaction; lastly, when love acts toward one of the opposite sex, it appeals to lust for help. The narrator believes many people exist who enjoy giving happiness to others and this is the highest form of love.

Chapter II

Back at Western's house, everyone celebrates Allworthy's recovery except for Sophia. Her father does not notice Sophia's melancholy, but Mrs. Western, who has "lived about the Court, and ... seen the World," quickly discerns that Sophia has fallen in love. Although Mrs. Western has not suffered this state herself, she is as well read in love as she is in politics. When Mrs. Western tells her brother that Sophia is in love with Mr. Blifil, Western is furious that Sophia has fallen in love without his permission. Mrs. Western pities his "Country Ignorance," while he scorns her "Town Learning." Mrs. Western eventually wins the Squire's approval of the match, but he worries that Allworthy will not agree to it, since "Money hath no Effect" on him. The Squire believes that "Petticoats should not meddle" in politics, but when Mrs. Western threatens to leave, the Squire remembers that he is to inherit her fortune, and tries to mollify her. She suggests that they "sign a Treaty of Peace."

Chapter III

Sophia suspects that her aunt has realised her affection for Tom, and she attempts to conceal her feelings by paying more attention to Blifil than to Tom. This baffles Mrs. Western, who reckons that Sophia's behaviour must be "extreme Art in Sophia" to deflect her from the truth. Mr. Western invites Allworthy to dinner and proposes a match between Sophia and Blifil directly afterward. Allworthy considers the "Alliance" to be a sensible one, and greatly praises Sophia. He appreciates Sophia's grand fortune, but will only ratify the plan only if Sophia and Blifil profess mutual tenderness. This answer upsets Western, who believes that parents have a better knack for choosing marriage partners than their children. The narrator suggests that Allworthy is an avatar of moderation.

Chapter IV

Allworthy proposes the match to Blifil, who admits he has not once entertained the thought of marrying Sophia. His appetites, the narrator confides, are so moderate that they can easily be supplanted with philosophy or study. Since Blifil does possess a healthy portion of "Avarice and Ambition," however, he gravitates toward the idea of Sophia's fortune. Allworthy disapproves of the cold answer from Blifil; Allworthy himself "possessed much Fire in his Youth, and had married a beautiful Woman for Love." Blifil subdues Allworthy's concern with a learned exposition on "Love and Marriage." Allworthy and Western, by letter, arrange a courtship opportunity for the young lovers.

Chapter V

Mrs. Western finds Sophia reading in her bedroom and they debate the merits of the book. Mrs. Western tells Sophia that she has long perceived the aura of love about her. Sophia need disclose her passion no further, since Squire Western has proposed the match to Allworthy, who has wholeheartedly complied. Sophia, overcome with surprise and joy, blurts out: "So brave, and yet so gentle; so witty, yet so inoffensive; so humane, so civil, so genteel, so handsome! What signifies his being base born, when compared with such Qualifications as these?" The words "base born" alert her aunt to the fact that they are talking about different men. Mrs. Western is enraged that Sophia can consider dishonouring the prestigious Western family line by marrying a bastard. Sophia begs Mrs. Western not to tell her father her secret. Her aunt agrees on the condition that Sophia will agree to meet Blifil that afternoon.

Chapter VI

Mrs. Honour finds Sophia in tears and begs Sophia to tell her what has happened, even though she has, in fact, been listening to the conversation through the keyhole. Mrs. Honour responds to Sophia's dire news with a long speech in her country dialect. She believes Sophia should be free to choose the man she finds "most handsome." After Honour mentions having seen Tom walking by the canal that morning, Sophia immediately dons her hat, but, deciding that the ribbon in the hat does not suit her, orders Honour to fetch her. The ribbon exchange results in Sophia's missing Tom by a few minutes. The narrator takes this opportunity to warn all female readers against vanity.

Chapter VII

Blifil and Sophia have an awkward courtship meeting. For the first quarter of an hour Blifil can hardly get a word out. Suddenly he breaks into a "Torrent of farfetched and high-strained Compliments." Sophia bears as much as she can, then exits the room. Blifil leaves perfectly satisfied with the meeting, since he does not care about possessing Sophia's heart, but only "her Fortune and her Person." Blifil entertains no idea that Tom loves Sophia because Tom has stopped confiding in Blifil since their brawl. Western begins to "caper and dance about his Hall" when he hears from Blifil how successfully the meeting went. Seeing that her father is so happy, Sophia decides this is the best time to break the bad news to him. Confirming first that her father does indeed "place all his Joy in his Sophie's Happiness," Sophia begs him not to force her to marry a man whom she utterly despises. Mr. Western damns Sophia and threatens to turn her out of the house. He agrees to let Tom try to talk some sense into the girl.

Commentary

Once again Henry Fielding thinks aloud about a concept. This time, in keeping with the current situation in the novel, the theme is love. Fielding analyses the elements that together constitute love. His analysis is interesting to read and he seems to use the archaic English style.

Now, as the history moves on, allied characters begin to perform important roles. Mrs. Western is responsible for giving rise to the entire Blifil affair. It is she who wrongly suspects that Sophia is in love with Blifil. She informs Sophia's father and he approaches Squire Allworthy immediately for the match. It is Mrs. Western's wrong suspicion that gives rise to this entire chain of events. Her insistence on Blifil as a match for Sophia finally edges the young lady on to reveal her secret liking for Tom.

If it hadn't been for Mrs. Western's role in the affair, Sophia & Tom would have continued in a neutral manner for a longer time. Sophia thinks that her aunt has guessed her liking for Tom. In order to reduce her aunt's suspicion, she tries to pretend that she has more interest in Blifil. Her aunt misunderstands her and thinks that Sophia loves Blifil. Squire Western is informed and she spares no time in approaching his neighbour Allworthy. When Aunt Western talks to Sophia about the latter's love life, Sophia thinks that the elder lady is referring to Tom. In reality Lady Western is referring to Blifil. So finally Sophia's secret passion for Tom is revealed.

Aunt Western is shocked by her niece's choice. The higher circles might consider Tom good company but their opinion ends there. They all still view him as the bastard who was adopted by the Squire and who will have no property to boast of. Therefore he is not a good match for any young lady. Sophia exhibits her good sense when she explains what it is that attracted her to Tom. She recognizes and values Tom's inherent humane qualities. She is able to see through Blifil's gentlemanly exterior. She has an instinctive knowledge of Blifil's selfishness and detests him.

As we can see, her understanding of human nature is quite accurate. Sophia combines beauty with intelligence in her own personality. Mrs. Western promises not to reveal Sophia's secret, if the latter promises to meet Blifil. So, Sophia does meet Blifil and is naturally, quite withdrawn. Blifil's obnoxious vanity makes him believe that he has been a success with Sophia. This is the biggest misunderstanding of them all. Squire Western is told that Sophia is happy with Blifil. You can imagine this father's surprise when Sophia refuses to marry Blifil. The Squire thinks that this refusal arises from womanly modesty and stubbornness. He had thought all this while that he had been fixing Sophia with the man, whom she loved. His natural instinct is to get angry and bully his daughter into doing what he thinks is right.

Tom learns about the Blifil Sophia match and is heart broken. But he displays a keen presence of mind and asks the Squire to let him see Sophia. Mr. Western has no clue that Tom too is attracted to Sophia. He suspects nothing and thinks that Tom will really be trying to persuade Sophia into marrying Blifil. Nothing could have been farther from the truth. It is not surprising then that Mr. Western loses faith in Tom. Later, he shuns the young man's company.

Fielding manages to build events in such a way that they excite the reader's interest. This is true of the incidents in the first half of Book Six.

Chapter VIII

Sophia trembles with fear when Tom appears in her room. Tom laments that he has been sent by Mr. Western to praise Blifil to Sophia. He declares his love for her and intimates that he hopes to have some in return. Sophia, however, warns of the terrible repercussions of crossing her father. It will be the ruin of Tom, and therefore of herself. Tom says that he fears nothing except losing Sophia. The lovers cannot draw their hands from each other. The narrator breaks the chapter, since some readers might think it has "lasted long enough."

Chapter IX

During the conversation in the previous chapter, Mrs. Western chanced to meet her brother in the hall. Hearing that Tom is with Sophia, Mrs. Western decides that Sophia has breached her trust. She divulges Sophia's secret to Squire Western, who cannot comprehend that Sophia would fall in love with a poor man. In his eyes, equality of fortune is as necessary to a marriage as difference of sex. Western descends on the two lovers, who are compared to two quaking doves. Finding that his daughter has fainted, however, Western ignores Tom and rushes to the assistance of Sophia. Western then curses Tom and the local parson urges Tom to leave.

Chapter X

Allworthy, satisfied with Blifil's account of the courtship, sincerely wishes for the match between his nephew and Sophia. Western suddenly appears and accuses Allworthy of "breeding up a Bastard like a Gentleman, and letting un come about to Vok's Houses." Allworthy reminds Western that he was averse to Tom's spending so much time at Western's estate. Allworthy asks if the Squire has observed any tokens of love between Sophia and Tom. The Squire has not.

Blifil declares that he will continue his pursuit of Sophia and calls Tom "one of the worst Men in the World." Allworthy asks what he means by this. Blifil tells Allworthy a completely distorted story about Tom's behaviour during Allworthy's illness. He says that Tom drank and danced every night, and that when Blifil tried to calm him, Tom beat him. Allworthy calls on Thwackum so as to "examine all the Evidence of this Matter." Thwackum confirms everything Blifil has said and displays his bruises from the fight.

Chapter XI

Allworthy confronts Tom with the story, omitting his own illness, which forces Tom to admit to his drunkenness. Tom is so stunned that he cannot excuse himself, and instead decides to confess to everything and beg mercy of Allworthy. Allworthy insists that he has given Tom too much forgiveness in the past, and thus sends him out in the world with some money to support himself until he finds a job to make an honest living. He particularly disapproves of Tom's behaviour toward Blifil, who has treated Tom with the utmost "Tenderness and Honour." The neighbours criticize Allworthy for his harshness to Tom, overlooking the fact that Allworthy sent Tom away with no less than five hundred pounds.

Chapter XII

The banished Tom sits by a brook and tears out his hair like a Homeric hero. His biggest quandary rests in how to deal with Sophia. He is worried about breaking his own heart by leaving her, but he cannot entertain the idea of "reducing her to Ruin and Beggary," or of betraying Allworthy's wishes. Tom decides the most honourable action is to leave Sophia, and he writes her a letter explaining this. He cannot find any wax to seal the letter, since, in a fit, he threw out everything, including the five hundred pounds from Allworthy. Black George has already found the book and pocketed it, but helps Tom search for it all the same. He promises to deliver Tom's letter to Mrs. Honour. Tom receives a letter from Sophia in return, promising that she will marry no other. Tom reads and kisses the letter one hundred times, then departs from the estate.

Chapter XIII

Sophia has passed the day listening to lectures from her aunt about how women should exercise Prudence and seek marriages for money. Western confines Sophia to her room and gives the key to Honour. Sophia weeps over Tom's letter, and Honour tries to console her by praising Blifil's appearance and manners. Sophia sends all her money—sixteen guineas—to Tom. Honour gives the money to Black George who, after some deliberation, gives it to Tom.

Chapter XIV

Mrs. Western chastises her brother for incarcerating Sophia and for ruining all the good she has done with her lectures on prudence. She reminds him of her superior knowledge of the world. When Western invokes politics in his rant, Mrs. Western says he should think about Sophia, who is "in greater Danger than the Nation." The Squire eventually agrees to turn Sophia's care over to his sister, but only because "Women arc the properness to manage Women."

Commentary

The eighth chapter is the first in which Tom & Sophia behave openly as lovers and confess their love for each other. Tom wants that Sophia should not give herself to Blifil. There is a tender scene between them. Tom & Sophia do genuinely love each other but there are many obstacles between them.

Mrs. Western had joined Squire Western outside the duo's room. She informs the Squire about Sophia's interest in Tom. The Squire's eyes are finally opened and he is furious. While Tom may be considered good company and a pleasant man, he would never have been considered as worthwhile husband material. The Squire immediately charges towards Tom and Sophia. Sophia, on hearing her father, faints again.

As we see, throughout the novel, Sophia faints at the opportune times. Her delicacy cannot handle excessive physical or mental strain. On seeing Sophia faint, the Squire forgets his anger for sometime. We see that he loves his daughter to distraction. When she is restored, the Squire pounces on Tom. The Squire forgets his previous friendship with Tom at this juncture. He insults the young man and Tom cannot restrain his anger either. It is Parson Supple, who prevents the hero from resorting to blows.

Squire Western goes and tells all to Allworthy. He complains that Tom had tried to mislead his daughter. Squire Allworthy listens attentively but does not pass a harsh judgment on Tom. If the matter had ended at Squire Waster's complaint, Tom would not have been thrown out of the house. But the matter doesn't end there. Blifil had been waiting for an opportune moment to reveal Tom's iniquities and he now finds it. He tells Allworthy about Jones' behaviour in the house when the former had been ill. Blifil paints a villainous picture of Tom as 'drunk and greedy'. Moreover, Blifil tells of Tom's violence to Thwackum as well as to Blifil himself.

The Squire's mind is poisoned by the tales that Blifil tells. The truth is that Blifil is a shrewd man who is able to say things in such a way that they have exactly the effect that he means them to have. In this case, the effect that he had sought was Squire Allworthy's anger directed at Tom. The Squire indeed is very troubled at his foundling's behaviour and he harangues him when they meet next.

Tom is often not able to defend himself properly. This happens because he tends to be very hard on himself and is not deceitful, as Blifil is. When the Squire throws many charges at Tom, the latter merely cries and feels bad, instead of pleading his own cause. We see that the villains - Blifil and Thwackum succeed in their endeavor to destroy Tom.

Tom is turned out of the house. He is a very desolate man. We see that he fights with his conscience where Sophia is concerned. He decides to give her up. But as soon as he gets a tender letter from her, he once again is encouraged to attain her. Tom is often capricious and vacillating. He is a young man who is yet to mature completely. By the end of the book, he does manage to, however.

Black George steals Tom's money. It is poverty that drives him to do this. At the same time, George does deliver Sophia's money to Tom. Sophia pities Tom's loss of Squire Allworthy's patronage. She therefore sends sixteen guineas across to the hero. She is indeed a generous woman.

Squire Western is an orthodox and chauvinistic man. He locks Sophia up when she refuses to marry Blifil. For all his love for Sophia, eventually, he likes to impose his own will on her.

Tom retires to another town and still hopes that Allworthy will change his harsh decision. Mrs. Western argues with her brother about his orthodox ways. She is an emaciated woman who believes in the freedom of women. But, later we see that despite all her thoughts on freedom, she tries to force Sophia into doing what she herself wants from the young woman. Mrs. Western at least manages to free Sophia from the prison of her own room.

The novel reaches a crucial stage in this book Tom and Sophia's love is out of the closet. Blifil's malevolency succeeds in getting Tom banished from Squire Allworthy's house.

BOOK VII

Chapter I

The narrator expounds on the analogy between world and stage, so often made in literature. From this, he says, we might applaud those who have been so good at mimicking the world that we cannot tell the copy from the original. He says, however, that the audience has always been forgotten in these comparisons. The narrator predicts how his spectators' reactions to Black George stealing Tom's five hundred pounds. He says that the people of worst character are the first to criticize.

Chapter II

Jones is sent his possessions by Allworthy, with an accompanying letter from Blifil telling him that Allworthy no longer wants to speak to Tom. Blifil urges Tom to change his lifestyle. Tom laments having to abandon Sophia, then, having decided to go to sea, hires horses to take him to Bristol. Here we will leave Tom's story, says the narrator, and return to Sophia.

Chapter III

Sophia is now released from her prison. She says that her refusal of Blifil is the only matter on which she will disobey her aunt and her father. She despises him. This confession makes Mrs. Western even more resolved to marry her off to Blifil. She asserts that in a marriage, the "Alliance between the Families is the principal Matter." Western swears at Sophia, causing Mrs. Western to remind him not to intervene. Western accuses his sister of filling Sophia's head "with a Pack of Court Notions." He says that she has "made a Whig of the Girl." Mrs. Western storms out of the house, leaving Sophia concerned and Squire Western enraged.

Chapter IV

Mr. Western moans to Sophia that men are always mistreated. He claims it was hard enough with Sophia's mother. Sophia's mother died when Sophia was eleven years old. She was a faithful wife to Mr. Western, who "returned that Behaviour, by making what the World calls a good Husband. He very seldom swore at her (perhaps not above once a Week) and never beat her." Western gets satisfaction out of complaining of Sophia's late mother since he is envious of the greater love Sophia bore for her mother than for him.

Chapter V

Sophia refuses to say a word during her father's invective against her mother. This makes him even angrier. He supposes that she will take her aunt's side too. Sophia does not want to seem ungrateful to her father, but she must remind him that her aunt loves him more than any sister loves a brother. He accuses Sophia of causing his sister such "violent Passions." Sophia encourages him to stop Mrs. Western from departing, to which Western finally agrees. Sophia rereads Tom's letter and cries over her muff. Mrs. Honour comforts her by recounting a list of the most eligible bachelors in the neighbourhood, which results in Sophia angrily dismissing Honour.

Chapter VI

Squire Western and Mrs. Western reunite as they plan the match between Sophia and Blifil. Blifil visits Sophia but the narrator says that he is going to omit the details of this scene. Blifil is happy with the courtship, but Western, who has eavesdropped with his sister on the meeting, is not, and wants the youths to tie the knot the following day. Blifil agrees with Western, since he was in fact not satisfied with the meeting. To stop the reader's suspense, the narrator confides that Blifil is not entirely devoid of Lust and now thinks of Sophia as "a most delicious Morsel." Moreover, Blifil savors the fact that he has triumphed over Tom. Allworthy gives his assent and the "Treaty" is closed. Sophia's actions will soon disrupt the Treaty, however.

Chapter VII

Honour tells Sophia she is to be married the following morning. Honour says she would not object to marrying Blifil, whom she thinks to be "a charming, sweet, handsome Man." Sophia announces her plan to run away from the house that evening and to stay with a lady relative in London, whom she met at her aunt's house, and who invited Sophia to her house whenever Sophia was in London. She says that if Honour really possesses the friendship she has always claimed, then she will accompany her. Honour expresses concern at the idea of them walking alone in the freezing cold of winter, but Sophia promises compensation. Together, they plot how Honour can get herself dismissed by Mr. Western.

Chapter VIII

Honour weighs up the pros and cons of running away with Sophia. She desires to see London, and Sophia's generosity promises more monetary rewards. Mrs. Western's maid provokes Honour by calling Sophia a "Country Girl," and Honour retaliates by saying that Sophia is "younger, and ten thousand Times more handsomer" than Mrs. Western. Mrs. Western's maid tells Mrs. Western that Honour called her "ugly." Mrs. Western refuses to sleep another night in the house unless Squire Western discharges her.

Commentary

With nearly every book in this novel, the tradition of the usage of the first chapter as 'comments on life' is common. In the first chapter of Book Seven, Fielding compares the world with a stage. In doing this he uses examples of the characters in the book.

Jones is now in a little town away from Allworthy's estate. He still hopes that the Squire will revoke his judgment but instead he receives a curt letter from Blifil, written on Squire Allworthy's behalf. The letter is condescending and Tom is hurt, angry and sad. It must have needled him further that the Squire did not write himself. Blifil ends the letter with the request that Tom should try and repent as a true Christian. Blifil's tone is always an elevated one. He believes that he is superior when in realty his 'morality' is hypocritical. Tom is much more of a Christian and this we learn as we go through the entire story.

While Tom is generous and humane, he is also a trifle childish. He is yet to grow up. Hurt and angry about Squire Allworthy's response, he decides to leave the country immediately and go to sea. Here he behaves like a little naughty boy, who has been reprimanded, for his rowdiness.

While Tom is making such plans, Sophia is having a tough time. Lady Western lectures Sophia on the concept of nobility and morality. Sophia is polite to her aunt and yet, very firm about the fact that she cannot marry a man she hates. Sophia's logic is simple and intelligent. She displays a keen mind and an open heart. Lady Western, on the other hand, for all her talk about emancipation is tied to hypocritical values and ways of life. She is greatly angered at Sophia's polite argumentativeness.

We notice that both the elder Westerns - the Squire and his sister are very demanding and authoritative. Both like to have their own way and are extremely restless when others do not agree to their particular opinions.

Lady Western vents her anger about Sophia, on Squire Western instead. Squire Western is equally rude and blunt, with the result that Lady Western leaves the house. Their basic ideas clash and more than that, each one thinks that he/she knows best. They keep forcing their own ideas on each other. Lady Western is especially tiring because of her snobbishness and her arrogance. It is apparent that she does not think much about her brother.

One whole chapter is devoted to Squire Western and also to a description of his late wife. Squire Western is a coarse man and it is quite surprising that he has such a delicate daughter. Fielding has a great understanding of human nature and the manner in which he describes Squire Western's affection for his daughter is accurate in psychological terms.

Sophia comes across as a 'proper' young lady who is rightly grateful and accurately thankful. She defends her aunt to Squire Western and urges her father to get her back home. We are told that Sophia lacks 'worldly' woman-sense though.

Squire Western values money and fortune. On hearing that Lady Western would have left her estate for him, he agrees to go after his sister. After retrieving his sister, the squire and she plan to be more rigid with Sophia. Sophia in the meanwhile mopes for her Tom in characteristic romantic style. Sophia is force to meet Blifil. Blifil is once again vain enough to think that Sophia is quite nice to him. He tries to paint a rosy picture to Squire Western and Squire Allworthy, because he does not want to lose the benefits he can gain by marrying Sophia.

The reader is allowed a peep into Blifil's mind and we see how selfish he really is. It is a pity that the two elder Squires cannot see through Blifil's ploy, but then the story would not have developed.

Mrs. Honour now starts playing a key role. It is she who informs Sophia about Squire Western's hurried plans. Sophia now makes a very bold decision to leave her father's house. For all of Sophia's sensitivity, she is really quite a strong woman. Mrs. Honour too decides to accompany her but not after she has weighed the pros and cons carefully.

Once again, Fielding triumphs in the way he builds a series of coincidences together. Mrs. Honour succeeds in getting herself thrown out of the house by picking up a quarrel with Lady Western's chambermaid. This is advantageous to Sophia as it fits with their plans to leave the house.

Chapter IX

After threatening to send Honour to Bridewell prison, Squire Western, who is also a Justice of Peace, merely dismisses her. Honour now has no qualms about running away with Sophia, and they pick a place to meet at midnight. Sophia consents to her father's wish for her to marry Blifil, and he rewards her with a generous bank bill. Sophia so enjoys making her father happy that she now has some doubts about leaving, but then Sophia's thoughts of Tom destroy all her filial obedience. The narrator hopes the reader is not disappointed with Sophia, but pleads that he cannot "vindicate the Character of our Heroine, by ascribing her Actions to supernatural Impulse."

Chapter X

Tom and his guide have lost their way. At the first village, Tom asks some men for directions. A Quaker by the name of Broad brim points out to Tom that he is on the wrong route and recommends a reputable public house to Tom, since it is dark and there have been robberies nearby. At this public house, the Landlord Robin tells Jones his history. He has nothing in the house because his wife and his wife's favourite daughter, who has just married, have taken everything. Broad brim tells Tom that his daughter ran away with a man, rejecting the prosperous marriage he arranged for her. Tom pushes Broad brim violently out of the room. Robin accuses Tom of being a bastard, and Tom is made to sleep in a chair. Robin cannot sleep, terrified that Tom will rob his bare house.

Chapter XI

During the night, a troop of soldiers arrives and demands beer from the landlord. Tom mingles with the men. Some soldiers leave the house without paying for their drinks and a dispute arises. Tom, who has been speaking to the Sergeant about becoming a volunteer in the army to confront the Jacobite rebels, offers to pay the bill. This wins Jones the appellations of "honourable, noble, and worthy Gentleman." Tom is attracted to the army by his love of liberty and the Protestant religion. He marches off with the Sergeant, who tells Tom made-up stories about his conquests. Tom is introduced to the Lieutenant, who marvels at Tom's "Air of Dignity."

Chapter XII

The Lieutenant, who is almost sixty years old, has not received many promotions despite his forty-year military career. It does as not help that his wife, whom his commander fancicd, refused to sacrifice her virtue for her husband's career. The Lieutenant is a "religious, honest, good-natured Man."

Commentary

Sophia may be simple but at the same time she can defend her own interests. She acts well while Mrs. Honour is being thrown out of their house. Inwardly, she is pleased as now Mrs. Honour can leave with her belongings and without raising any suspicions.

Sophia is soft hearted too. When her father is kind to her she repents having to hurt him. She even toys with the idea of sacrificing herself for her father's wishes. But, love overrules eventually and she decides that she must flee from her father's house.

Now, we meet Tom and accompany him on his adventures. Beginning in this book, there are a series of adventures that take place on the highway. Tom puts up in a public house. He is looked at suspiciously here. News of him being a foundling travels fast and the landlord suspects that Tom might not be able to pay his bills. So, he keeps a watch over Tom and does not even give him a room to stay in.

But, Tom's generosity of spirit wins him well wishers and friends every where. The Quaker pleads for Tom's cause to the landlord. Tom generously agrees to pay the bill of a group of arguing soldiers, who become his friends.

Tom is spontaneous and responds to situations emotionally. Being with the soldiers, he is enthused to join them in their 'glorious cause.' He decides to become a volunteer with them.

The group of soldiers and their commander is described. Fielding's novel is a minor epic in the way it includes a wide variety of other minor characters. The lieutenant of this group of soldiers is described as a good man.

One night, Tom and one of the soldiers get into an argument. Theirs is an ego clash and the soldier who fights with Tom is a petty man. Tom is even more angered when his love, Sophia is insulted. We see that women are often the cause for fights amongst men.

Northerton hits Tom's head with a bottle and the latter is injured badly. Our poor hero is not going through very good times. He is going through a bad phase. The lieutenant is kind to Tom, while he is convalescing in the public house.

Tom is such a self-respecting man that despite his injured condition, he hungers to get even with Ensign Northerton. He makes quite a ghastly spectacle with his sword in hand and the sentry guarding the Ensign is frightened. Tom finds that Northerton has already escaped. The sentry is held to blame for the escape, but in reality, the landlady had helped Northerton to get away.

Tom exhibits his humane spirit yet again. He calls the lieutenant and tells him that the sentry had not helped the Ensign to escape.

Most of the chapters here are devoted to Tom's adventures. The poor young man is now lying terribly wounded in a public house. We feel piteous towards him.

BOOK VIII

Chapter I

The narrator distinguishes his genre as that of the "Marvelous" but not "Incredible." Writers should confine themselves not only to possibility, but to probability, and should not invoke the aid of "supernatural Agents" as Homer unfortunately did. "Man" is the highest subject and writing should not be sullied by the inventions of "Elves and Fairies, and other such Mummery."

Chapter II

The landlady visits Tom Jones, thinking he is a gentleman, and asks him why a decent man like himself is spending time with army ruffians. She mentions that Sophia has "lain" in her house many a time. Enraptured, Tom tells her his story. He shakes out his purse to indicate the reason he has joined the army—he has no money. As soon as the landlady perceives this, she snubs Tom.

Chapter III

In fact, the landlady knows nothing of Sophia, and is only repeating what she overheard the Lieutenant saying. Tom injures his head in a fight with Broad brim, and a surgeon arrives to bleed his head. The landlady warns the surgeon that Tom has no money with which to pay him for his services, and the doctor leaves in a rage.

Chapter IV

Refreshed from sleep, Tom rises with an appetite. He manages to win back the landlady's affection with his sweet-natured temper. A barber by the name of little Benjamin comes to shave him. Warming to the barber's sense of humour, Tom invites him to share a drink with him. Freshly dressed and shaven, Tom wins the love of Nanny, the chambermaid, who is pretty and coy. In Tom's absence, however, the landlady tells the barber and company a contorted story about Tom's past. The barber says he has heard that Tom is the son of Allworthy. The landlady asks why Tom does not then go by his father's name.

Chapter V

The conversation of the previous chapter occurs while Tom eats his dinner. Eventually the barber arrives to drink with Tom, and tells Tom he has heard from many people about Tom's kind deeds to Black George. These deeds, says the barber, have made Tom "beloved by every body." Jones tells the Barber his "whole History." The narrator warns that a man's recounting of his own story differs greatly from his enemy's depiction of the same events. The barber desires to hear the name of Tom's beloved. Tom decides to tell him, since Sophia's name has already been made public.

Chapter VI

Little Benjamin reveals to Tom that he is in fact the very Partridge with whom Jenny Jones was reported to have had an affair. Partridge assures Tom, however, that he is not his father. He has nevertheless loved Tom Jones ever since he heard about his kind treatment of Black George. He asks Tom to make amends for the misfortune Tom's existence has caused him. Tom agrees to this, but admits that he can do nothing at present since he is penniless. Partridge says that, since he is presently wealthier, he will share everything he has with Tom. Satisfied with each other's company, Tom and Partridge set off for war together.

Chapter VII

Partridge is shocked to hear that Allworthy banished Tom, since he truly that Tom is Allworthy's own son. He secretly believes that Tom ran away from home, and begins to devise a plan to send Tom back to Allworthy so that he can, in turn, be restored to Allworthy's favor. Jones has bonded with the landlord, who is bed-ridden from gout, over horse-racing. This man spends much of his time fighting with his wife, who constantly invokes her first husband. Tom and Partridge leave for their expedition. The landlady does not condescend to say farewell.

Chapter VIII

Tom Jones and Partridge head for Gloucester and, on arriving there, decide to lodge at the Bell, which the narrator recommends to his readers. The landlord's wife, Mrs.

Whitefield, is beautiful and good-natured and generally free of silly notions. She notices "in the Air of our Heroes something which distinguished him from the Vulgar" and invites Jones to dine with her that night. At dinner, Jones meets Dowling, the attorney from Salisbury who conveyed the news of Mrs. Blifil's death, and a petty-fogger, a term for a lawyer willing to take any case. Displeased with the paltry conversation, Tom leaves the table as soon as the food has been cleared. After he has left, the petty-fogger proceeds to tell a distorted history of Tom's life. He claims that Tom is "the Bastard of a Fellow who was hanged for Horse-stealing." When the Petty-fogger says the man's name is "Thomas Jones," Dowling gets excited, saying he has heard about many good things about him. The landlady no longer likes Tom and refuses to drink tea with him. She is so rude to him that he pays his bill and leaves the house.

Commentary

The author is omniscient. He is also one who likes to discuss his art - that of writing. Fielding's masterpiece, 'Tom Jones' is rich because it is more than the history of a foundling. Fielding builds it in such a way that this novel adopts epic proportions. Not only are there many characters and events, Fielding often adds his own comments that add to the depth of this narration.

Once again, in the beginning of book 8, he writes about the supernatural element in any written work. The landlady had kept a distance from Tom so far. She finally visits him and goes on to say that she has met Sophia. Tom is told that Sophia had lain in the same bed, where he lay now. This makes Tom happy and fills his head with romantic thoughts. When he is filled with such sweet notions, his surgeon visits him. Tom is stubborn and does not want to be bled. The surgeon learns from the landlady that Tom is short of money.

This is true and in his anger with the surgeon, Tom does not pay him. Tom is definitely an impetuous and spontaneous young man. After sleeping for a long while, Tom feels much better and decides to get dressed. He calls for a barber. The barber knows Latin and gets along with Tom very well. The landlady in the meanwhile defames Tom in the kitchen. Tom was generally known as a bastard and now, after having been banished from Squire Allworthy's house, he is criticized even more. The barber too hears Tom's history in the gossip session at the inn.

Being of a friendly nature, Tom befriends the barber after taking a liking to him. He invites the barber for a drink after dinner. The barber is shrewd and he extracts Tom's entire history from him. We can see that the barber must be having a motive behind questioning Tom. We learn the barber's secret in the next chapter.

The next morning Tom is worried about the state of the wound on his head. So he talks to the drawer about it, the drawer suggests that the barber who had met Tom the previous day is an equally good surgeon. Tom is surprised but he calls him and discovers that he is indeed a skilled surgeon. He is indeed an extra ordinary man!

Now we learn the truth. This barber surgeon is in reality Partridge, the supposed father of Tom. But he tells Tom that he is not his father. He relates his unlucky past. He goes on to plead with Tom to allow him to travel with him. Tom displays his honesty once again when he tells him frankly that he has nothing to pay him. But, Partridge is convinced that Tom will be rich soon and in his predictions we see that he is right. Tom is too innocent to realise that Partridge is not accompanying him merely out of love.

Partridge is undertaking to go with Tom, with the hope that eventually he shall benefit a lot from Squire Allworthy. Partridge does not realise the depth of Squire Allworthy's anger at Tom. The two undertake to travel together. They make a Don Quixote and his squire sort of pair!

Soon they reach Gloucester and lodge at an inn. Mrs. Whitefield, the landlady is told many negative things about Tom and she consequently starts despising him. We see that

Tom becomes an unfortunate victim of malicious gossip. He doesn't even realise that he is being criticized by many. Tom is strangely innocent many times. But he has a great degree of self respect and when he sees that Mrs. Whitefield despises him, he decides to leave the inn as soon as possible.

Later, Sophia shall pass through the very same route as she follows Tom. At the moment though things don't seem to be going well for Tom and fortune is not by his side. The tragedy of Tom is that his fortune depended on him being adopted by Squire Allworthy. Now that Squire Allworthy's aegis is not with Tom, the latter finds himself defamed as well as friendless.

Chapter IX

Tom and Partridge depart from Gloucester early in the morning. It would be dark if it were not for the full, red moon. Tom launches into quotations about the moon, but Partridge complains of the cold. Partridge wishes to return to Gloucester, since they are unsure of their route. Tom wants to go forward and Partridge is forced to comply. As they walk, Tom wonders whether Sophia might be watching that same moon. Tom asks if Partridge was ever in love. Partridge says not only has he experienced the enjoyments of love, but the nastiness too, for his wife was very unkind to him. Partridge says he knows a way for Tom to be in Sophia's arms. Tom claims that at present his greatest desire is to effect "a glorious Death in the Service of my King and Country." Partridge suddenly realises that he and Tom are on opposing sides of the conflict—whereas Tom supports King George, he himself supports the Jacobite rebellion.

Chapter X

Tom and Partridge arrive at the base of a sheer hill. Through the trees on the hill, they see lights shining and approach to investigate. No one answers their knocking, but eventually an old woman appears at a window. Partridge promises her that Tom is a gentleman and she lets them in for half a crown. The woman, whom Partridge thinks is a witch, warns the men that her Master, the Man of the Hill, will be home soon and that he is a hermit who "keeps no Company with any Body." Suddenly there is hollering outside of the door and voices demanding money. Tom grabs a sword from the wall and scares some robbers away from the Man of the Hill, who was returning home. The Man of the Hill, at first suspicious, now calls Jones his "Deliverer" and "Preserver."

Chapter XI

The Man of the Hill begins his history. Born in the village of Mark-in- Somersetshire in 1657, he is the younger son of a "Gentleman Farmer" and his "arrant Vixen of a Wife." The Man of the Hill's older brother cares for nothing but hunting. The Man of the Hill, however, advances rapidly in his studies and attracts the attention of learned men in the neighbourhood. He is sent to Exeter College at Oxford where he meets a rich, debauched man called Sir George Gresham, who corrupts him. He becomes so rebellious that he is almost expelled by the vice chancellor. His father refuses to loan him more money, so he steals forty guineas from a friend. The Man of the Hill escapes punishment by running away with a lady to London, where he continues his wild lifestyle. This lady informs on him and soon he is thrown into jail, where he reflects on his behaviour. He is allowed to return to Oxford, where he finds that his friend has dropped the charges. Partridge interrupts, telling a story about a man who was hanged for stealing a horse and came back as a ghost to torment the plaintiff.

Chapter XII

The Man of the Hill continues his story. Now that he has ruined his reputation at Oxford, he returns to London. He has no money and no friends. One night he meets up with an old Oxford friend named Watson, with whom he eats and gambles.

Chapter XIII

The Man of the Hill now becomes part of Watson's gambling gang and lives a life of roller-coaster fortunes. One night, he assists a man who has been robbed and beaten in the street—it turns out to be his father, who came to London specifically to search for him. The Man of the Hill goes home with his father and immerses himself in Philosophy and the Scriptures. Four years later, his father dies and life becomes difficult as his older brother runs the household and often entertains "Sportsmen" in the house. On the advice of a doctor, he leaves home to drink Bath waters. There he saves a man who attempts suicide by throwing himself into a river. The Man of the Hill, on visiting this man, discovers that it is his old friend Watson.

Chapter XIV

The Man of the Hill gives Watson one hundred pounds on the condition that he use it to set himself up in an honest profession. He catches Watson gambling some of the money away, however. Watson and the Man of the Hill talk politics. The Man of the Hill is anti-Jacobite, and is worried about what the Protestant religion will suffer under a "popish Prince." Tom interrupts and informs the Man of the Hill that two rebellions aimed at putting the son of King James on the throne have taken place. The Man of the Hill returns to his story. He and Watson join the army, but Watson betrays the Man of the Hill to the Jacobite forces trying to restore King James to the throne. The Man of the Hill manages to escape, but resolves in the future to avoid all humans. He visits his brother, who gives him a stingy payment, then settles on his hill. He has, however, traveled to most places in Europe.

Chapter XV

The Man of the Hill gives a brief summary of the people of various nations. He says his main purpose in traveling was to see nature. He says that people are the one creation of God that "doth him any Dishonour." Jones argues for the diversity of humanity and expresses surprise that the Man of the Hill can fill up so many hours in solitude. He strongly opposes the Man of the Hill's hatred for humankind, arguing that he has generalized the behaviour of the worst men, when he should have generalized the behaviour of the best. Partridge has fallen asleep during this debate. The narrator invites the reader, like Partridge, to rest, since this is the end of the eighth book.

Commentary

We learn more about Partridge's nature and his conversation amuses us too. While Jones is romantic and philosophical here, Partridge is concerned about the basic necessities of life. He wants to satisfy his hunger and needs a shelter for himself.

The way Partridge proclaims of his basic wants is entertaining. Jones can only think of Sophia while Partridge tries to persuade him into going back to Gloucester. We can note a key difference between the two: while the younger Jones is romantic and impractical, Partridge is older, more practical and realistic. The contrast adds colour to the narrative and makes the duo's adventures more entertaining. Reading about Tom and Partridge, we are reminded of Don Quixote and his accompanying Squire.

Tom & Partridge travel on the highways too in the same manner as Don Quixote and his Squire had. Partridge's mind is presented to the reader. His motive in accompanying Tom is a selfish one. He wishes to win back the favor of Squire Allworthy. Partridge did not have the facts of Tom's banishment right.

Fielding is able to explain how coincidences develop for certain characters to take particular decisions. He is a master in the art of outlining the intricacies of human social behaviour. Fielding must have had an excellent psychological understanding of situations. Jones, on reaching, the bottom of a hill, wishes to climb up the summit. This response is characteristic of his nature as he is spontaneous and alive. His animal instincts dominate. Partridge is scared to climb a hill in the dark. On seeing a light, he urges Tom towards it. Partridge is desperate for some shelter, warmth and food. There is an old woman in the house. But, she is reluctant to let them in because she feels that her master would not like to find strangers in the house. Jones as we see is not only adventurous but also extremely curious.

On hearing the old woman housekeeper's tale about the 'Man of the Hill', Jones insists on satisfying his curiosity by seeing him in reality. Tom is forever alive and youthful. The old man is lucky that Tom had exhibited such curiosity. As Tom delays his departure he sees some bandits attacking the old man and is able to rescue him. If Tom had left the house when the old woman wanted him to, be would never have been able to rescue the 'Man of the Hill. We admire Tom's spirit that he does not hesitate even once, in going to the old man's aid. These are some of the several reasons because of which he is the 'hero' of the novel.

The old man is surprised that a human creature has helped him. His opinion of humans is not good and that is one of the reasons why he stays so far away from civilization. Fielding succeeds in maintaining the reader's interest by adding episodes such as these. The old man relates his history in epic style. While Tom listens very attentively, Partridge asks silly questions in between.

The old man's history spans four chapters and is told in detail. There seems to be a lesson to be learnt from this man's fortunes. He had been guilty of excess in youth and of being carried away. He has to experience many misfortunes before he finally tires of human civilization and retires to a forest.

Both Jones and the old man take to each other and are very pleased with each other's company. The old man realises that Tom too has been hurt by fate. Tom is frank enough to tell the old man that the latter is himself responsible for some of the unfortunate things that happened to him. Tom and the old man talk through the night while Partridge sleeps off.

In the character of the old man may be warning to Tom that he might land up like that if he is not careful. The next morning, the above two decide to take a walk, while our practical Partridge dozes off.

BOOK IX

Chapter I

These prefatory chapters have been inserted as a gauge for readers to sort out "what is true and genuine in this historic Kind of Writing, from what is false and counterfeit." The narrator sets himself apart as a "Historian." This brand of author requires genius, learning, conversation, and "a good Heart."

Chapter II

Tom and the Man of the Hill climb Hazard Hill at dawn. They hear a woman screaming and Tom slides down the hill to investigate. He finds a man forcing a woman, who is half naked, against a tree. Tom knocks the man out with his stick and beats him until the woman begs him to stop. On her knees, she thanks him profusely. He lifts her up, expressing joy that he was able to save her from the terrible situation. She likens him to an angel. Even though the woman is middle- aged and not possessed of a beautiful face, her voluptuous and very white breasts attract Tom's attention. The two spend a couple of moments staring at each other until the attacker on the ground begins to move. Tom now realises that this man is Northerton, a low-ranking soldier with whom Tom joined the army. Tom bids the Man of the Hill farewell and carries the woman to Upton. He offers the woman his coat but she refuses to accept it.

Chapter III

Tom Jones carries the woman into an inn, where he appeals for clothes from the landlady, who threatens him with her broom, telling him her house is a reputable place. Partridge arrives just in time to prevent Tom from being clobbered. Soon the naked woman and Susan, the landlady's Chambermaid, join the brawl, which is interrupted by the arrival of a lady and her maid. Susan has straddled Partridge, whom she is beating with all her might. The naked woman tells Tom she hopes to see him soon so as "to thank him a thousand Times more."

Chapter IV

A Sergeant and his musketeers arrive in the kitchen with hails for beer. Tom is comforting the naked lady, who has been covered by a pillowcase. One of the soldiers approaches her and asks if she is the lady of Captain Waters. She says that she is indeed that "unhappy Person." When the landlady hears that the woman is actually a gentlewoman, she apologizes profusely, using the title "your Ladyship" an inordinate number of times. After some haughty resistance, Mrs. Waters deigns to accept the landlady's offer of a gown. Partridge and Susan make peace, and the Sergeant urges that a toast be made.

Commentary

Fielding is a learned man with an excellent knowledge of psychology. He often practices and fine-tunes his learning in the first chapters of new Books. Once again, the first chapter of Book Nine is devoted to Fielding's own meditations and comments.

Tom had left for a walk with the old man of the Hill. He had scarcely begun to enjoy his walk when he was lunged into another new adventure. He hears screams of a woman and immediately goes to her rescue. Tom is consistently portrayed as a brave, gallant, large hearted young hero. He is never scared of jumping into the thick of fights or of saving someone from distress. In this case it is a middle-aged woman who has her clothes torn off her body by a vicious man. Tom deals with the man quickly and lays him onto the ground within minutes. Tom is a well-muscled hero! The aggressor turns out to be none other than Ensign Northerton. This is good fortune for Tom who had always wanted to take revenge on the Ensign for hitting him wrongly.

Tom ties up the Ensign's hands but not his legs. So despite being heroic, Tom is a trifle careless at times. When Tom goes to see the Old man of the Hill, the Ensign runs away. From the minute the rescued lady lays her eyes on Tom, she gets attracted to his handsomeness and vitality. There are certain things that she does that are questionable. When Tom offers her his coat so that she may cover herself, she refuses. Logically speaking she could have accepted the offered cover for her breasts but she does not. One of the reasons could be that she enjoyed the attraction that they offered to the potent Tom.

Tom, being the gallant he is leads her to an Upton Inn. His farewell to the old man of the Hill is not elaborated. Tom merely wants that Partridge be told where Tom has gone.

On reaching the Inn, Tom ensures that the lady is safety sent to a room. Her disheveled appearance and her ragged clothes immediately raise suspicions in the mind of the landlord and landlady. Both Tom and the rescued woman appear to be a couple, who have come to the public house in order to find a room to indulge in sensuous pleasures. This raises the anger of the keepers of this so-called respectable inn. The landlady insults Tom and a grand fight proceeds.

This big showdown is described in quaint comic terms by Fielding. The scene of the battle includes quite a few warriors - landlord, landlady and the chambermaid, Susan on one side, with Tom & Partridge on the other side.

A sergeant and a file of musketeers arrive at the Inn. The sergeant recognizes the distressed lady to be Mrs. Waters a Captain's wife. All this while we see that Mrs. Waters plays the role of the damsel in distress very well. We feel that she is all out to seduce young Tom and we see that we are right in the next chapter. The weakness in Tom is that his large heartedness and tender heartedness make him especially susceptible to the pointed, purposeful flirting of women. We question why he cannot exercise more restraint.

We learn in chapter four that a young woman and her maid arrive at the Inn. At this moment we do not pay much attention to this arrival but these guests are crucial to the narrative as we later learn

Chapter V

Heroes are more mortal than Divine. While Minds may aspire to the highest principles, everyone's bodies are subject to the same natural desires. In other words, everyone needs to eat. Tom is presently consuming three pounds of ox in the room of Mrs. Waters, who is preening herself for Tom. The narrator apologizes for being spare with descriptions of Tom's appearance and calls him "one of the handsomest young Fellows in the World." The narrator calls on a Muse of War to help him describe Mrs. Walters's attempted seduction of Tom, who cannot succumb until he has finished his food.

Chapter VI

While Mrs. Waters and Tom are engaged upstairs, the Sergeant entertains the rest of the company with the history of Mrs. Waters. She is the wife of Mr. Waters, a Captain of the Regiment. The Sergeant is not sure if they were lawfully married or not. At their last station, Mrs. Waters developed an intimacy with the ensign Northerton. The interest turns to Tom, whom Partridge declares to be the heir to the renowned Allworthy. The young lady staying in the inn wishes to depart, but her coachman is too drunk. The landlady joins Jones and Mrs. Waters upstairs for tea and praises the young lady's beauty. Tom sighs, inducing Mrs. Waters' to believe she has a rival. However, since she cares only for his body, she is not greatly concerned.

Chapter VII

The narrator imagines that the reader must possess some curiosity as to the relationship between Mrs. Waters and Northerton. Mrs. Waters has assumed Captain Walters's name after living for some time with him. She was indeed intimate with Northerton and, after Northerton was released from jail, the two began to plan an escape to Wales. On the morning they set out, Northerton decided to rob Mrs. Waters of her money and diamond ring. This is the incident from which Tom so heroically saved Mrs. Waters.

Commentary

Fielding is a learned man with an excellent knowledge of psychology. He often practices and fine-tunes his learning in the first chapters of new Books. Once again, the first chapter of Book Nine is devoted to Fielding's own meditations and comments.

Tom had left for a walk with the old man of the Hill. He had scarcely begun to enjoy his walk when he was lunged into another new adventure. He hears screams of a woman and immediately goes to her rescue. Tom is consistently portrayed as a brave, gallant, large hearted young hero. He is never scared of jumping into the thick of fights or of saving someone from distress. In this case it is a middle-aged woman who has her clothes torn off her body by a vicious man. Tom deals with the man quickly and lays him onto the ground within minutes. Tom is a well-muscled hero! The aggressor turns out to be none other than Ensign Northerton. This is good fortune for Tom who had always wanted to take revenge on the Ensign for hitting him wrongly.

Tom ties up the Ensign's hands but not his legs. So despite being heroic, Tom is a trifle careless at times. When Tom goes to see the Old man of the Hill, the Ensign runs away. From the minute the rescued lady lays her eyes on Tom, she gets attracted to his handsomeness and vitality. There are certain things that she does that are questionable. When Tom offers her his coat so that she may cover herself, she refuses. Logically speaking she could have accepted the offered cover for her breasts but she does not. One of the reasons could be that she enjoyed the attraction that they offered to the potent Tom.

Tom, being the gallant he is leads her to an Upton Inn. His farewell to the old man of the Hill is not elaborated. Tom merely wants that Partridge be told where Tom has gone.

On reaching the Inn, Tom ensures that the lady is safety sent to a room. Her disheveled appearance and her ragged clothes immediately raise suspicions in the mind of the landlord and landlady. Both Tom and the rescued woman appear to be a couple, who have come to the public house in order to find a room to indulge in sensuous pleasures. This raises the anger of the keepers of this so-called respectable inn. The landlady insults Tom and a grand fight proceeds.

This big showdown is described in quaint comic terms by Fielding. The scene of the battle includes quite a few warriors - landlord, landlady and the chambermaid, Susan on one side, with Tom & Partridge on the other side.

A sergeant and a file of musketeers arrive at the Inn. The sergeant recognizes the distressed lady to be Mrs. Waters a Captain's wife. All this while we see that Mrs. Waters play the role of the damsel in distress very well. We feel that she is all out to seduce young Tom and we see that we are right in the next chapter. The weakness in Tom is that his large heartedness and tender heartedness make him especially susceptible to the pointed, purposeful flirting of women. We question why he cannot exercise more restraint.

We learn in chapter four that a young woman and her maid arrive at the Inn. At this moment we do not pay much attention to this arrival but these guests are crucial to the narrative as we later learn.

BOOK X

Chapter I

The narrator likens critics to reptiles and tells the reader not to judge the work too soon. The reader should not mind if he finds characters too similar. It is natural for characters—like humans—to be akin in many aspects. In fact, there is more refinement in the critic who can distinguish between more closely aligned characters.

Chapter II

An Irish Gentleman, Mr. Fitzpatrick, arrives at the inn that night looking for his wife. The maid leads him to Mrs. Walters's room. Fitzpatrick breaks down the door and Tom leaps out of bed. The man apologizes for making a mistake, but then sees the room strewn with women's clothing and attacks Tom. Another Irishman, Mr. Mack Lachlan, who knows Fitzpatrick, runs in and points out that the woman is not Fitzpatrick's wife. The landlady arrives and Mrs. Waters accuses all three men of breaking in [illegible] room to violate and kill her. Fitzpatrick asks pardon for his mistake and leaves. Tom tells the landlady that he was trying to save Mrs. Waters.

Chapter III

A brief history of Mr. Fitzpatrick is given. He married for money and spent his wife's fortune, then treated her so badly that she ran away from him. A post-boy arrives at the inn with a young lady and her maid. The lady very politely asks if she may retire for a couple of hours. Her manners are magnificent, and she does not want any one to be disturbed. The landlady tells the maid Susan to light a fire in the Rose room. Once the lady and her maid leave, the company falls to praising the beauty of the lady's face, dress, and manners.

Chapter IV

Mrs. Abigail, the young lady's maid, demands a hearty feast. She does not act with the gentility of her mistress, but greedily occupies most of the space before the fire. She asks the landlady whether it is true that her house is filled with "People of great Quality." The landlady cites the young squire Allworthy as an example. Mrs. Abigail expresses great surprise, saying that she knows the squire Allworthy very well, and he has no sons. Partridge says the young man is not generally acknowledged to be the Squire's son, but that he is most certainly the Squire's heir, and that his name is Jones. Mrs. Abigail drops her bacon and hurries to tell her mistress.

Chapter V

The young lady eulogized in the previous chapter is Sophia Western herself, and the so-called Mrs. Abigail is Mrs. Honour. Honour scurries to tell Sophia that Tom is in the house. Sophia sends Honour to request Tom's presence, but Partridge, who is tired and drunk, tells Honour that Tom is in bed with a "wench." Sophia bribes the maid Susan to see whether Tom is in his own bed, and Susan discovers that he is not. She tells Sophia that Partridge has told everyone that

Sophia is madly in love with Tom, who is heading to fight in the wars to escape her. In tears, Sophia tells Honour it is now easy for her to leave. She can forgive Tom's behaviour with the wench, but not his misusing her name. Sophia leaves her muff with her name on a piece of paper pinned to it in Tom's bed as "some Punishment for his Faults."

Chapter VI

Partridge tells Tom he would rather not fight in the rebellion, but that if they must, Tom should at least let him steal horses so they do not have to walk. They argue and Partridge lets slip that the previous night he had to bar two women from getting to Tom. He points out that one of the ladies has left her muff on Tom's floor. Frantically, Tom demands to know where the women have left for and orders the horses. Mac Lachlan suggests that the lady who arrived the previous night might have been Fitzpatrick's wife, who he has yet to find. A gentleman enters the kitchen just as Fitzpatrick is returning.

Commentary

The author converses with his reader often. He is aware of his novel as a work of art that may be criticized by others. He does not wish for his story to be criticized unnecessarily. In the first chapter of Book Ten the author hits out at the entire exercise of futile criticism. Fielding satirizes social conventions quite often through his novel. He seems to be parodying social, artificial and futile conventions.

The Upton Inn is a scene of much drama. Late in the night, a frantic Irish gentleman arrives looking for his wife. Fielding builds up a series of coincidences and chance meetings at the Upton Inn. This Irish gentleman is Lord Fitzpatrick who has come in search of his wife. Susan, the chambermaid assumes that the 'searched for wife' is Mrs. Waters and leads Lord Fitzpatrick to her room. The Lord finds Tom Jones with a lady unknown to him. There is much chaos in the room. Mrs. Waters is a woman of the world who knows how to put on an act in order to protect her reputation. She starts screaming for help when several gentlemen arrive in her room. Fate introduces yet another Irish character in the narrative. This Mr. Mach Lachlan knows Mr. Fitzpatrick and points out that Mrs. Waters is definitely not Mrs. Fitzpatrick. When the landlady comes up to Mrs. Walters's room, Tom pretends to have entered the lady's room on hearing all the commotion.

In reality Tom had been in bed with Mrs. Waters. Our hero is quite a promiscuous young man, who is unable to refuse the pleasures of lovemaking. Tom too is ingenious enough to fabricate a lie in order to protect his own interests, as well as those of Lady Waters'.

When Susan and the landlady converse, Susan points out that Tom & Mrs. Waters had been in bed together. But the landlady refuses to listen to Susan. It is clear that the landlady is a worldly-wise woman. She respects all who are wealthy and now that she knows that both Tom & Mrs. Waters are from decent backgrounds, she defends them both. She would rather maintain a good relationship with Squire Allworthy's heir than spoil things by gossiping about him.

Fielding is indeed a good presenter of the strengths and weaknesses of humans. He has a wonderful understanding of 'human nature' and succeeds in presenting it in all its diverse forms.

Other events take place during this fateful night at the inn. Two young women arrive and the lady amongst the duo is charming and beautiful. The landlady leaves no stone unturned in looking after aristocratic looking guests. So the young lady in the riding habit is cared for well. It comes as a surprise to the reader that this young lady is none other than Sophia herself. The chambermaid Susan plays a key role here. It is she who tells Sophia about Tom deriding her even though this is not true. What is true however is that Tom had had a one-night stand with Mrs. Waters. One can empathize with Sophia's concern when she learns this. She is very angry and hurt.

If it hadn't been for Tom's affair with Mrs. Waters, things would have stood very differently. Tom would have met Sophia and they might have formulated joint plans together. But Fielding had to create exciting situations and he succeeds in holding the reader's interest. Sophia leaves the Inn but not without resorting to a characteristic lover's reaction. She leaves a well-recognized muff of her own on Tom's bed. We wait to see Tom's reaction on seeing his beloved's muff on his own bed.

Upton Inn and its events are placed in the centre of this history and thus it gains in relevance. The incidents in this inn have a far-reaching effect on the course of the novel. Most key characters visit this Inn. Fielding manages the various threads of the novel quite well.

Chapter VII

Squire Western has arrived in pursuit of his daughter. The kitchen is filled with confusion as Western asks for Sophia and Fitzpatrick searches for his wife, who is also Western's niece. Tom enters holding Sophia's muff. Western attacks Tom and Parson Supple, who has accompanied Western, points out that Tom has Sophia's muff. Western charges the house and bursts into Mrs. Walters's room. Fitzpatrick argues that the stolen muff represents a felony, and a "trial" ensues. Tom's witnesses are Susan and Partridge, and he is acquitted. Western departs to follow Sophia, as do Tom and Partridge.

Chapter VIII

The narrator retraces his steps to the morning after Sophia made her escape. A serving-man, sent to summon Sophia to meet Blifil, returns to say that Sophia cannot be found. Mrs. Western launches into a grand speech in which she blames her brother for Sophia's disappearance. She says that English women are not to be bullied in such a way.

Chapter IX

The night before these events, Sophia courageously escapes at midnight. She meets Mrs. Honour at their prearranged place of rendezvous, a town five miles away. Honour wishes to head straight for London, but Sophia, hearing from her guide that Tom journeyed to Bristol, pays the guide to take her there. In Ham brook, Sophia and Honour meet Mrs. Whitefield, who tells them how much Jones has spoken about Sophia. Honour wrathfully calls Tom a "saucy Fellow." Mrs. Whitefield advises Sophia not to chase any man, but the narrator says he can forgive her due to her tumultuous state of mind, which is torn between her duty to her father, her hatred of Blifil, and her love for Tom. En route to London, Sophia and Honour happen to rest at the Inn at Upton, where the uproar of Chapter V occurs. Western has been able to track down his daughter by following Tom's trail, which Partridge has made as public as possible by announcing Tom to everyone he meets.

Commentary

The situation reveals 'dramatic irony' used by Fielding—the readers know that Sophia has been at the Inn but Tom doesn't. Thus here the reader is one up on the protagonist! Tom returns to his own room after a night with Mrs. Waters. Partridge talks to Tom, urging him to a point of view that would be beneficial to him. Partridge does not want Tom to join the army because he has his own selfish motive. He would rather accompany Tom and have him reconciled to Squire Allworthy, so that his own fortune is made too.

Partridge is not a villain, but is quaintly a man of the world. He is bothered about his own well being and wouldn't mind lying to ensure it. Partridge is a man who adds much interest to Tom's travels on the highway. The narration would not have been as enjoyable without Partridge's presence.

Tom finds Sophia's muff and is quite shocked. He now regrets his short affair with Mrs. Waters. The lesson that Tom has to learn in this history is that he cannot afford to keep getting carried away by the attractions of flirtatious women.

The two Irish gentlemen too decide to leave the inn. Fielding builds such a setup that the characters arrive at the Inn together and leave together too.

Now there is another twist to the Upton events. Squire Western arrives there looking for his daughter. He argues with Tom on seeing him. Their previous friendship holds no value, as now they are on war footing.

Every individual is after his own interest. There are two characters who wish to restore their relationship with Squire Allworthy. They are - Partridge & Jenny Jones. The other two characters who want to be in the good books of Squire Western are Lord Fitzpatrick and Lady Fitzpatrick. All the four above-mentioned characters work in a manner that can ensure the completion of the goal. Thus Lord Fitzpatrick in this book endeavors to reconcile himself with Squire Western by condemning Tom and by trying to help him find his daughter. He assumes that the lady he had seen with Tom is the lost daughter and urges Squire Western to her room. The Squire bursts into Mrs. Waters' room only to find that she is not Sophia. The squire then goes down and confronts Tom again.

Fate had endeavored to bring a commission of peace to this same Inn. Lord Fitzpatrick continues to try and humour Squire Western. He announces that Tom could be legally tried for committing a robbery. Tom held Sophia's muff. Surprisingly, Susan comes to our hero's rescue and confesses that she had delivered the muff herself to Tom's room. Tom seems so good and handsome that women go out of their way to help him. Partridge of course supports his master and says that he was with Tom when the muff was found. Tom is thus acquitted.

Our misbehaving Tom hurries after Sophia now. He is a highly emotional man who makes promises and takes oaths at the spur of a moment. He now takes an oath that he will never let Sophia go again and that he will be faithful to her. We see later that he breaks this highly motivated oath.

In their hurry to look for Sophia, both her lover and father overlook the common niceties. Tom does not bid adieu to Mrs. Waters and Squire Western doesn't bother about Lord Fitzpatrick. Squire Western is a childish man who forgets everything and everybody else when he is involved with any burning issue.

The two Irish gentlemen leave the Inn along with Mrs. Waters. We are given to believe that Mrs. Waters might have begun yet another liaison with Lord Fitzpatrick.

The eight and ninth chapters take a peep back into the past. Inter penetration of past and present is a common feature throughout the novel. We read how Sophia's absence had caused tumult in the Western household and how she herself had managed to escape from her house. Sophia is desperately in love with Tom. When she learns about the route Tom had taken, she followed him to Upton. In this book, key characters reach Upton and a great drama takes place. The Upton events are wrapped up in the same Book and all the characters leave this little Inn.

BOOK XI

Chapter I

The word "critic" is Greek and denotes "Judgment." Most critics are slanderers since they only find fault with the books and authors they read. There have, however, been some fine critics—for instance, the ancient critics Aristotle and Horace, or the French critics Deicer and Boss. Critics need to have mercy, and not condemn an entire work if they only find fault with one part of it.

Chapter II

On the road to London, Sophia and Mrs. Honour meet up with another young lady and her maid on horseback. They exchange compliments and civilities. As daylight breaks, Sophia recognizes that the lady is her cousin Harriet, the wife of Fitzpatrick. They eventually arrive at an inn, where Sophia can barely muster the strength to dismount from her horse. The landlord attempts to help her, but they both fall over backwards, to the amusement of all on-lookers. This landlord convinces himself that Sophia and Harriet are "Rebel Ladies," and that Sophia is in fact Jenny Cameron, whom the Whigs allege is the lover of the Jacobite leader Bonnie Prince Charlie. The landlord does not support the Jacobites, but when he hears that the rebels are making headway in London, he decides to flatter Sophia and Harriet in the hopes that they will later reward him. The landlady cannot believe that Sophia is a gentlewoman since she is courteous to people of all classes.

Chapter III

Mrs. Fitzpatrick would be deemed beautiful if she were not with Sophia, who looks more radiant now than ever before. Harriet has agreed to accompany Sophia to London. The landlady has become a "staunch Jacobite" since Sophia, who she also believes to be Jenny Cameron, has treated her with such deference. Sophia and Harriet agree to relate their histories in turn.

Chapter IV

Mrs. Fitzpatrick reminisces about the days when she and Sophia lived at their Aunt Western's house. She was "Miss Giddy" while Sophia was "Miss Grave airs." She tells Sophia that she met her husband in Bath on a trip with their aunt. Her husband, although he had no title, was the envy of all the men because he was much admired by the ladies. He was one of the favourites of Mrs. Western, with whom he shamelessly flirted. He flirted with Harriet too, however, and eventually revealed that he was only feigning interest in her aunt in order to win Harriet's love. Flattered, Harriet agreed to marry him, much to the fury of Mrs. Western, who departed immediately from Bath. Harriet laments to Sophia that she based her opinion of Mr. Fitzpatrick on the opinions of others.

Chapter V

Mrs. Fitzpatrick continues her story. Mr. Fitzpatrick wanted to return to his native Ireland after the wedding, but she did not care to leave England. One day she discovered a letter lying on the floor, from which she learned that her husband had married her only for her money. When she confronted him, however, he mollified her by means of caresses and protestations of love. In Ireland, she grew more and more depressed, and her husband attempted to drag her down further with snide remarks. She became pregnant by him—the man she "scorned, hated, and detested."

Commentary

The author goes to great lengths to explain his point of view. He now explains why he disapproves of critical critics. The author is a learned man who is able to support his views with able examples and reasonable logic. What makes Fielding a great writer is his excellent understanding of human nature and his wide knowledge and in depth learning.

Sophia continues her travel along highways. A mysterious incident occurs. She is pursued by three horse riders who do not let go of their chase. They overtake her finally. The readers' curiosity and interest increases as to the identity of these mysterious followers. The lady turns out to be Harriet - a cousin of Sophia's. The two young ladies are very glad to see each other. In fact Harriet too had been at Upton Inn for some time. Mr. Fitzpatrick is her husband and on learning that he was looking for her, she manages to make her escape. Thus the Upton Inn threads continue in this book too.

The description of the two young ladies and their waiting women taking a nap is a quaint one. Fielding's sense of humour ranges from the subtle to the loud. His vivid range of writing helps him create epical scenarios.

The landlord of this Inn is shown to be an inquisitive man with great faith in his own worldly understanding. He cannot believe that Sophia is just another ordinary woman. He believes her to be the mistress of the rival general. He is sure that she is the beautiful Madam Jenny Cameron herself. Fielding brings in a little bit of history here by referring to the revolution and the war within England.

The two cousins are refreshed after their sleep. Both of them decide to share their experiences with each other. Mrs. Fitzpatrick relates her history here. This narration occupies the whole of the fourth and the fifth chapters. Sophia is completely engrossed in the tale and feels sad for the tragedies in Harriet's life.

Mrs. Fitzpatrick plays a crucial role in the narrative. It is she who later informs the elder Westerns where Sophia could be found. She is presented in contrast to Sophia. Both are pretty and young, but Sophia is much more scrupulous and principled compared to Harriet.

By including sub Themes and sub stories in this novel, Fielding succeeds in elevating the novel to an epical scale. All the varying views are ultimately joined to create an entertaining network of society and life.

Chapter VI

Distraught from her cousin's story, Sophia has lost her appetite. Harriet has not. The landlady interrupts their conversation to impart some "good News." Mrs. Honour suddenly bursts in, shouting "they are come, they are come!" Sophia thinks Honour means her father. She is secretly relieved to discover that it is the Jacobite rebels who have arrived.

Chapter VII

Mrs. Fitzpatrick concludes her story. In Ireland, she made friends with a lieutenant and his wife, of whom Mr. Fitzpatrick grew jealous since he did not share their intellect. Mrs. Fitzpatrick lived in utter solitude most of the time after her child died, and her husband frequently traveled to Dublin and London. One day, a lady relation of Mr. Fitzpatrick's informed Mrs. Fitzpatrick that her husband was having an affair. Mr. Fitzpatrick returned from London having lost all his money, and demanded that they sell one of her estates. She refused, and accused him of having a mistress. He locked her in her room, but she managed to escape and has been running away from him ever since.

Chapter VIII

Sophia tells Mrs. Fitzpatrick her story without saying a word about Tom. At the conclusion, they hear an awful screeching noise—Mrs. Honour has learned that the landlord believes Sophia to be Jenny Cameron and has begun to scratch him indignantly. The landlord now believes Sophia to be of even greater consequence than Jenny Cameron. He announces to Sophia and Mrs. Fitzpatrick that an Irishman has arrived to see them. This man happens to be the person who helped Harriet escape from Ireland. This friend denounces the institution of marriage and offers to take Sophia and Harriet to London in his coach.

Chapter IX

Having settled their bill at the Inn, Sophia and Harriet prepare to leave for London with Harriet's friend. Sophia discovers that she has lost the one hundred pounds her father gave her. The narrator praises Sophia's ability to present a cheerful face to others while she feels dismayed inside. Moreover, Sophia leaves a present for the landlord, over which he rejoices. After a journey of two days, Sophia and Harriet arrive in London.

Chapter X

Out of propriety, Harriet will not stay her friend's house since his wife is out of town. She and Sophia therefore find lodging for the night. The next morning, Sophia seeks out her relation since she is a little suspicious of Harriet's behaviour. Sophia suspects that Harriet seeks a man to rescue her from her dire situation. Sophia tracks down her relation Lady Bellaston, since "there was not a Chairman in Town to whom her House was not perfectly well known."

Commentary

We see that Sophia has a tender heart for all around her. She is very upset for Lady Fitzpatrick because of the latter's misfortune in marriage. Sophia's sensitivity is questionable sometimes. She comes across as being too sissy. So, while Mrs. Fitzpatrick eats heartily, Sophia is too preoccupied to eat well.

Now a conversation takes place in which both the parties misunderstand each other. Sophia thinks that the landlord has guessed who she is whereas he believes that she is Jenny

Cameron. Judging her scared look the landlord believes that Sophia is guilty and that she has guessed that he knows the truth. In reality both are conversing in two completely divergent strains.

Mrs. Honour's entry into Sophia's room is described very dramatically. Fielding has a flair for melodrama. Mrs. Honour is exaggerated in her reactions and is furious at the fact of Sophia being insulted. She learns that the landlord believed Sophia to be Jenny Cameron. Mrs. Honour is loyal to Sophia and we see that she respects her mistress a great deal.

An analogy is made between Mrs. Honour's anger and Nell Gwen's footman's furiousness at his mistress being insulted. Fielding often resorts to comparisons to enrich his writing. He has all the arts under his command, which make his writing attractive. Mrs Honour's extreme reaction is truly funny.

Mrs. Fitzpatrick concludes her history. Sophia herself is very discreet in her own narration. She does not mention Tom's name at all while stating the reasons of her departure from her home. She is the diametric opposite of Tom. While he is open and indiscreet, she is guarded and secretive.

Sometimes Tom's spontaneity is much more attractive than Sophia's priggishness. Another minor character is introduced. He is a noble Irishman who knows Harriet (Mrs. Fitzpatrick). He comes up to meet Sophia and Harriet as he happened to be in the same inn. We suddenly have a host of Irish characters in the novel.

The ladies journey to England with this lord. Before leaving, the generous Sophia gives a large tip to the landlord. She is indeed a large hearted young lady. The group reaches London. The equation has changed somewhat by now. Harriet and Sophia are not too eager to remain in each other's company. Sophia suspects that Harriet is having an affair with the Irishman. Sophia is prudish and does not hesitate in ticking Harriet off for being wanton. Harriet is equally self-willed and independent and reiterates that she can look after herself well.

Thus, Sophia and Harriet go their separate ways. Harriet stays in a London lodge whereas Sophia goes on to join Lady Bellaston.

Sophia's reaching England is a major step. Now the rest of the drama will unfold in London. Sophia had pursued Tom for a part of the journey. Now Tom shall pursue Sophia and will follow her to London.

We are not told much about the lady, who Sophia puts up with. We learn about her later and see how she is not much of a protector to Sophia. Infect, she becomes jealous of this young lady because she herself falls in love with Tom.

BOOK XII

Chapter I

The narrator has made quotations without citing books or their authors throughout this history. He believes that the "Ancients" to the "Moderns" are as the rich to the poor.

Chapter II

Squire Western, tracking Sophia on the Worcester Road, bursts into a volley of oaths and curses the fact that hunting for his daughter is preventing him from hunting on this fine morning. At this moment, to Western and Parson Supply's great surprise, a pack of hounds races by. Western leaps into action and joins the hunt. However, since nature always conquers reason in every character, we should not "arraign the Squire of any Want of Love for his Daughter." The master of the hunt, impressed with Western's skills, invites him to dinner. Western wishes to hunt the following day, but his host and Supple discourage him from it.

Chapter III

Finally, the narrator returns to the story of Tom Jones and Partridge. After departing from the Inn at Upton, Partridge wants to go home. But Jones laments that he has no home and wishes only to join the army. Partridge argues that perhaps the Man of the Hill was a spirit who was sent to warn them against entering the military. He peppers his speech with non-sequitur Latin quotations, which Tom brings to his attention. Although Partridge preaches that no Christian should kill another man, he is terrified of losing an arm or leg, or even his life, in battle.

Chapter IV

At a crossway, Partridge shoos away a beggar, but Tom hands the man a shilling, chastising Partridge for his hypocrisy. The beggar gives Tom something that he has picked up—to Tom's elation, it is Sophia's pocket-book, which was a present from Mrs. Western. Unfortunately, the beggar cannot read, or he might have realised that inside the pocket-book lies one hundred pounds that Western entrusted to his daughter. Tom gives the beggar a guinea for his honesty, and the man leads them to the place where he found the pocket-book. He then demands more money, but Tom insists that the money must be given to its rightful owner. He writes down the man's name and address so that he can compensate him in the future.

Chapter V

Tom and Partridge hear the noise of a drum, and Partridge fears that the rebels are advancing. Partridge is eager to see a puppet show they pass by, "The Provoked Husband." The show fetches high acclaim from the spectators and from the puppet-master himself, who praises his show for its ability to "improve the Morals of young People." A clerk agrees that everything base should be excluded from theaters. Tom offends the puppet-master by saying that he would rather have watched the merry pranks of Punch and Joan.

Chapter VI

The landlady is in a frenzy after finding her maid, Grace, backstage with the puppeteer who played Merry Andrew. She reminisces about the old days when puppet shows staged Bible stories, silencing the puppeteer's boasts. Tom is prevailed upon by Partridge, the puppet-master, and the landlady to sleep at the inn before continuing his journey—he has hardly slept since the "Accident of the broken Head" at Bristol. Partridge prefers eating to sleeping or drinking. The uproar caused by Grace has passed and calm has been restored among hosts and guests.

Chapter VII

Although Partridge's pride prevents him answering to the title of "servant," his constant bragging about Tom's superior status leads people to believe that Tom is his master. Indeed, Partridge greatly embellishes Tom's fortune, convinced that Tom is Allworthy's heir. Now Partridge tells the company at the inn that he thinks Tom has gone mad. Some say that Tom should not be allowed to roam the countryside in such a state, as he might cause trouble. Partridge perks up at this idea—he is still keen to induce Tom to return to Allworthy. The landlady cautions that no one should treat Tom with violence, admiring Tom's pretty eyes and modesty in the process. The rest of the company debates how they can prove Tom's insanity to a jury. The landlord enters the kitchen and announces that the rebels are almost in London. The conversation now turns to the rebellion and whether a right descends to a son if a father dies. The landlord fears that the rebel leader Bonnie Prince Charlie will try to convert everyone into Catholics.

Commentary

As usual the first chapter of a new book begins with the author's comments. The author is quite self-conscious of his own work. He confesses that he might have borrowed some material from others. He rationalizes this confession. He believes that any author's work is distinctive and in that sense the work is restorable to the original owner whenever perceived.

We are now back with Squire Western as he searches for his daughter. He is a man who is naturally accompanied by harshness and bustling. He travels down the highway with many hounds and a desperate looking priest. There is an amazing incident here. While the Parson thinks that the Squire is sad about the loss of his daughter, in reality that is not so. The Squire is more concerned about the fact that he is missing out on excellent weather for hunting. The Squire adores his daughter but can still get distracted from her pursuit by the thought of a challenging hunt. Squire Western joins another Squire in a hunt and forgets all about his daughter. It is interesting to know that a genteel person like Sophia has a loud and dominating father.

Tom's animal instincts dominate his reactions when he is desperate, he gives into a startling fit, he nearly beats up Partridge and is melodramatic for quite some time. In that sense Tom has yet to grow up into a calm headed man. He is still boyish in his reactions. On the other hand his love Sophia is mature and responsible to an irritating length. Tom and Partridge have very entertaining conversations while they travel like the one they have now. The next incident contrasts the characters of Tom and Partridge. While Partridge keeps quoting the Bible, he does not really follow its precepts. He does not want to help the beggar, who approaches them. Tom teases Partridge and then gives some money to the beggar. Tom's goodness comes back to him in typical karmic fashion. The happy beggar gives Tom a pocket book that he had found on the road. This book belongs to none other than Sophia herself. Tom starts kissing the book with gusto and behaves in characteristic romantic style. Sometimes, when a 21st century reader reads about Toms and Sophia's reactions, they are skeptical about such romantic actions and exaggerations.

Tom also finds some money inside the pocket book, we had read in an earlier book that Sophia had lost this money on the highway.

Tom and Partridge now arrive at an inn where there is a puppet show, we see that Tom is an open man who does not hesitate in speaking his mind. He clearly tells the puppet master what he had enjoyed in the show, even thought the rest of the company thinks that Tom's likes are vulgar.

Fielding seems to be a very open author where sexual relations are concerned not only do many affairs occur in the narrative, Fielding creates a believable, promiscuous hero i.e., Tom. Tom might love Sophia but he does naturally get attracted to a lot of other women. These women are usually elder to Tom, more sexually aggressive and always succeed in seducing the hero.

Partridge does Tom much good by praising Tom's fortune. But the others at the Inn think that Tom is quite mad. Tom is fired and looks a little crazy. He is also very stubborn and as we said before, extremely frank. His frankness is often misunderstood by those around him. Partridge's behaviour at the Inn is questionable. He seems to agree with the others that his master is a lunatic. But Fielding does not develop this strain. He puts an end to it by writing that the inmates of the Inn give up the idea of trying to catch hold of Tom.

Chapter VIII

Jones rescues the Merry Andrew puppeteer from the puppet-master, who is beating him for his misconduct with Grace. Merry Andrew accuses the puppet-master of wanting to violate "one of the prettiest Ladies that was ever seen in the World." Tom perks up at these words and has a private conference with Merry Andrew, who tells him that he saw Sophia ride through the town the day before. Tom and Partridge set out along the route Merry Andrew points out, but a violent rainstorm rises and they have to take shelter in an inn. Here they find the boy who acted as Sophia's guide. Tom does not mention Sophia's name in public—it is Partridge who has been bandying about stories of her.

Chapter IX

Tom manages to get the boy to take them to London by horse. Jones insists on sitting in the side-saddle—usually reserved for ladies—since this is where his beloved Sophia sat. Partridge is delighted that Tom's thoughts are no longer tending towards the rebellion. At three in the morning, Tom is trying to convince the boy to take them to Coventry, when they are interrupted by Dowling, the lawyer from Salisbury with whom Tom dined in Gloucester. Dowling urges Tom to halt for the night, but he will not, even if it means traveling on foot. Tom accepts Dowling's invitation to share a bottle of wine.

Chapter X

Dowling drinks to Allworthy and Blifil. Tom warns him not to confound the names of the best and worst of men, shocking Dowling. Dowling in fact has never met Allworthy, but has only heard reports of his goodness. His opinion of Blifil is based on the boy's "pretty behaviour on the news of his mother's death." Tom explains that recently he has realised that Blifil has the "basest and Blackest Designs." He does not elaborate on the details of these designs, however. The narrator reminds the reader that even Tom Jones does not realise how dark these designs in fact are. Tom admits that he is not a relation of Allworthy. Dowling wishes to hear Tom's history. Dowling has much empathy for Tom in spite of his being a lawyer. Tom avows that he has no interest in Allworthy's fortune—he prefers the enjoyments of benevolent thoughts and acts to material goods.

Chapter XI

Tom, Partridge, and the guide boy lose their way. Partridge, who has a wild imagination, is terrified. He thinks a witch has cast a spell on them. When the guide boy and his horse fall over, Partridge's believes his fears are confirmed. Jones helps the guide boy recover while Partridge gripes.

Chapter XII

Tom and Partridge spot a light and, as they approach, notice music and lanterns. Partridge's superstition leads him to think it must be a witches' den. It is in fact an Egyptian gypsy wedding in a barn. The King of the Gypsies welcomes Tom, who has such an "open Countenance and courteous Behaviour" that he makes an astounding first impression on everyone that he meets. Partridge has now relaxed and has been decoyed by a young female gypsy pretending to tell his fortune. The gypsy's husband catches them, and a trial ensues. The husband demands two guineas from Partridge, but the king chastises him for putting a price on the virtue of his wife. The king sentences the man to wear horns and his wife to be called a "whore." The narrator expresses his support for the institution of monarchy.

Chapter XIII

The narrator chides himself for his didactic digression in the previous chapter. Tom Jones and Partridge travel from Coventry to St. Albans, which Sophia left two hours earlier. Partridge wants to borrow some of Sophia's one hundred pounds—he says that Fortune must have sent it for their use. Jones calls this dishonest. Partridge, garbling some Greek into his speech, says that Tom will understand life better when he grows older. They have offended each other, but Partridge apologizes and Tom forgives him.

Chapter XIV

A stranger asks to join Jones and Partridge to London. They speak about the dangers of robbery. Partridge alludes to the hundred pounds in Jones's pocket. Near High gate, the stranger suddenly whips out a pistol and demands the money from Jones. Jones grabs the pistol and restrains the man, who calls for mercy—he says that the gun is not loaded and that this is his first robbery. Partridge, terrified, is still yelling. The man tells Jones that he has five children and a pregnant wife and does not have money to feed them. Jones gives the man a couple of guineas. Partridge says that Jones should have punished the man—stealing deserves death by hanging. Jones reminds him that not long ago Partridge stole some horses.

Commentary

Jones plays the gallant once again. When he sees the puppet master beating up the Merry Andrew, he comes to the latter's rescue. He manages to separate Merry Andrews and the violent puppet Master. We notice that throughout the novel, Jones wins many friends by his generosity. Merry Andrews now agrees to take Tom to the place where he had seen Sophia. Jones is very happy to hear about Sophia. He behaves like a mad lover who rejoices on hearing news of his beloved. He is further enthused to follow Sophia's trial. He does not care about the storm that is developing outside.

The author often follows the habit of commenting on previous developments, later in the narrative for instance, he tells us that Tom is not at fault for defaming Sophia. It had been Partridge all this while, who had been talking about Sophia openly, though initially Fielding had let us believe that it was Tom who had been defaming Sophia. She had become the source of gossip in all the Inns that Tom and Partridge stayed in. We can see that the author is quite fond of his hero and defends him on more than one occasion. Tom might be careless and might even get carried way with women but he is essentially a man of honour, who would never defame his beloved.

Dowling, the lawyer makes an appearance once again. Dowling is famous for his busy schedule. He travels much and thus meets Tom often at various Inns. Dowling tells Tom that Blifil is now the heir of Squire Allworthy's estate. By now Tom does not have a good opinion of Blifil. He knows him to be devious and openly says so. Tom is an emotional man. He does not take long to open up his heart to strangers. He tells Dowling about his birth. Tom is the kind of man who impresses others with his large heartedness. Good people always stick to him. This is the kind of personality that impresses people who love benevolence. Dowling is completely on Jones' side by the end of their conversation.

The author often comments on the different professions and the variety of women. He makes reference to the profession of law and goes on to say that not all lawyers are unscrupulous.

Tom seems determined for a change. Even though he is requested to stop at many inns, he does not. He persists in his pursuit of Sophia. The problem with Tom is that he is sometimes too careless about the sensitivity of the sensible Sophia.

Partridge is portrayed as a superstitious old monk, he had been frightened of an old man of the hill in a previous book. In this book, he is terrified of strong lights and loud noises that he perceives at a distance. Tom laughs at Partridge's fears.

Fielding inserts an interesting bit about the gypsy way of life. Fielding must have had an excellent knowledge of different kinds of people. The amazing thing about this is that he can write about society aristocrats, lowly maids and even gypsies in the same breath.

Fielding is supportive of the gypsies' sense of justice. Partridge gets away with his little fling with a female gypsy. The fact that Tom sympathizes with the King's sense of justice shows that he himself is a fair-minded person. Tom's nobility is made to shine through at all times. At St. Alban's, Partridge and Tom stop to get some food and rest. Tom is more or less peaceful, but Partridge has a way of infuriating him, Partridge nags Tom often. Thus Toms looses his temper with the old man. These little starts serve to make the Tom-Partridge relationship interesting. The two can be compared with Don Quixote and his squire. Fielding himself makes a reference to Cervantes' famous pair.

In the last chapter of this Book we get a glimpse of Tom's large heartedness once again. A highwayman threatens Tom and Partridge. Tom is quick enough to overpower the robber. He does this while Partridge behaves in an extremely cowardly manner. Partridge tries to run away, whereas Tom defends himself; the robber pleads for mercy, saying that his pistol had been empty. Tom finds that this is true and he believes the highway man, when he says he was desperate enough to commit a robbery. Not only does Tom let the man go he also gives him some money. Later in the novel, Tom meets this very same man in London and finds out the he had indeed told the truth. Tom succeeds in creating a well wisher yet again. It is the charm and his large heart that finally enables him to win Sophia.

BOOK XIII

Chapter I

The narrator creates his own Muse of the "Love of Fame." He has been tempted by Fortune and Money to write this novel, which he hopes will achieve fame for posterity. He implores the assistance of genius, humanity, learning, and experience.

Chapter II

Jones and Partridge have never been to London before. They search for the house of the Irishman who brought Sophia to London. He has returned to Ireland. The following day Tom searches for Sophia, but he is turned away from the Irishman's door by the porter. Tom bribes the porter to lead him to Mrs. Fitzpatrick's doorstep. He arrives ten minutes after Sophia has left. Tom strikes the waiting woman with his civility and comeliness. She agrees to approach Mrs. Fitzpatrick with Tom's request to see Sophia. Mrs. Fitzpatrick, who suspects that Tom is one of Squire Western's party, sends a reply that Sophia has left. Jones believes that Sophia is there but is still offended over the Upton affair. That night, after Tom has kept vigil near the door all day, Mrs. Fitzpatrick deigns to meet with him. She thinks that he is Blifil. Her maid Abigail believes that the visitor is Jones, since Mrs. Honour has been "more communicative" than Sophia. Mrs. Fitzpatrick agrees with Abigail.

Chapter III

Mrs. Fitzpatrick plots to return Sophia to her father, in order to reinstate herself in the favor of Mrs. Western and Squire Western. Mrs. Fitzpatrick is also distantly related to Lady Bellaston, whom she for help in dissuading Sophia from pursuing Tom. Lady Bellaston receives her with a smile and asks if Tom is as handsome as she has been told by her dressing lady, Setoff. Mrs. Fitzpatrick says that he is, so that Lady Bellaston begins to think of him as "a kind of Miracle in Nature." She desires to see Tom.

Chapter IV

Tom, having watched Mrs. Fitzpatrick's door all day, meets her an hour early. Lady Bellaston swoops in, curtseying to Tom. The women show Tom some attention until Mrs. Fitzpatrick's Irish friend arrives. The conversation now becomes too dainty for the narrator to describe to vulgar ears. Jones retires after entrusting Mrs. Fitzpatrick with his address. Lady Bellaston declares that Sophia can be in "no danger" from such a fellow.

Chapter V

Tom knocks at Mrs. Fitzpatrick's door five times the following day, but every time the maid says that she is not at home. Tom and Partridge lodge themselves at a house in Bond street. A young man is residing on the first floor. He is one of those privileged "Men of Wit and Pleasure" who spend their days and nights in coffee-shops. That night, Jones hears an uproar downstairs. He runs downstairs and saves a young man, who is being beaten by his footman. A young woman stands nearby, wringing her hands. This woman is in fact Nancy, the boarding-house landlady's daughter, and the young man is Nightingale, who lives on the first floor. Nightingale asks Tom to drink with him, and Nancy joins the men. Nightingale explains that his footman referred to a young lady in a manner that enraged him.

Nancy's mother and sister return from a play. Although Tom is feeling despondent, he puts forward a gracious and entertaining front. Nightingale, Nancy, and Nancy's mother are delighted with Tom and invite him to breakfast. He is similarly pleased with them—Nancy is a pretty girl, as is her mother, who is almost fifty. Jones admires Nightingale for his "Generosity and Humanity" in spite of his foppishness. The man professes complete disinterestedness in affairs of love.

Chapter VI

Partridge tells Jones that Mrs. Fitzpatrick has left her house, and that he does not know where she has gone. Jones cannot conceal his disappointment at breakfast, where the conversation revolves around love. A maid arrives with a parcel for Tom—it holds a domino mask and a masquerade ticket. Nightingale declares that Tom has a female admirer. Nancy and her mother, Mrs. Miller, now agree with Nightingale, but Tom secretly thinks that Mrs. Fitzpatrick must have sent the billet since she is the only woman who knows his address. Nightingale offers to accompany Jones to the ball. He invites Nancy and Mrs. Miller to join them, but Mrs. Miller says such an event is too extravagant for women who have to earn their living. Nightingale, who likes Tom's company, invites him to dinner in a tavern—Tom, not wanting to admit he has no money, says that his dining clothes have not yet arrived. Tom is ravenous and Partridge urges him to use Sophia's bank bill. Tom absolutely refuses. Partridge cries and begs Tom to take him home to Somersetshire. Tom tells Partridge that Allworthy never wants to speak to him again.

Commentary

Fielding was definitely influenced by the classical strain. In the first chapter he invokes various muses in order to help him write. Fielding manages to personalize his writing by referring to it often. He does this mostly in the first chapters of new books, like he does in Book thirteen.

Partridge and Jones finally reach London in pursuit of Sophia, Tom must have loved her a great deal to be able to follow her so judiciously. He reaches the Lordships house. This is the same Lordship who had accompanied Sophia and Mrs. Fitzpatrick to London. But, Tom finds out that the ladies are not in this house. He now goes searching for Sophia all over London. He manages to reach Mrs. Fitzpatrick's house. There is a misunderstanding here. Mrs. Fitzpatrick thinks that Squire Western, Sophia's father, has sent Tom. She therefore does not entertain his request for a meeting. Jones suspects that Sophia is within the house and doesn't want to meet him. Jones is truly desperate to see his beloved. The pragmatic reader might think that Tom deserves to suffer now, after having been disloyal to Sophia at Upton Inn.

Tom is very patient and keeps standing outside Mrs. Fitzpatrick's house. He is finally granted a meeting with the lady but she refuses to divulge Sophia's whereabouts as she thinks he is the odious Blifil. Till now Mrs. Fitzpatrick thinks that she has been acting for the well being of Sophia. It is only after Tom leaves that Mrs. Fitzpatrick realises that it was Tom and not Blifil. So far she had not known about Tom and Sophia's love. She learns of this from her waiting woman. She is adequately surprised at her cousin Sophia's secrecy.

In the Third chapter Mrs. Fitzpatrick meets Lady Bellaston. Her purpose is entirely selfish. As we have mentioned before, both Lord Fitzpatrick and his wife wish to reconcile themselves to Squire Western and Lady Western. Mrs. Fitzpatrick hopes to achieve this end by informing the elder Westerns about Sophia's whereabouts. Fielding has an excellent understanding of human nature and knows that most of the actions of humans are driven by selfish motives.

There are only a few characters in the novel who act unselfishly, among them are Tom, Mrs. Miller and to some extent Squire Allworthy. Sophia might be generous and charming but she is no less concerned about her own affairs.

When Lady Fitzpatrick goes to meet Lady Bellaston, we see that the latter is very curious about the personality of Tom. Tom's fame has already spread wide and far. People in London too have heard of his rakish reputation. Lady Bellaston is a middle-aged woman who is greatly attracted to young men. We can make out that Lady Bellaston is expressing a more than a normal curiosity regarding Tom. On learning that Tom is charming and handsome, she expresses a wish to see him. She is smart enough not to reveal her true intentions to Mrs. Fitzpatrick. She tells Mrs. Fitzpatrick that she wants to see Tom only because she can then recognize him and keep him away from innocent Sophia.

Tom visits Mrs. Fitzpatrick's house and it is here that Lady Bellaston sees him for the first time. Apart from the above three people, another Lady and yet another gentlemen are present. Fielding had promised to show us various kinds of human nature and he succeeds. In the first half of the novel, he had shown us the country way of life. Now, he represents the hypocrisy of society in cities. Tom is a stranger to the conversation that takes place in Mrs. Fitzpatrick's house.

Jones finds a lodge for himself in London. It belongs to a lady who is known to Squire Allworthy. Tom is once again the rescuer when he delivers a young gentleman from the blows of a servant. Tom thus makes one more friend and his name is Nightingale. Jones impresses Mrs. Miller - the lodge landlady, and her two young daughters. Tom is consistently portrayed as a likeable protagonist.

The next morning, Tom receives a mysterious package that includes an invitation to a masquerade. Fielding succeeds in adding intrigue and mystery at occasion. The reader too is curious as to who could have sent the invitation. We later learn that it is from none other than Lady Bellaston.

Chapter VII

Nightingale immediately walks off with a woman at the masquerade, and encourages Tom to do the same. Tom searches the place for Sophia, but neither sees nor hears a sign of her. A Lady in a Domino mask suddenly slaps him on his shoulder and leads him to a separate room. She tells him he should end the affair with Sophia. Tom maintains that his love is a selfless one—he wants only the best for Sophia. This adds to the Domino lady's affection for him. Jones's gallantry emerges as he realises that he needs to win this woman's favor in order to get to Sophia. An old lady interrupts their conversation and begins to follow them around the room. Nightingale saves Tom by deflecting her. Jones offers to chaperone the Domino lady home. She says that she has to visit a friend, and that she hopes he will not follow her—which puts that very idea in his head. He follows the lady into a house and, since her friend is nowhere to be seen, she asks Jones what people would think of the two of them being alone in a house at that time of the night. Then she unmasks herself—it is Lady Bellaston. She will contrive an interview with Sophia for him if he promises then to quit all thoughts of her.

Chapter VIII

Jones sends Partridge to change a fifty-pound note that he received from Lady Bellaston. Jones and Nightingale wait for Mrs. Miller to return for dinner. She arrives two hours late. She says that she has been to visit her cousin, who is giving birth in a cold house with no fire. Mrs. Miller warns her daughters not to marry into such poverty. Tom takes Mrs. Miller aside and, with tears in his eyes, wants to give her the fifty pounds he received from Lady Bellaston. Mrs. Miller compares him to Mr. Allworthy and takes ten guineas from him for the family. At the table, Nightingale offers to give the family a guinea. Nancy turns pale. The narrator remarks that some people regard charity as voluntary, and some regard it as a duty.

Chapter IX

Jones meets with Lady Bellaston many times, but she does not fulfill her promise of fixing an interview with Sophia for him. Indeed, she begins to balk whenever Sophia is even mentioned. Jones sends Partridge to try to discover Sophia's whereabouts from the servants. Jones still worries about how to deal with Squire Western, who will disinherit Sophia if she marries against his will. Lady Bellaston has set Tom up in a "State of Affluence." He feels burdened by his obligations to her for her financial support. One night he receives a letter from her saying that they cannot meet at their usual place. Then a second epistle arrives, telling Tom to meet her at her home at seven o'clock that night. The lady owner of the house in Hanover Place has refused to provide cover for Lady Bellaston and her male friends any longer. Lady Bellaston decides to send Sophia to the play to get her out of the way for her rendezvous with Tom.

Chapter X

Jones has just dressed to visit Lady Bellaston when Mrs. Miller invites him to take tea with her cousin, Mr. Anderson. Jones and the man recognize each other instantly—it is the man who tried to rob Jones on the highway. The man thanks Jones profusely for saving his family, calling him an "Angel from Heaven." Mrs. Miller says that Jones will meet a great reward one day for his generosity. Jones says that witnessing the man's happiness has been the greatest reward. Mr. Anderson almost tells Mrs. Miller about the robbery, but then decides against it.

Chapter XI

Tom arrives early at Lady Ballston's house and waits in the drawing room. She has been held up on the other side of town. Sophia leaves the play after the first act and returns to the house. Unaware that anyone else is in the drawing room, Sophia walks up to a mirror and contemplates her face. Then she notices Jones, who has frozen in a corner.

After a couple of mutual exclamations of surprise, Sophia asks Tom if he has any business at Lady Ballston's house. Tom says he has brought her pocketbook for her. On his knees, he begs pardon from her for his misbehaviour in Upton with Mrs. Waters. Sophia says she does not mind this as much as the fact that he has bandied her name about the countryside. He clears himself of this accusation by informing her that it was Partridge who misused her name. Tom mumbles a marriage proposal, but Sophia says that she cannot disobey her father. Jones thumps his breast and says that he will never ruin her. Sophia starts crying into Jones's bosom, and he kisses away her tears.

Sophia asks him how he came to be in Lady Ballston's drawing room, at which point Lady Bellaston herself enters the room. Realizing that Tom has not admitted to Sophia that he knows her, Lady Bellaston pretends not to know Tom. Sophia pretends that Tom is simply some man who has delivered her pocketbook. Lady Bellaston thinks that Sophia must have secretly prearranged the meeting with Tom. Tom, feigning ignorance of Lady Bellaston, tells her that he was given her address by a lady at a masquerade. Tom begs that his honesty in delivering the pocketbook be rewarded by his being allowed to visit Sophia again. Lady Bellaston consents. On the stairs Jones passes Mrs. Honour and tells her his address.

Chapter XII

Once Jones has departed from Lady Ballston's house, the woman exclaims to Sophia how good-looking he is. Sophia says that she did not take much notice of him and that she found him rather ungentlemanly. Lady Bellaston agrees, and decides aloud that she will not admit him to visit. Lady Bellaston makes a snide comment about Tom's clothing. Sophia upbraids her for her cruelty and lets slip that the man is Tom Jones. She attempts to cover up her mistake. Lady Bellaston enjoys tormenting Sophia. Sophia cannot sleep from her guilt at lying.

Commentary

At the masquerade Tom meets a masked lady, who mentions the name 'Ms. Western'. Jones follows the lady only because he wants to know more about Sophia. He thinks that the lady is Mrs. Fitzpatrick. But he is soon proved wrong, the lady is in fact Lady Bellaston. She now proceeds to flirt with Tom. Throughout the novel women chase our hero Tom, we wonder why he cannot brush them off. This is the lesson that Tom has to learn before he can become worthy enough to marry Sophia.

The problem with Tom is that he is too generous to refuse the kindness of women. In being polite to them, he sometimes unknowingly starts a romantic affair. Lady Bellaston knows that Tom is without money and obliges him with her favors. Tom could be said to be actually kept by an elder lady. Even though our hero is noble, generous, gallant, straightforward, yet the reader has doubts as to his integrity. He could have refused to be under the heavy obligations of Lady Bellaston. We would have had more respect for Tom if he were able to maintain his independence. But, Fielding is not creating a unbelievably perfect hero. He creates a hero who has more chances of being real, than an imaginary paragon of virtue. In the eighth chapter, Tom meets the highwayman, whom he had forgiven on the highway to London. The highwayman is none other than Mrs. Millar's cousin. Tom wins yet another admirer. We see later that these friends stand by Tom in his time of need.

Jones continues to meet Lady Bellaston and she starts wooing him with love letters. It is not Tom who chases the elder lady, but the other way round. She seems to be a completely spoilt woman. We don't approve of her behaviour.

Our dear lovers finally get to meet each other in chapter eleven. Sophia as usual is too delicate and cannot handle the excitement of being next to Tom. She is very angry with him for having insulted her and for having an affair with Mrs. Waters. But, despite all these complaints, Sophia is still in love with Tom. Lady Bellaston arrives at the tender scene where our lovers are having a re-union. She is very jealous to see Tom with Sophia. Tom is flabbergasted in Lady Ballston's presence. He is scared of being exposed to Sophia. He does not want her to know that he has been having an affair with Lady Bellaston too. Sophia, for the matter is quite shrewd, she pretends that she does not know Tom and that he is there only to return to return her pocket book to her.

Sophia is not entirely innocent, she is a woman of the world. She pretends that Tom is a stranger to her. She tells Lady Bellaston that she would never get married contrary to her father's wishes. Lady Bellaston knows who Tom is but she, too puts on an act. The hypocrisy element is stronger in the cities, unlike the innocence of smaller towns and villages.

The reader is glad that Tom and Sophia have at least meet each other now. But the lovers never get much time together alone. We are curious to know what will happen next. Events are moving ahead and the novel seems to be working steadily towards the climax. The novel would have held no interest, if all these obstacles had not been placed between Sophia and Tom.

BOOK XIV

Chapter I

Since some gentlemen have recently made their literary mark without having any learning, modern critics are now claiming that a writer does not require learning. However, the narrator believes that writing—like any art—requires knowledge and study. A writer especially needs to have knowledge of their subject&mash;for instance, if one brought together Homer, Virgil, and Aristotle, they would not write a very good book on the art of dance.

Chapter II

Jones receives two letters from Lady Bellaston. The first asks him whether he arranged to meet Sophia in the drawing room of her house. She warns him that she can hate as passionately as she can love. The second urges him to come and visit her at her house immediately. As Jones is preparing to leave, Lady Bellaston walks in with her dress in disarray. She asks if Jones has betrayed her, and he promises her on his knees that he has not. Suddenly Partridge prances into the room announcing Mrs. Honour's arrival. Tom hides Lady Bellaston behind his bed before Honour enters. Honour prattles on about how Lady Bellaston meets men at a house where she pays the landlady's rent. Then she hands Jones a letter from Sophia. Once Honour leaves, Lady Bellaston emerges from behind the bed, enraged that she has been "slighted for a Country Girl." Lady Bellaston now realises that Sophia will always occupy first place in Jones's affections, but resigns herself to the second prize. She and Jones decide to camouflage the purpose of his visits by pretending that Tom has come to visit Sophia.

Chapter III

Jones receives a letter from Sophia saying that if he cares for her at all, he should not visit her that day—she is worried that Lady Bellaston suspects something. Jones pretends to be ill so as not to offend Lady Bellaston—he writes an explanatory letter to her ladyship, as well as a letter to Sophia. Lady Bellaston sends a note announcing that she will visit Jones at his room at nine that night. Mrs. Miller asks Tom, very courteously, to leave her house, as she does not approve of him entertaining strange women in his room from ten at night to two in the morning. She is worried about the virtue of her daughters. Jones, slightly annoyed, says that he will not defame her house, but he needs to see whomever he pleases. Tom learns from Mrs. Miller that Partridge has told her about the highway robbery and of Tom's relation to Allworthy. Tom is furious. Partridge blames Mrs. Honour for disclosing these facts.

Chapter IV

Nightingale tells Tom that he is also planning to leave Mrs. Miller's house, but without saying farewell. Tom insinuates that he knows this surreptitious mood has some relation to Nancy. He accuses Nightingale of using too much gallantry in order to make Nancy fall in love with him. Nightingale professes that he likes Nancy more than any woman he has ever met, but that his father has prearranged a marriage for him with a woman he has never seen before. He begs Tom not to reveal his secret. The narrator praises Nightingale's honourable character—although this honour, he says, does not extend to affairs of love.

Chapter V

Mrs. Miller invites Tom to tea—she does not wish to part on bad terms with him. She tells him her story, saying that, without Allworthy's assistance, her family could not have survived. Mrs. Miller's father left his three daughters poverty-stricken, and Mrs. Miller was the only daughter to survive. She married a clergyman, who died five years after their wedding. Mrs. Miller reads Tom the generous letter that Allworthy wrote to her at this time. He sent her an initial twenty guineas, then bought her a furnished house, and bestowed a fifty-pound annuity on her. Tom relates his history to Mrs. Miller—without mentioning Sophia. That night Jones waits in his room from nine until midnight, but Lady Bellaston makes no appearance.

Commentary

As usual, the first chapter does not have any direct relation with the proceedings within the novel's story. Sometimes, the modern reader tires of the comments that the author makes at the beginning of each book. One needs to have a wider knowledge of literature, to understand exactly what Fielding has to say. The lay man might have a problem with all the analogies and references that Fielding makes.

Jones has such power over women that Lady Bellaston cannot stay away from him, even though she is furious with him. She is an excitable and emotional woman. She sends Tom contradictory letters within a short span of time. Now the reader really begins to wonder, why Tom had to get into such an amorous mess.

Lady Bellaston is so desperate that she lands up in Tom's room. There is an element of the 'Comedy of Humours' in Fielding's novels. In this chapter, Tom has to hide Lady Bellaston, when Mrs. Honour comes up to Tom's room, with a letter from Sophia. Mrs. Honour criticizes the reputation of Lady Bellaston and the latter hears all. Tom tries to quieter Mrs. Honour, but to no avail. Tom is in a trying situation, when he has too many sides to please. Mrs. Honour too is suspicious of Tom's doings. She knows that he had an affair at Upton and she hopes for her mistress's sake, that he is not having another.

The affair between Lady Bellaston and Tom remains an ambiguous one. We never quite learn whether theirs is a truly physical relationship or no.

We see that Sophia trying to remain true to the promise, she made to her aunt and uncle. She had decided that she would not marry against her elders' will, and she tries to remain true to this promise. She decides to avoid Tom for this very purpose. She is always trying to maintain an honourable position and by the end of the novel, we start equating her name with 'principle' and 'discipline'. Tom is sad that Sophia does not want to meet him and now he does not feel like meeting Lady Bellaston. Tom is in a fix where his relation with the bossy Lady Bellaston is concerned.

Mrs. Miller is concerned about her lodge's reputation and this is quite natural. She does not approve of ladies visiting gentlemen in their rooms late in the night. Tom, we see is understanding and sympathetic towards her point of view. Mrs. Miller by now has learnt who Tom really is and this increases her affection for him. She greatly respects Squire Allworthy and remembers the Squire having praised Tom earlier.

Tom may have had affairs with many women but he is not a vicious character, or out to hurt women. He talks to Nightingale and says that he has noticed the latter flirting with Nancy. He wants that Nightingale should not break the poor girl's heart. He knows that Nightingale had no intention of marrying her, though he enjoys 'making love' to her. Now, both these young men decide to leave the lodging.

Squire Allworthy has been the benefactor of many people. We learn that it was he who sheltered the support less Mrs. Miller when she was younger and her girls were but kids. It is no wonder then that she greatly respects the Squire and is obliged to him for his various favors to her. The secret that Tom is related to the Squire is now out and Tom sees that there is no point in hiding it from Mrs. Miller.

Tom too tells Mrs. Miller about his own experiences. He is an emotional man, but at the same time, he is careful enough not to say anything about Sophia. Tom, it seems is finally learning the lesson of discretion.

Chapter VI

Jones is woken by an uproar. He summons Partridge, who relates that Nancy, Mrs. Miller, and Betty are crying in the kitchen. He jokes that there is a new delivery for the "Foundling-Hospital." Mrs. Miller tells Jones that Nightingale—"that barbarous Villain"—has deflowered her daughter, who is pregnant with his child. She shows Tom the letter Nightingale left for Nancy, in which he promises to provide for her and the child. Nancy's reputation might have been preserved if she had not fainted in public after receiving the letter. Nancy has twice attempted suicide, says Mrs. Miller. She admits that she noticed Nightingale's attentions to Nancy but sincerely thought that he would marry her daughter. Tom resolves to find Nightingale.

Chapter VII

Jones finds Nightingale sitting despondently beside the fireplace in his new dwelling—he is worrying about Nancy. He says that he is upset she showed the letter to others—if she had not, her reputation would still be intact and he would not have to worry. Tom tells Nightingale that he should marry her, and Nightingale now admits that he had given Nancy a promise of marriage. He worries, however, about what people will think of him for marrying a "whore." Tom argues that Nightingale's "Honour" will not be reinstated by his rejection of a woman whom he corrupted. Nightingale now argues that he is obliged to uphold his duty to his father. He is to meet the woman his father has arranged for him to marry the following day. Jones insists on meeting with Nightingale's father, and orders Nightingale to visit Nancy. Nightingale suggests that it will be easier for Jones if he tells his father that he is already married.

Chapter VIII

When Jones arrives at the house of Nightingale's father, the latter is meeting with the father of Nightingale's prospective wife. He thinks that Tom has come to claim a debt from his son. Jones begins by praising Nancy, but without mentioning her name. Nightingale's father, believing Tom to be talking about the lady he wishes his son to marry, is pleasantly surprised by the new attractions of this lady—her beauty, her education, her sweet temper. Tom slowly suggests that it would be silly for Nightingale's father to reject the woman simply because she has no fortune. At this point Nightingale's father asks whether Tom is speaking about Miss Harris. Tom replies that he is speaking of Miss Nancy Miller. Nightingale's uncle enters the room and argues that a parent should have the prerogative to veto a marriage partner, but not to prescribe one. Nightingale was raised more by this uncle than by his father.

Chapter IX

Jones returns to Mrs. Miller's house to find everyone rejoicing. Nightingale and Nancy are to be married the next day. Mrs. Miller calls Tom her good Angel. Nightingale's uncle arrives and, in private, congratulates his nephew on his recent marriage. Nightingale admits that he is not actually yet married, and his uncle rejoices at this news. He advises Nightingale to leave Nancy, since he does not have any formal obligations to her until the matrimony. Nightingale tells his uncle that honour demands that one carry through one's promises as well as one's actions. Moreover, he loves Nancy. He reminds his uncle that he always promised to let his daughter, Harriet, choose her own marriage partner. Nightingale's uncle tells Nightingale to accompany him to his lodging so that they can debate the matter more.

Chapter X

Downstairs, Nancy, Mrs. Miller, and Tom are wondering why Nightingale and his uncle have taken so much time for their conference. When the two men emerge, everyone feigns that nothing is amiss. Mrs. Honour arrives with awful news about Sophia. Tom can think of nothing but his "unfortunate Angel."

Commentary

A sub theme is given due attention in this Book. Nightingale leaves a farewell note for Nancy and this greatly upsets the poor young girl. The truth is that Nightingale had gone to a great length with Nancy. He had impregnated her. On receiving the news that he was leaving because his father intended to get him married to another woman, she is obviously extremely harried. This creates much tension is poor Mrs. Miller's life. More than anything, she is worried about her daughter's reputation.

When Tom learns of this terrible disaster, he consoles Mrs. Miller and then decides to go and meet the careless Nightingale. Tom plays the guardian angel yet again. He convinces Nightingale that he must marry Nancy. Tom himself an upright man helps Nightingale to take an upright decision regarding a defenceless girl.

Nightingale does really love Nancy and is convinced by Tom's arguments. He is not a city gallant for no reason. It is he who decides that his father must be told that he is already married to Nancy. Both Tom and Nightingale feel that this ploy shall work better with Nightingale's strict father.

The young men that Fielding writes about seem to have no fortunes of their own. This is true for both Tom and Nightingale. One of the major obstacles in their love-life is the fact that they are not self-reliant. Both have no money of their own!

Tom now pleads with Nightingale's father on his behalf. When the father learns that his son is married, he is obviously very angry. We are told about the lady, whom he had chosen for his son. Her only attraction is that she had a good fortune and the qualities begin and end there. Mr. Nightingale, in the novel represents the greedy worldly men of the cities.

Nightingale's uncle is somewhat more understanding but as we learn later, he is just as callous about the concept of honour. Initially, the uncle is reconciled with his nephew's decision to marry a poor woman, who he loves. But, later when he learns that Nightingale is not yet married to Nancy, he persuades his nephew to forget about her, as well as the promise he made to marry her. Fielding's represents urbane characters to be more selfish and money minded, when compared to the country folk.

The evening at Mrs. Miller's house had been a jolly one, till the nephew and the uncle go to another room to talk. When they come back, everyone looks a little tense. They can make out that the Uncle is eager to take away the nephew to his own lodging. Tom notices that the Uncle is also artificially polite to Nancy. Tom is worried that the Uncle might have persuaded Nightingale not to marry Nancy. We see that Tom is perceptive and is right on this occasion.

But, now Fielding brings back a reference to the major theme of the novel and that is Tom and Sophia's love affair. Mrs. Honour comes to Tom with some upsetting new regarding Sophia and Tom can now think of nothing else.

So far Tom had been getting involved in other's concerns too, but now we see that events take such a turn that Tom is forced to think about his own predicaments too. We hope that this helping hero will get help in his own time of need. We learn that he does and the friends that he makes by his good deeds stand by his side in his times of trouble.

BOOK XV

Chapter I

The narrator disagrees with "Moral Writers" who believe that virtue leads to happiness and vice to grief.

Chapter II

Lord Fellamar, a nobleman who brought Sophia home from the play, is a frequent visitor at Lady Ballston's house. He has fallen in love with Sophia. One morning he visits Sophia for two hours before realizing that he has stayed too long. Lady Bellaston is pleased with Flamer's lengthy visit—she is hoping to deflect Sophia from Tom through Fellamar. Lady Bellaston advertises Sophia to Fellamar by telling him about her great fortune. She complains, however, that Sophia is in love with "one of the lowest Fellows in the World ... a Beggar, a Bastard, a Foundling." She invites Fellamar to dine with them the following day so that she can prove to him that Sophia is attached to such a man.

Chapter III

Lady Bellaston is a member of the "Little World," a high-class club. She devises a plan for the dinner that night with Fellamar and calls on the assistance of Edwards, another member of the club. Specifically, Edwards has to say that a certain Colonel Wilcox was killed by Tom Jones in a duel.

Sophia faints on hearing the news, proving to Fellamar that Lady Bellaston was correct in her assertions about Sophia's love for Tom. Lady Bellaston contrives to have Fellamar and Sophia meet at seven the following evening. She has secretly been encouraging Fellamar to rape Sophia so that Sophia will be obliged to marry him. Fellamar is tortured by the thought of the crime, and resolves that his "Honour" will subdue his "Appetite." The following day Sophia begs Lady Bellaston not to admit Fellamar. Her aunt chastises her, and snidest that country girls think every man who is courteous to them intends to make love to them.

Chapter IV

Lady Bellaston distorts literary examples of rape to try to convince Fellamar to ravish Sophia. It is ultimately for Sophia's good, she argues, since Fellamar will be a fine husband for her. Fellamar agrees to carry through with Lady Ballston's plan, extolling Sophia's beauty and fortune.

Chapter V

Lord Fellamar enters Sophia's room and throws himself at her feet, offering her the world. She rejects him in harsh terms. He grabs hold of her and she screams out, but Lady Bellaston has removed everyone from earshot. At this moment Sophia hears her father's voice as he thunders up the stairs. She calls out to her father, and Fellamar releases her. Squire Western explodes into the room, drunk and verbally abusive. Western orders Sophia to marry Blifil. Fellamar thinks that Western is speaking of him, and thanks him for the honour of considering him as his son-in-law. Western curses Fellamar, who departs as quickly as possible. Lady Bellaston chastises Western for his rudeness to so great a man. Western declares that he wants a country man, not a city fop, for Sophia. He violently drags his daughter down to his coach, swearing to lock her up.

Chapter VI

Mrs. Fitzpatrick is the one who betrayed Sophia's whereabouts to Squire Western and Mrs. Western. The narrator presents her fawning, obsequy letter to Mrs. Western.

Commentary

The author once again begins the Book with his own comments. By doing this he places the immediate events of the narrative against the larger background, of the universe. This book is not just another narrative-it also imparts a moral lesson at occasions. Life's profundities are condensed into a few lines expertly by the narrator. We enjoy the story because it has a 'slice of life' to offer.

In the second chapter, we see Lady Ballston's viciousness at work. She is jealous of Sophia and so she plots to remove her from her way. Lady Bellaston encourages Lord Flamer's romantic feelings towards Sophia. She does this by telling the Lord about Sophia's fortune and by praising her person. Lady Bellaston is a woman who knows how to drive a man into doing what she wants. She is able to use the triggers of ego and pride effectively, to her advantage. Her sole aim is to remove Sophia from the path of her love for Tom. Lord Fellamar on the other hand is smitten by Sophia's charms. Lady Bellaston makes up a story to urge Lord Fellamar to use force with Sophia. Lady Bellaston claims that Sophia is only infatuated with Tom and she would be destroying her own life, if she would insist on running away with him. Lord Fellamar is fooled. Moreover Lady Bellaston thinks up a heinous way of claiming Sophia. This so-called genteel woman of society propounds rape. She even goes so far as to suggest that women sometimes enjoy rape and are not averse to men being forceful. Thus, Lord Fellamar decides to rape Sophia in order to win her. We see that Lady Ballston's circle of society is an unscrupulous one. In this circle comic jests are played often and without any remorse.

So on Lady Ballston's insistence when a whist group settles down to play, Tom Edwards one of the players, jests that he had seen Tom Jones dead. Sophia is shocked and faints. She is a tender woman who is not familiar with such cruel jokes. There is a great contrast in her behaviour and in that of Lady Ballston's London friends. Sophia is always faithful to Tom and rarely ever approves of another man. She does not like Lord Fellamar paying compliments to her. She tells Lady Bellaston to keep the Lord away but the Lady teases Sophia, saying that she has sweethearts in her head. Lady Ballston's hypocrisy is apparent in contrast to Sophia's straight forwardness.

Lord Fellamar does try and force himself on Sophia one evening.

Lady Bellaston arranges the scene in such a way that none of the servants can hear Sophia's screams. Sophia is lucky in that, her father enters the house at just that moment. He had come from the country to London to look for his daughter. Squire Western charges in his usual blustering style. He calls for Sophia loudly and the daughter is thus saved from Lord Flamer's clutches.

She is taken away by her father-Squire Western. Fielding uses the past-present interpolation technique in his narrative. The Squire is already in London, but in the sixth chapter of this Book, we learn how he came to be in the city.

Squire Western is a source of wry humour in the novel. He entertains us all with his bluntness and his loud hollers and bellows. This Squire's behaviour adds colour to the narrative, along with Partridge's contribution. Squire Western is the quintessential countryman and his characterization is excellently done

Chapter VII

At Mrs. Miller's house, Mrs. Honour laments losing Sophia. Jones, thinking that Sophia must have died, frantically begs Honour to tell him what has happened. When Jones finally extracts the news that Western has locked up Sophia and dismissed Honour, Tom is thankful that Sophia is alive. Honour chides Jones for not having compassion for her misfortune, since she says that she has always taken his part against Blifil. Honour is scared that Western will hurt Sophia. She says she wishes Sophia had some of her courage—if her father withheld her from the man she loved, she would tear out his eyes. Partridge runs into the room to inform Jones that

Lady Bellaston has arrived. Jones hides Honour behind the bed. Lady Bellaston plops herself on the bed and scolds Jones for not contacting her. Then she flirts with him. Lady Bellaston waits in surprise as Jones stands awkwardly, not knowing what to do. A very drunk Nightingale suddenly bursts into Tom's room, mistaking it for his own. Partridge manages to lead Nightingale away. While Tom was occupied with Nightingale, Lady Bellaston tried to hide herself behind the bed, coming face to face with Honour. The ladies are horrified. Lady Bellaston implies that she will bribe Mrs. Honour, after which Honour calms down. Lady Bellaston leaves, shunning Tom's attempts to hold her hand. Honour is upset about Tom's infidelity to Sophia, but Tom "at last found means to reconcile her."

Chapter VIII

Mrs. Miller gently scolds Tom for the upheaval in his room the previous night. Nightingale and Nancy are married that day, with Tom acting as father to Nancy. Before the wedding, Nightingale's uncle tries to intoxicate him and dissuade him from marrying Nancy. News arrives during this meeting that Harriet, the daughter of Nightingale's uncle, has run away with a neighbouring clergyman. This destroys his case with Nightingale.

Chapter IX

Tom receives three letters from Lady Bellaston summoning him immediately. Nightingale enters the room while Tom is reading and reveals that he knows about Tom's affair with Lady Bellaston. Tom asks for more details on the affairs of Lady Bellaston, but the narrator refuses to repeat Nightingale's words for fear of being accused of spreading scandals.

Nightingale's stories greatly reduce Tom's gratitude to Lady Bellaston and he realises that he has been in "commerce" with this lady rather than in "love." Nightingale advises Jones that the easiest way for him to rid himself of Lady Bellaston is by proposing marriage. Together they compose a letter of proposal, to which Lady Bellaston replies that she is offended that Tom is so covetous of her fortune. Tom responds that he is insulted by her suspicion and will return her gifts to him. At the wedding dinner that night, Mrs. Miller devotes more attention to Tom than to Nightingale and Nancy.

Chapter X

Mrs. Miller has received a letter from Allworthy informing her that he and Blifil are coming immediately to London. He wishes to reserve the first and second floors of her house. The truth is that when Allworthy started paying Mrs. Miller an annuity of fifty pounds, it was on condition that he could occupy the first floor of her house whenever he came to town. Mrs. Miller thus has to comply with Allworthy's wishes, but she is distressed that Jones and Nightingale have to leave. Jones says that he does not mind at all. Honour sends Jones a letter saying that she is sure he will attain Sophia in the end, but she can no longer be of service to him. Lady Bellaston has hired her.

Chapter XI

Mrs. Arable Hunt, a friend of Mrs. Miller's, sends Tom a marriage proposal. She is twenty-six and a little plump, but otherwise attractive. She has recently been widowed by a turkey merchant who left her a rich woman. Tom is at first excited by the prospect of having so much money, but—thinking of Sophia—writes a courteous refusal.

Chapter XII

Partridge capers into Jones's room with good tidings. He has found out that Black George is now a servant in Squire Western's apartment in London, by which means Tom may send letters to Sophia. Much to Tom's frustration, however, Partridge cannot remember the name of the street on which Western lives.

Commentary

Mrs. Honour is in a problematic situation. She no longer enjoys the favor of Squire Western and she is not allowed to serve Sophia. In this anxious state of mind she comes to inform Tom, what had been happening with Sophia. When Mrs. Honour comes to meet Tom, a classic case of hide and seek takes place. Lady Bellaston too comes to meet Tom and Tom does not display presence of mind. In his confusion he hides Mrs. Honour, when Lady Bellaston enters the room. It would have been better for Tom to have let Lady Bellaston and Mrs. Honour meet than letting Mrs. Honour see Lady Bellaston speak endearments to Tom. Tom is in a tricky spot-he cannot respond to Lady Ballston's overtures as Mrs. Honour is there in the room too. Just then a drunk Nightingale too enters the room. So the situation is akin to one in a Comedy of Manners play.

On seeing Nightingale, Lady Bellaston tries to hide in Mrs. Honour's place and discovers the old maid. The situation is truly funny. Lady Bellaston handles herself well though and is civil to Mrs. Honour.

Mrs. Honour is shocked by Tom's unfaithfulness to Sophia and reprimands him. He for that matter bribes Mrs. Honour into keeping quiet about the affair. Tom's history is quite murky, unlike Sophia's spotless reputation.

Apart from Tom-Sophia's love theme, there are other sub Themes in the novel. One such sub theme is Mrs. Miller's family. Her daughter Nancy is married to Tom's friend, Nightingale, with Tom's help. Tom is the kind, who helps others by his large-heartedness.

The main theme of Tom-Sophia is interpolated with other affairs, such as that of Mr. Nightingale. The young Nightingale escapes from the older one, because the latter's daughter runs away. We often see in life that those who preach against something have exactly the same unfortunate thing happening to them. This is true in the Mr. Nightingale's case, i.e. the younger Nightingale's Uncle.

Lady Ballston's letters to Tom are passionate and she seems quite desperate for him. She keeps asking him to 'come to her'. Nightingale advises Tom to keep a distance from Lady

Bellaston as she has a very bad reputation. He suggests that Tom can do this by proposing marriage to the Lady. Ladies such as Lady Bellaston would flee such a serious alliance. Nightingale is right about Lady Bellaston. She does shy away from marriage. But at the same time she is so attracted to Tom that she woes him again later.

Tom solves Mrs. Miller's small problems for her. He agrees to leave her lodging along with the newly married couple so that Mrs. Miller can give that place to Squire Allworthy and Blifil. Tom wins Mrs. Miler's heart by these kind gestures. We later see how Mrs. Miller's friendship helps Tom in his time of trouble.

Tom is worried about Sophia. Partridge gets him good news. Black George would like to help his friend Tom and he can do so as he has access to the Western family. There is some humour in this part. Partridge's reference to himself being 'cunning' is funny. The word 'cunning' is then repeatedly used by Tom too. This makes for interesting reading.

BOOK XVI

Chapter I

The narrator claims that it is difficult to write introductory chapters. They are not ordered in a particular manner—any of them could grace the beginning of any chapter. Their purpose is simply to whet the critic's appetite.

Chapter II

Western and Sophia—who is still confined to her room—argue about Blifil. A messenger arrives from Lord Fellamar, who intends to pay his respects to Sophia that afternoon. Western answers that Sophia is already "disposed of." The messenger asks whether Western knows what kind of man he is declining. Western rudely retort that he hates all lords and begins to caper angrily about the room. Sophia joins in her father's rancor by stomping her foot on the floor and running screaming from her room. Once Flamer's messenger has departed, Western heads straight for Sophia's room, where they weep together and express their love for each other. Sophia says that she promises not to marry at all—she will devote herself to her father. This refuels his anger.

Chapter III

The narrator confides in the reader that Western "really donated on his Daughter, and to give her any Kind of Pleasure was the highest Satisfaction of his Life." Black George carries up a pullet with eggs for Sophia's dinner. Although Sophia has been refusing food, Black George manages to entice her with the pullet, which is her favourite dish. She finds a letter from Tom inside its belly. The letter labours the point that Tom only wishes to see Sophia happy. While she reads the letter, Sophia hears a fracas downstairs between her father and her Aunt Western, who has just arrived in London.

Chapter IV

Mrs. Western asks for her niece. When Squire Western reports that he has locked the wayward Sophia in her room, Mrs. Western reminds him of his promise not to take such drastic actions against his daughter's disobedience. She stresses the ideal of female liberty, and the narrator compares her to Tapestries, that Amazonian champion of women. Eventually Squire Western tosses down the key and Mrs. Western departs to find Sophia. No sooner has she left than her brother damns her and invites Parson Supple for a drink. Squire Western allows Mrs. Western to take Sophia to her own lodging. Mrs. Western begs her brother not to see Mrs. Fitzpatrick if she seeks him out.

Chapter V

Black George delivers a letter to Tom from Sophia. She tells Tom that she is with her Aunt Western and has promised not to write any further to Tom. She does give her word, however, that she will marry no other man. Tom is torn by happiness and grief. Tom spends three hours reading and kissing the epistle, after which he joins Mrs. Miller, Betsey, and

Partridge at the playhouse to watch a performance of Hamlet. Partridge becomes fully immersed in the play and trembles at the ghost of Hamlet's father—whom he believes to be a real ghoul. He shouts out to Hamlet when the latter picks up the skull of Orrick, and amuses all the spectators around him with his running commentary on the play. After the performance, Mrs. Fitzpatrick approaches Jones and invites him to meet with her the following afternoon.

Commentary

Fielding has a very informal style of writing at times. In the first chapter of this Book he impresses his opinion about prologues. It's almost as if he is conversing with himself.

In the second chapter Squire Western and his daughter Sophia alternate between arguments and reconciliations. They both love each other tenderly but Sophia cannot seem to reconcile herself with the idea of marrying Blifil.

Lord Fellamar continues to pursue Sophia. He sends a Captain to Sophia's father to acquire a meeting with the Squire. But there is a large gap between the sophistication of the Lord's manners and the coarse bluntness of Squire Western's country up bringing. Squire Western has no patience with polite language and courtly manners. He is childish in his immediate expression of dislike. The Captain & the Squire have a verbal argument and Sophia is worried about her father's safety. When he comes up to her room she makes a significant promise to him. She says that she will not marry without his consent. Sophia does have tender feelings for her father.

Now that Black George is in London he does his friend Tom favors by agreeing to serve as a messenger. In dramatic movie style, George brings up a letter for Sophia hidden inside a bird for her eating. Tom's letter is a dramatic one characteristic of a lover's. There is little common sense and more of bombastic in the letter. Sometimes Tom is too simple to use artful words.

Sophia finds some relief when her aunt comes to London and decides to take her niece under her own wing. Sophia is freed from her locked jail.

The altercation between Squire Western & his sister is amusing. Lady Western comes across as a pompous, condescending person. The reader tends to not like her. But at least Sophia has more freedom while she is with her aunt.

Now Sophia sends Tom a letter. Sophia's letters are very different from Tom's. They are not as open and passionate, she is retrained but her anger and irritation are apparent in the letter.

Sophia makes it a point to be very judicious about her promises. For her a promise is a sacred thing. She is more careful about aspects of honour than Tom. She tells Tom not to write to her anymore. Tom is happy that at least his love is in safe hands as she is now with her aunt.

Tom attends a play with Mrs. Miller, her daughter and Partridge. Partridge entertains all with his comic responses to the horror on the edge. In the midst of serious development Fielding provides comic relief with the inclusion of this trip. Partridge is really lovable and provides wholesome entertainment. We laugh at him but still love him.

At the end of the fifth chapter, Mrs Fitzpatrick approaches Tom. We are surprised and are curious as to why she would want to meet tom. Fielding manages to keep our interest excited by frequent developments in the plot.

Chapter VI

The narrator considers all the characters in the novel as children. He harbors an "extraordinary Tenderness" for Sophia. Soon after Mr. Western departed for London, he sent a note to Blifil encouraging the lad to come to London as soon as possible to be married to Sophia. Blifil's motive for marrying Sophia has become pure hatred. Since Sophia ran away from home, Allworthy has suspected Sophia's dislike for Blifil. Blifil and Thwackum tried to convince Allworthy that Blifil should still pursue the young lady. Allworthy's tenderness eventually conquered his prudence and he agreed to accompany Blifil to London. Allworthy and Blifil arrive in London while Jones is watching Hamlet. Western insists on taking Blifil to Mrs. Western's residence immediately.

Chapter VII

Mrs. Western is reading Sophia a lecture on the prudence and politics of marriage when Mr. Western barges in with Blifil. Mrs. Western chastises him for not following the principles of a decorous entrance and sends Sophia—who she claims has been shaken by the event—to her bedroom. Blifil blubbers and blunders in fear. Mrs. Western says that he may leave a message for Sophia. Blifil leaves, less pleased with the meeting than Western. Western puts their failure down to Mrs. Western's mood, but Blifil suspects something more lurks beneath the surface.

Chapter VIII

Fellamar is still passionately in love with Sophia and, inspired by Lady Bellaston, has commissioned Captain Egg lane to force Tom onto a ship. Mrs. Western sent a greeting card to Lady Bellaston on her arrival in London. Lady Bellaston, delighted to have a female partner in crime, runs to Mrs. Western with her news about Lord Fellamar. Mrs. Western dubs Blifil a "hideous kind of Fellow" like "all country Gentlemen." Lady Bellaston now gives Mrs. Western the marriage proposal she received from Tom. She says she hopes the letter will change Sophia's mind. It was directly after this conference that Western and Blifil made their appearance, which explains Mrs. Western's icy behaviour to the latter.

Chapter IX

Jones meets with Mrs. Fitzpatrick, who suggests that Jones should try to get access to Sophia by flirting with Mrs. Western. She reminds him that this is what Mr. Fitzpatrick did in order to court her, and it worked. Jones politely declines the suggestion, infuriating Mrs. Fitzpatrick. Jones attempts to assuage Mrs. Fitzpatrick, who now takes a fancy to Jones. Out of vanity she believes herself to be one of the finest ladies in the world. As Jones leaves, Mrs. Fitzpatrick gazes at him seductively and invites him to visit her the following day. Jones's thoughts, however, tend only toward Sophia and he resolves not to call on Mrs. Fitzpatrick.

Chapter X

Mr. Fitzpatrick, who has tracked his wife to London, arrives at her doorstep as Jones is departing. Jones recognizes him from the inn at Upton and greets him amicably, but Fitzpatrick punches him and draws his sword out. Jones knows nothing about fencing but manages to retaliate and plunges the sword into Fitzpatrick. Jones, calling for assistance for Fitzpatrick, is apprehended by a gang of men employed by Lord Fellamar. Jones lands up in jail after a trial. Partridge visits Jones at the prison with news of Fitzpatrick's death. Sophia sends Tom a letter saying that she has seen his proposal letter to Lady Bellaston and wishes to have nothing more to do with him.

Commentary

Squire Western is faithful to Blifil. As soon as he realises that he has not sent word to Blifil regarding Sophia, he does the needful. Blifil will do anything to attain Sophia but genuine love for her is doubtful. He is more impressed by her father's fortune and by her external beauty. Blifil is eager to go to London on hearing news of Sophia. It is Squire Allworthy who notes that Blifil's passion may be a false one, he also realises that Sophia must hate Blifil very much, if she took the step of running away to London. But Blifil and his supporters are shrewd enough to convince Squire Allworthy into letting Blifil pursue Sophia. Blifil swears he would never use violent means with a woman. Blifil's selfish villainy is seconded by the equally evil Thwackum. Together they persuade the Squire into letting Blifil go to London. We wonder why the Squire is unable to see beneath all their pretences. The problem is that the Squire often condemns the honest people, without realizing the treachery of the evil ones, such as Blifil.

On reaching London Blifil is quick to attend upon Squire Western. The Squire upholds Blifil's cause and hurries him to Sophia. Squire Western has loud blustering ways and he often over runs decency and courtesy in the bargain. Lady Western on the other hand, dislikes having her privacy disturbed without prior notice. She reprimands her brother for having barged in so boisterously. Sophia behaves like a delicate darling yet again and is shocked to see Blifil. Blifil too is at a loss of words for a change. He is flabbergasted. The Squire insists that Lady Western appoint a time for their meeting with Sophia. The Lady however does not oblige.

When Lady Western learns of Lord Flamer's proposal, she entirely forgets Blifil. Lady Western values nobility and she encourages Lord Flamer's proposal for her niece. Sophia on the other hand is completely unaffected by these attractions. Lady Western now proves as tiring to her niece as the her father has been. She berates young Sophia with long lectures on honour & chastity. From Lady Bellaston, Lady Western gets a love letter that the former had received from none other than Sophia. This is to be shown to Sophia one day to shock her out of her love for Tom. Lady Bellaston is unscrupulous enough to giver her private love letters to another. She has no scruples whatsoever. And her only desire is to attain Tom at whatever cost.

Tom goes to meet Mrs. Fitzpatrick; she is a jealous woman, who desires to have her revenge on Lady Western. She therefore encourages Tom to flirt with the elder Western lady, in order to have access to the younger that is Sophia. Lady Fitzpatrick's intention is clearly to hurt Lady Western. But Tom refuses to listen to her suggestion of courting Lady Western. Mrs. Fitzpatrick too is attracted by Tom's charms. We see that there are very few women who can resist Tom, all are drawn to him at one point or the other. It is his good looks that prove to be the bait.

We see that Tom gets into trouble when he is coming out of Lady Fitzpatrick's lodging, Mr. Fitzpatrick sees him. He is jealous of Tom and his jealousy results in a duel between the two. Tom is a young man who knows how to defend himself, he does not lack spirit and he wounds Mr. Fitzpatrick seriously Tom is arrested and jailed. Since Mr. Fitzpatrick is in danger of dying, Tom too is in danger of being tried for murder. Partridge hears this dismal news and runs to his master. Tom's grief is made more intense by a letter that he receives from Sophia. In this she expresses great disdain at his writing love letters to Lady Bellaston. Tom's state of mind is an unhappy one full of remorse and regret. He is in a tricky situation now and we are eager to see how he will be extricated.

BOOK XVII

Chapter I

A comic writer concludes when his characters reach the happiest of states; a tragic writer concludes when his characters descend to the most wretched of states. If this were a tragedy, the narrator's work would be finished. He provides a possible tragic ending: Sophia could be given in marriage to Blifil or Fellamar, and Jones could be hanged at Tiburon. The ancient writers had the benefit of bringing Divine Intervention to their assistance in saving their characters; he has to rely on natural methods. Jones still has worse news to face.

Chapter II

Blifil finds Allworthy and Mrs. Miller at breakfast and tells them that Tom is a villain. Mrs. Miller vehemently stands up for Tom, surprising Allworthy, who tells her not to treat Blifil so rudely. Mrs. Miller says that although she has to acknowledge that Tom has faults, they are merely the "Faults of Wildness and of Youth." She promises to tell Allworthy stories of Tom's humanity and generosity. Blifil now recounts that Tom has killed a man. Mrs. Miller argues that Tom must have been provoked. A visitor arrives for Allworthy.

Chapter III

Squire Western arrives in Mrs. Miller's kitchen and tells the company about Mrs. Western's plan for Sophia to marry Lord Fellamar. Allworthy has to translate Western's dialect. After listening to Western's speech, Allworthy strongly discourages Western from forcing Sophia into any marriage. Western bellows that he begat Sophia and thus has a right to govern her. Blifil begs that he may be allowed to persevere with Sophia. Allworthy is concerned that he is pursuing Sophia out of lust rather than love and encourages Blifil to examine his heart. When Blifil alludes to the fact that Tom has committed a "murder," Western sings and dances about the room in joy. The narrator promises to return to Sophia's story, since he "can no longer bear to be absent" from her.

Chapter IV

The narrator compares Sophia, pursued now by Lord Fellamar as well as by Blifil, to a hunted doe. Mrs. Western threatens to take Sophia back to her father if she does not agree to meet with Fellamar.

Sophia tells her aunt that Fellamar attempted to violate her—the proof of which she still has on her left breast. Mrs. Western is horrified—no man has ever treated a woman of the Western family in such a way before. Sophia reminds her aunt that she herself has turned down many suitors. Sophia wants to know why she cannot do the same. This sets Mrs. Western boasting of her love "conquests" and "cruelty" for half an hour. Mrs. Western's mood improves to the point that she agrees that some distance between Sophia and Fellamar is appropriate.

Chapter V

Mrs. Miller, Nightingale, and Partridge—the most faithful of friends—visit Jones in jail. Partridge announces the happy news that Fitzpatrick has not died. Relief washes over Jones—until he begins to think of the helpless situation with Sophia. Mrs. Miller, who has learned about Sophia from Partridge, offers to speak to Sophia on behalf of Jones. Tom thus entrusts a letter for Sophia with Mrs. Miller, who has already been "so warm an Advocate to Mr. Allworthy" on account of Tom. Nightingale promises to investigate Fitzpatrick's state of health, and to discover who else was at the duel.

Commentary

In the first chapter of the book, Fielding states that he wishes to maintain the reality of the adventure, by not resorting to supernatural means to resolve Tom, as well as Sophia's predicaments. The author seems to enjoy putting his characters in difficult situations. He does an equally good job of extracting them from these tricky spots later. But Fielding has to be commended, as no situation looks false or contrived. The tricky spots are realistic and the resolutions are earthy too. The author refers to the reader as a friend and bids him farewell.

In the second chapter we return to the narrative. Blifil is forever ready to condemn Tom. He now hears about the duel between Tom and Mr. Fitzpatrick and the fact that Tom is in jail. Blifil comes eagerly to the Squire with this news. Mrs. Miller defends Tom faithfully. She proves to be a loyal friend, one who never forgets the favor that Tom had done to her. The Squire is surprised to note Mrs. Miller's affection for Tom but she explains it to him while praising Tom all the time.

The Squire as we can see, still has his doubts about Tom's character and is more convinced of Blifil's goodness. He is wrong in this but he does not realise it till much later.

The Squire is sad to hear that Tom has nearly killed a man.

Squire Western pays Allworthy a visit, in his characteristic loud style. He criticizes Lord Fellamar. Squire Allworthy behaves like a perfect gentleman insisting that if Western has found a better match for Sophia, Blifil is ready to withdraw his proposal. But Western will have none of that. He is like a stubborn child who has fixed his mind on an object, in this case-Sophia. Western never really bothers to study Blifil's character, to see whether it is worthy of Sophia. Squire Western is too rough sometimes and throws up the idea of forcing Sophia into marriage. But Allworthy will have nothing of brute force and insists that Sophia be left alone to make up her own mind. Allworthy praises Sophia amply. She is such a person that everyone has a good word for her. The Squire is an excellent judge of situations and he rightly advises Blifil to examine his 'love' for Sophia and to see whether it is truly genuine.

On the other hand Lady Western insists that Sophia meet Lord Fellamar. Aunt and niece have an argument and the latter reveals Lord Flamer's violence to her person. If it hadn't been for this revelation, Lady Western would have forced Sophia to meet the Lord. When the Lord visits he is surprised to meet cold behaviour-both from aunt and niece.

As for Tom his friends stand by him in his hour of need. Mrs. Miller and Mr. Nightingale go and visit him in jail. Tom the hero, is a nobleman, whose intrinsic value is greatly respected by people such as Mrs. Miller and Nightingale.

Thus both hero and heroine are in uncomfortable situations.

Chapter VI

Sophia and Mrs. Western have been on great terms since Sophia allowed her aunt to brag about her ex-suitors. Sophia may thus admit whomever she pleases to the house. She permits Mrs. Miller to visit her, but when she sees that Mrs. Miller has a letter from Tom, she refuses to accept it. Mrs. Miller falls to her knees and tells Sophia the stories of Tom's goodwill to Mr. Anderson and to her daughter Nancy. She surprises Sophia with her vehemence on Tom's behalf. Sophia says that since she cannot prevail over Mrs. Miller, she will have to accept the letter. She opens it as soon as Mrs. Miller leaves the room. In his letter Tom says that he can account for the marriage proposal to Lady Bellaston and that he did not wish to marry her at all. However, he does not provide any details in his letter that mollify her anger towards him. Sophia is obliged to attend a party with Lady Bellaston and her aunt that evening, at which she struggles to maintain a cheerful countenance.

Chapter VII

Mrs. Miller tells Allworthy about her many obligations to Tom. Allworthy accepts that even the worst villains have some goodness in them, but he begs her never to mention Tom's name to him. Moreover, he resents the fact that Mrs.

Miller compares Blifil unfavorably to Tom. Mrs. Miller, however, cannot say enough about Tom's beauty, goodness, and generosity. Allworthy is moved by her speech, but changes the topic of conversation to Nancy. He visits Nightingale's father to try to reconcile him to the family. Blifil and the lawyer Dowling arrive. Blifil, greatly pleased with his new friend, has made Dowling his steward.

Chapter VIII

Mrs. Western's good spirits continue, but she has not abandoned her plan for Sophia to marry Fellamar. She is further encouraged by Lady Bellaston, who argues that most marriages are arranged. Sophia agrees to a visit from Fellamar, who showers her with compliments and professions of love. Sophia asks him how he can reconcile such sentiments with his violent behaviour to her in the past. He pleads madness from love. Sophia says that if he truly wishes to attune himself to her happiness, he should leave. He asks whether she has another suitor—she retorts that it is not her responsibility to tell him. A flushed Mrs. Western enters the room and begins to chide Sophia for her "silly Country Notions of Bashfulness."

Mrs. Western's fury stems from more than one reason: her new maid, warned by Mrs. Honour to keep a close eye on Sophia, has told Mrs. Western all about Sophia's conversations with Mrs. Miller. Sophia refuses to hand over the letter that Mrs. Miller brought her from Tom, and Mrs. Western threatens to evict Sophia from her house and take her back to Squire Western's house.

Chapter IX

Jones has spent twenty-four hours alone in prison before Partridge and Nightingale return. Nightingale has tracked down two of the men who claim to have witnessed the start of the duel. He bears bad news: both of the men say that they saw Tom provoke the fight. Mrs. Miller arrives with news of Mrs. Western's rebuff. Once his friends have left, Jones receives a surprise visit from Mrs. Waters. The narrator updates the reader on all that has happened since Tom parted with Mrs. Waters at the inn at Upton: Fitzpatrick courted her in the coach on the way to Bath, where they were married. He did not tell her that he was already married. When Mrs. Waters learned that the man who wounded her husband was none other than Jones, she decided to visit him in prison. Mrs. Waters tells Tom that Fitzpatrick is beyond danger of dying and that he has admitted to initiating the duel. This information improves Jones's spirits dramatically. He suffers, however, over the thought that Sophia has abandoned him.

Commentary

Mrs. Miller is devoted to Tom and goes as soon as possible to Sophia with Tom's letter. Sophia had promised herself not to entertain Tom's correspondence so she refuses to accept the letter. But Mrs. Miller is equally insistent and finally Sophia agrees to letting Mrs. Miller leave the letter in the room. Sophia's natural instincts cannot let her remain away from the letter for long. She reads it and not once, but again and again. We see how Tom is always willing to accept his guilt if it is his fault. In this letter he is very apologetic and that gets him nowhere. He tells Sophia that he can explain the letters written by him to Lady Bellaston, if given a chance. We see that Sophia loves him by the attention she gives to his billet dour.

A day of Sophia's in London is described. She does not like a frivolous life especially in the company of the jealous Lady Bellaston. Moreover, Lord Fellamar attends upon Sophia and our poor little heroine is grossly tired. She is a sensitive creature and she does not enjoy seeing plays or playing cards in such company. While Sophia is thus struggling Tom's faithful friends do him some service. Mrs. Miller pleads Tom's cause to Allworthy and even he admits that Tom couldn't entirely be a debase or vicious character. Squire Allworthy continues his benevolence when he promises to plead the young Nightingale's cause to the older father. Allworthy is genuinely fond of Mrs. Miller.

We meet Dowling again and we see how the smart Blifil gets his Uncle to get him a steward. This steward is none other than Dowling. Blifil seems to be in the process of consolidating his own affairs. This Dowling will play a key role now, as we shall soon see.

Sophia is still having to combat with force. First it was Mr. Western forcing her to wed Blifil. Now Lady Western, the Squire's sister wants that she pay attention to Lord Flamer's proposals. Thus, the poor young woman is trapped from either side. Lady Western admonishes Sophia for not having kept her promise. Sophia tries to manage the sticky situation though. She bluntly informs the Lord that he should stop bothering her.

But the Lord is too enamored by the charming Sophia. Unlike Tom Sophia's loyalty to him never falters. While Tom has affairs, Sophia shuns all male attention.

While Sophia's fortune becomes messy Tom's fate improves. None other than Mrs. Waters visits him in jail and gives him the good news that Lord Fitzpatrick shall live and that he also will confess that it was his own fault not Tom's. While Tom's life is out of danger, his heart is still weary at the news that Sophia had refused to read his letter.

Mrs. Waters who brings Tom some good news herself seems to be a wanton woman. It is mentioned that she is now living with Mr. Fitzpatrick as his wife. We learn more about her interesting history in the forthcoming chapters and are surprised.

BOOK XVIII

Chapter I

The narrator wishes the reader farewell. He compares the reading process to a journey in which he and the reader are fellow passengers in a coach. He hopes that he has been an entertaining companion.

Chapter II

Partridge visits Jones at the prison to break the horrifying news that Mrs. Waters is Tom's mother. Tom receives a letter from Mrs. Waters in which she alludes to this fact and says she has been greatly affected by it. She adds as a postscript that Fitzpatrick is on the recovery. Black George arrives next at the prison, and he and Tom exchange warm greetings. Black George reports that Squire Western and Mrs. Western have had a vicious argument that has concluded with Mrs. Western declaring she never wants to see her brother again. The Squire has been reconciled with Sophia, however. The narrator retraces his footsteps to describe how this reunion came about. Sophia took her father's side when arguing with her aunt about Lord Fellamar—this delighted Squire Western and endeared Sophia to him once more.

Chapter III

Allworthy visits Nightingale's father and, after three hours, convinces the old man to see his son. On his entrance to the house, Allworthy spots Black George, but takes no notice of him. Later, he asks Nightingale's father what business he had with Black George. Nightingale's father shows him five bank bills of one hundred pounds each that Black George has given him to invest. Allworthy recognizes the bills as those he gave to Tom.

Mrs. Miller is depressed about Tom's situation, but Allworthy cheers her somewhat by telling her he has no doubt there will soon be a reconciliation between Nightingale and his father. Allworthy summons Dowling from Blifil's room to ask him what should be done about the case of the bank bills. Mrs. Miller interrupts their conversation and introduces Allworthy to Nightingale, who brings the tidings that Fitzpatrick has recovered and admitted provoking the duel. Mrs. Miller urges Nightingale to remind Allworthy in what great esteem Tom holds him. Tears come to Allworthy's eyes and he reminisces briefly about the time he discovered the infant Tom between his sheets. The narrator hints that Allworthy's tears have been partly caused by a letter that he received from Square.

Chapter IV

The narrator presents Square's letter to Allworthy. Square writes that he is terminally ill, and that he has been reflecting on his past behaviour. He feels worst about his behaviour to Tom, who is innocent of the crime for which Allworthy condemned him. In fact, during Allworthy's illness, Tom was the only person who showed any real concern and compassion. Tom's mirth was motivated by Allworthy's recovery. Square hints at the dark designs of "another Person." The narrator also presents a letter from Mr. Thwackum to Allworthy, in which Thwackum haughtily and arrogantly tells Allworthy to consider him for the position of Vicar of Alder grove if the current vicar should die.

Chapter V

Mrs. Miller tells Allworthy that Nightingale discovered that the men who accused Tom were commissioned to do so by a Lord who wanted Tom sent off on a ship. Nightingale also happened to see Mr. Dowling with these men in the tavern. Shocked, Allworthy calls for Dowling, but he has already left. Allworthy asks Blifil if he knows whether Dowling has seen the eyewitnesses of Tom's duel. Blifil does not speak for some moments, which leads Mrs. Miller to shout "Guilty!" Allworthy asks Blifil why it is taking him so long to answer. Blifil answers that he sent Dowling to mollify the evidence of the witnesses. Allworthy now feels even more tenderness for Blifil. He proposes that they all pay a visit to Tom in prison. Partridge arrives and privately tells Mrs. Miller that Mrs. Waters is Tom's mother. Allworthy, hearing that the man with Mrs. Miller is Tom's servant, summons him. He immediately recognizes him to be Partridge. Surprised, he asks if he is indeed Tom's servant. Allworthy asks Partridge many questions about Jones.

Chapter VI

Allworthy asks Partridge why he has been serving his own son. Partridge tells Allworthy that he is not actually Tom's father. He tells Allworthy what has happened in his life since he was found guilty. First Partridge worked for a lawyer in Salisbury. Then he moved to Limington, where he worked for a lawyer for three years, after which he set up a school. One day, one of his pigs broke into his neighbour's yard and Partridge was taken to court. Allworthy tells him to get to the point. After seven years in the Winchester jail, Partridge taught at Cork in Ireland. He then moved to Bristol, where he met Tom. Partridge now tells Allworthy that Mrs. Waters, with whom Tom has had a relationship, is Tom's own mother. As Allworthy expresses his horror at the situation, Mrs. Waters walks in and asks to talk to Allworthy alone.

Chapter VII

Mrs. Waters tells Allworthy the story of Tom's conception and birth: his father, Mr. Summer, was the son of a clergyman whom Allworthy raised and even sent to the university. Mrs. Waters is not Tom's mother, although she did put the baby Tom in Allworthy's bed. She reveals that Bridget Allworthy, Allworthy's own sister, was Tom's mother. After Allworthy left for London, Bridget approached Jenny's mother and confided her secret in her. Together they contrived to send Deborah Wilkins, the maid, to Dorset shire to have her out of the way. Allworthy is shocked that his sister did not tell him the truth. Jenny exculpates her, however, by saying that she intended to tell Allworthy one day. Bringing the conversation back to the present, Mrs. Waters tells Allworthy that Dowling approached her and promised her money from a "very worthy Gentleman" if she continued her prosecution of Tom. Allworthy guesses that this gentleman must be Blifil.

Chapter VIII

Squire Western arrives. He has discovered Sophia's letters from Tom. Allworthy offers to speak to Sophia after he has spoken to Dowling. Once Western has left, Jenny tells Allworthy that she spent twelve years with a man who swore to marry her but never actually did. She fled to Captain Waters for protection, and lived with him for many years under the alibi of being his wife. She met Tom when Captain Waters left to oppose the Jacobite rebels.

Mrs. Waters falls to her knees and praises Tom's goodness in saving her. Dowling interrupts them. Motioning to Jenny, Allworthy asks Dowling if he knows "this Lady." Dowling has to admit that he does. Allworthy now carries out a kind of trial by which he finds out that Blifil was indeed responsible for trying to bring further prosecution against Tom. Allworthy asks how Dowling could have been Blifil's accomplice. Dowling confesses that he already knows that Tom is Allworthy's nephew—on her deathbed, Bridget Allworthy took Dowling's hand and bid him tell Allworthy that Tom was her son. She also wrote a letter to Blifil explaining the story. Dowling entrusted the letter and story to Blifil, who promised to pass on the information to Allworthy.

Mrs. Miller returns and Allworthy tells her the shocking news. Mrs. Miller is overjoyed that Tom has been proven innocent. Before she leaves, Mrs. Waters tells the company that Tom will soon be released from prison. Allworthy summons Blifil and tells him to produce the letter that Bridget wanted him to deliver to Allworthy. Blifil's situation is "to be envied only be a Man who is just going to be hanged."

Chapter IX

Allworthy reads Tom's letter to Sophia. The beauty of it brings tears to his eyes. Allworthy visits Sophia and congratulates her on her refusal to marry Blifil, which shows foresight on her part. Allworthy says that he has a different proposal for her—he has another nephew, whom he would like her to marry. Sophia expresses surprise at never having met this mysterious nephew, and Allworthy tells her that it is Tom. Sophia says she can appreciate that Tom must be a worthy nephew, but she cannot accept him as a husband. Squire Western suddenly bursts in and chastises Sophia. In his country dialect, Western bellows that he has a letter from Lady Bellaston relating that Tom is out of prison and on the loose. Western warns Sophia to stay away from the man. Allworthy takes this opportunity to acquaint Western with recent events. Squire Western now begs Allworthy to bring Tom to court Sophia that afternoon.

Chapter X

Allworthy apologizes to Tom for his past behaviour. Tom says that there is no need for retribution; the joy he is experiencing now atones for his suffering. Tom laments his follies and vices, but Allworthy brushes them away, praising Tom for not being a hypocrite. Allworthy tells Tom that he has visited Sophia, and urges Tom to submit to Sophia's will. Mrs. Miller meets with Tom and tells him that she has explained to Sophia that Tom's proposal letter to Lady Bellaston was not meant seriously. Sophia still complained that Tom was a "Libertine," but Mrs. Miller told her that Tom turned down Mrs. Hunt. Mr. Western arrives, extremely impatient for the afternoon courtship festivities.

Chapter XI

Jones tells Allworthy and Mrs. Miller how he gained his liberty from the prison. Mrs. Waters assured Fitzpatrick that Tom did not have an affair with his wife and, consequently, Fitzpatrick admitted that he initiated the duel. Moreover, Fitzpatrick is so delighted with what Mrs. Waters has told him that he praises Tom to Lord Fellamar, who decides that he should assist this man whom he affronted by his advances to Sophia.

Allworthy wishes to punish Blifil, but Tom argues for forgiveness. Mrs. Miller and Allworthy want Blifil to leave the house as soon as possible. Tom asks that he may be the messenger of the news. He finds Blifil bawling on his bed, although Blifil is frightened rather than contrite. Tom tells Blifil the news—he comforts Blifil and offers to provide for him. Blifil thanks Tom profusely, then departs. Allworthy reveals Black George's corruption to Tom. Tom tells Allworthy of Black George's generosity to him while he was in prison, but Allworthy is determined to punish Black George for his dishonesty. Partridge and Tom are reunited.

Chapter XII

Tom meets Sophia at Western's house. They are both finely dressed and look breathtaking. At first they remain silent. Sophia suggests that Tom judge his own behaviour—she tells him that only time will prove whether he can cast aside his wild desires. She does not understand how he could have been unchaste in Upton. Tom argues that the delicacy of women prevents them from imagining how sordid men can be. He argues that amours of the body do not affect the amour of the heart. Sophia accepts his reply, but says that she will only marry him after twelve months. They kiss. Mr. Western bursts in and, after teasing the lovers with bawdy jokes, orders Sophia to marry Tom immediately. Sophia says that she cannot disobey her father. Western looks forward to having a grandson in nine months.

Chapter the last

The wedding is filled with mirth, and those who were unhappy before are happy now. The narrator summarizes the future. Tom makes Allworthy agree to give Blifil an annuity of 200 pounds, even though Allworthy refuses to speak to Blifil. Blifil converts to Methodism in the hopes of marrying a rich Methodist widow who lives near to him. Mrs. Fitzpatrick separates from Fitzpatrick. Mrs. Waters marries Parson Supple, and Allworthy grants her an annuity of sixty pounds. Partridge sets up a school with the help of Tom. He is engaged to Molly Seagrim. Sophia and Tom now live on Western's estate and have two children, a boy and a girl. Western has retired to a smaller estate, but visits the couple frequently. Tom has conquered his cheeky streak. He and Sophia are still very much in love, and hold each other in the highest esteem. They show kindness and respect to all around them.

Commentary

Fielding is a dramatic narrator, who often appears in the story himself to comment on some behaviour or to merely point out something. In the first chapter of the book, he makes an appearance to bid farewell to the reader. He hopes that the reader has enjoyed the narrative, for that was the author's objective. Fielding makes these comments in a unique, humourous style that is especially his. He endears himself to the reader with his frankness and warmth.

From the next chapter, the narrative is continued. We notice that the pace is brisk now and many events take place, which finally draw the history to an end.

Partridge has Mrs. Deborah Wilkins's habit and that is of overhearing. When Jenny (Mrs. Waters) visits Tom in jail, Partridge learns that the two had slept together at Upton. He is shocked by this news as he had thought all this while that Jenny is Tom's mother. The reader too is shocked at this news. Tom is now guilty of incest too, apart from the other follies that weigh on his shoulders. This is the first time we see Tom in absolute despair and are able to sympathize with him. Mrs. Waters brings news, which is a source of happiness to Tom and that is that Mr. Fitzpatrick who is now her consort, is out of danger. So Tom will not be tried of murder. But he feels guilty of incest and considers it equal to having been hung.

Black George proves to be a faithful friend despite having been guilty of minor crimes before. He comes to reassure Tom in jail and to give him money if required. Little does he know that the despair that Tom feels cannot be solved by financial aid. Black George assumes that Tom is unhappy because of Sophia. He gives Tom some positive information, regarding his beloved. Through Black George's character, Fielding illustrates the fact that it is poverty sometimes that makes us evil. Black George is faithful and a worthy friend, but previously it had been poverty that had driven him to commit small offences.

Squire Allworthy is a man who helps others. Now he undertakes Mrs. Miller's cause and goes to meet the elder Mr. Nightingale. He persuades this gentleman to be reconciled with his son and Mr. Nightingale agrees. Fielding develops the story through a variety of coincidences-one such incident happens when the Squire goes to meet old Mr. Nightingale. He sees Black George there and discovers the money that George had stolen from Tom. This is indeed a very strange coincidence and Mr. Allworthy tells of this to Mrs. Miller. He knows that Mrs. Miller is concerned about Tom and she would be happy to know that Tom would have some money of his own now.

Many important disclosures are made in these chapters. The Squire learns that Tom is not guilty of attacking Mr. Fitzpatrick and that Dowling had been sent by someone to talk to the men who witnessed the Tom-Mr. Fitzpatrick fight. We see how the Squire's eyes are slowly opened to the treachery of Blifil and to the innocence of Tom. These disclosures also come about in coincidental ways. Mrs. Waters comes to meet the Squire and condemns him for sending a lawyer who seeks to destroy Tom. The Squire had not send Dowling and realises that Blifil is behind this. Blifil had tried to make sure that Tom would be out of his way. While Tom would never ever have stooped so low, Blifil does. As readers, we are glad that the Squire finally starts learning the truth about Blifil.

Other relevant disclosures are made. We finally learn the identity of Tom's parents. His mother is none other than Miss Bridget and his father had been Mr. Summers. Thankfully for Tom, he is not guilty of incest, as Mrs. Waters (Jenny) is not his mother. The story behind Tom's birth is recounted by Mrs. Waters-how Miss Bridget hid the secret and how even Mrs. Wilkins was not allowed to know.

Indeed, Miss Bridget turns out to be an altogether different character than we had imagined. Beneath all the prudence is a passionate woman. Her brother, the Squire is surprised to say the least. He recalls that when Mr. Summers was home, he had noted an attraction between him and Bridget but the latter had denied it. Miss Bridget, indeed, had lived a hypocritical life.

Thus we see how Fielding gets together all the key characters, while drawing the history to an end. Many skeletons of the past are revealed and we have a better understanding of why certain characters behaved the way they did.

The commendable quality of Fielding's writing is the way he draws coincidences and surprising incidents to seem natural. The pace here is a hurried one, but at the same time, it never seems forced or artificial.

Chapter 7

Study Questions

Q1. Discuss the elements of Satire and Sentiment in Henry Fielding's novel.

Or

Q. Henry Fielding is considered as the most valuable English influence for the novel writing of the new century. Do you agree?

Satire and Sentiment

Both in his writing and in his world view, Henry Fielding serves as a bridge between the satiric writing which achieved triumphant expression in the third and forth decade of the 18th century, and the sentimental writing toward which British taste was moving. Thus, for example, Fielding's rewriting of Richardson's Pamela, first in Shamela (1741) and then in Joseph Andrews (1742), is often aligned with Fielding's participation in the satiric traditions most famously practiced by Swift, Pope, Gay, and Hogarth. Indeed, Fielding's first great success, the drama Tom Thumb (1730), is written in the bright and brittle language of Pope's The Rape of the Lock (1717). In the last act of the play, the tiny Tom wins a great military victory, but, on the way to claim the hand of the princess Huncamunca, he is swallowed by a cow. Like The Rape of the Lock and Swift's voyage to Lilliput (from Gulliver's Travels), the conjunction of grand language and diminutive size becomes a satiric device for exposing vanity to ridicule. Fielding's editorial expansion of Tom Thumb into Tragedies of Tragedies (1731), edited by

H. Scriblerus Secundus, is an explicit tribute to Martin Scriblerus, the editor of the Dunciad, and other satiric works. Fielding's Jonathan Wild (1743, revised in 1754), by taking up the history of the fence and thief-taker Jonathan Wild, updates the stage sensation of 1728, John Gay's The Beggar's Opera. These literary influences on Fielding's writing allow us to take account of a satiric strain in Fielding's work: urbane and skeptical, the satirist's moral aim is to cleanse the world by exposing vice and folly to view. But, Fielding is a satirist with a difference. By embedding satire in an inclusive and generous social commentary, he softens the tone and pluralizes the directions of satiric critique, Thus, Fielding's narrator is sociable, garrulous and playful; his works seem conceived as much to sustain as critique social life; and, certain passages of his writing, like the "Man of the Hill" episode in Tom Jones, diagnose the misanthropy of satire's assumption of the posture of the alienated outsider.

While the traditions and devices of satire—from the mock epic style to the literary caricature—flow into the English novel through Fielding (Paulson, 1968), a productive commingling of satiric and sentimental impulses can be read across the arc of Fielding's major fictional works, from Joseph Andrews (1742) and Jonathan Wild (1743) to Tom Jones (1749) and Amelia (1751). While all the novels have a rich economy of sentimental motifs, critics have found Amelia to be Fielding's most domestic, personal, and sentimental novel. Throughout these novels, Fielding manipulates the emotions of the reader by staging moments of endangered innocence, sudden loss, and touching acts of selfless generosity. Thus, for example, in writing Joseph Andrews, Fielding clearly intends to disperse the solemnity with which Richardson invests Pamela's sturdy but sanctimonious defence of her virtue. However, when we read the scenes in which Joseph Andrews protects his own virtue, first from the rapacious Mrs. Slipslop, and then from the importunate Lady Booby, Joseph sounds a good deal like his "sister" Pamela. He tells his mistress Lady Booby, "I can't see why her having no virtue should be a reason against my having any.

Or why, because I am a man, or because I am poor, my virtue must be subservient to her pleasures?" (I: VIII, 35) So, what at first seems like a satiric device—a reversal of genders so as to mock Richardson's cult of virginity—modulates in both Joseph Andrews and Tom Jones into something more nuanced: an exploration of the way a character balances the temptations of the moment and the weakness of the flesh against the social value of faithful love. Fielding's distinctive approach to novel writing arises from his class, his education, and his experience. While Defoe and Richardson still suffer a puritanical distrust of the mendacity of story-telling, and worry the deleterious moral effects of the new entertainment of novel reading, Fielding heartily embraces the restorative value of entertainment. Seven years of play writing and directing the Haymarket Theater had given Fielding practical insight into how to please contemporary audiences. His turn to novel writing, like the playwright Aphra Behn's recourse to writing novels in the early 1680s, was precipitated by a forbidding political climate.

The boldly literal satire of Fielding's plays stirred the ire of the Walpole regime, and the Licensing act of 1737 closed the theater to him. Fielding understood the entertainment value and enlightenment potential of his prose histories through the classical apology for literature. The literary author, according to Horace's Ars Poetical, must strive to balance delight and instruction (dulcet et utile). By contrast, in Pamela, Richardson exploited the absorptive powers of the novels of amorous intrigue to draw young readers toward the conduct book lessons he would teach them. Success for Richardson would mean that young readers would not want to read any more novels. (Warner, 1998) By contrast, Fielding understands Pamela to be a novel masquerading as a guide to moral life. In Joseph Andrews, Fielding writes his alternative history of modern life in "the manner of Cervantes." The Spanish master gives Fielding a template for fiction centreed upon a critique of the dangerous effects of absorptive romance reading. Fielding also follows Cervantes by translating vast learning in ancient and modern literature and classical rhetoric into a "history" of contemporary English life. In writing Joseph Andrews, Tom Jones, and Amelia, Fielding's avowed aim is to teach readers to be skeptical, wise, and generous critics of the social world of which they are a part. Some of Fielding's contemporaries, like Francis Coventry, agreed that Fielding had succeeded in practicing a "new species of writing," one that elevated the ethical purposes of novelistic writing while expanding its literary resources. Fielding also helped to raise the market value of novels.

His publisher, Andrew Millar, paid Fielding unprecedented fees for the copyrights to his three novels, and, after Fielding's death, Millar published an elegant posthumous collection of his novels in the quarto format, to which he appends a "life of Fielding," especially commissioned for the edition and written by Arthur Murphy. When, in the nineteenth century, Walter Scott anthologizes the most important novels of the previous century for Galantine's Novelist's Library, he gives pride of place to Henry Fielding, as the most valuable English influence for the novel writing of the new century.

Q2. Fielding constructs Tom Jones so that it offers an encyclopedic view of society. Discuss.

Or

Q. How does Fielding most inventively exploits the possibilities of the comedy.

Comedy and the Novel

Among the eighteenth century novelists, it is Fielding who most inventively exploits the possibilities of the comedy. In The Anatomy of Criticism, Northrop Frye offers a general account of the plot of comedy, from Greek new comedy to the novels of Charles Dickens, which applies particularly well to Fielding's major novels. In the Joseph Andrews and Tom Jones, the romance of the two lovers is interrupted by one or more blocking figures; their happiness is delayed by a journey full of incidents that are at once comic and instructive; the narrative climaxes with the surprise discovery of the true paternity of the hero; the plot's resolution takes the form of marriage and the prospect of a happiness that is at once erotic and moral; the narrative ends with a festive meal, itself an emblem of a communal celebration of life.

But what gives Fielding's comedy its distinctive flavour is his inventive interweaving of the diverse speech genres he finds in his social and literary world. I can illustrate this idea by discussing the scene, at the very end of Tom Jones, where the eponymous hero asks Sophia Western to marry him. Here, Fielding composes one of the oddest proposal scenes in literature. While Tom speaks the language of a penitent lover, asking forgiveness for his many transgressions, Sophia turns the language of personal injury into a judicial examination: "Mr. Jones, have I not enough to resent? After what past at Upton, so soon to engage in a new amour with another woman, while I fancied, and you pretended, your heart was bleeding for me!—Indeed, you have acted strangely. Can I believe the passion you have protest to me to be sincere?

Or if I can, what happiness can I assure myself of with a man capable of so much inconstancy?" (XVIII: xii, 972) Pressed so strictly on his infidelities, Tom has recourse to a libertine alibi: "The delicacy of your sex cannot conceive the grossness of ours, nor how little one sort of amour has to do with the heart." Sophia's reply has the dialectical finesse of a lawyer: "I will never marry a man who shall not learn refinement enough to be as incapable as I am myself of making such a distinction." (XVIII: xii, 973) The scene seems in danger of ending with the hero consigned to the extended probation necessary to prove his reform to Sophia. However, more hopeful words from Sophia make Tom "mad with joy," and he "kissed her with an ardor he had never ventured before." Sophia's father Squire Western, who is listening outside the door, "burst into the room, and with his hunting voice and phrase, cry's out, 'to her boy, to her, go to her.—That's it, little honeys, O that's it.'" When he finds that Sophia has not "appointed the day" for marriage, Western demands Sophia's consent to marry "not a minute longer" than the day after tomorrow.

When Sophia firmly declines, Western rants, "When I forbid her, then it was all nothing but sighing and whining, and languishing and writing; now I am for thee, she is against thee. ...She is above being guided and governed by her father...It is only to disoblige and contradict me." When Sophia suddenly consents to be guided by her father ("What would my Papa have me do?") and when she agrees to marry "to-morrow morning," "Jones then fell upon his knees, and kissed her hand in an agony of joy, while Western began to caper and dance about the room."

The distinct art of Fielding's comedy comes from the collision of radically different characters, sensibilities, and the language proper to each. In this scene Tom's impatient desire to get on with loving must enter into extended dialogue with Sophia's very sensible reservations about the implications for their future of Tom's all too recent infidelities. This proposal scene gets its power to represent social reality not from its plausibility—it is difficult to imagine real lovers talking this way—or as an analysis of a consistent character—we have not heard Sophia speak this sort of closely reasoned moral discourse before. Instead, the dialogue in this scene interweaves social languages for talking about love. Tom speaks the casuistic excuses of the libertine and the impatient enthusiasm of the lover.

Sophia brings to bear upon his behaviour the strict standards of the wise moralist. Finally, Squire Western interrupts their colloquy with the language of the hunt, of the indignant patriarch, and, finally, of the leader of the revels. Fielding develops a literary method that sustains the diversity of the social reality that he references. Fielding's most crucial literary technique is what we see in this scene: the incorporation within the boundaries of the comic novel of a diversity of genres, derived from the social world, which Bachchan calls heteroglossia—"another's speech in another's language" (The Dialogic Imagination, 324). While Fielding's comic novels give free reign to social passion (from conviviality to lust) they resist the coercive demands for sincerity, purity of sentiment, and ideological closure that Fielding associated (whether fairly or unfairly) with the novels of Samuel Richardson.

To offset the abstracting and rationalizing tendency of both characters and narrators, expressed in this scene by Sophia's critical assessment of her Tom's moral shortcomings, Fielding's comedy reminds us of the tenacious centrality of the body, asserted in this scene by the venturesome "ardor" of Tom's kiss and the sudden physical intrusion of Squire Western. Literature and the Law: Conceptualizing Society as a Complex Totality The only major English novelist who was also a practicing lawyer and magistrate, Fielding's study of the law (1737-1740) precedes his novel writing and deeply suffuses his fiction. (Bender, 1987) His day to day grappling with the problem of modern vice may have intensified his skepticism of moral formulas, like "virtue rewarded," the subtitle of Richardson's novel Pamela. Fielding offers his retort to this idea in the first lines of Book XV of Tom Jones.

There are a set of religious, or rather moral writers, who teach that virtue is the certain road to happiness, and vice to misery, in this world. A very wholesome and comfortable doctrine, and to which we have but one objection, namely, that it is not true. (XV:1: 783) Written in one elegantly balanced period, this passage at first seems to extend support to the doctrine of 'virtue rewarded,' until, with a sudden turn, like the prosecuting attorney at court, the author raises his one, devastating "objection", "namely, that it is not true." Fielding's rejection of the moral idealism of Richardson's exemplary characters, and Fielding's defence of his own use of ethically "mixed characters" (like Tom Jones and Captain Booth), reflects the empiricist underpinnings of legal practice. While the law may be grounded in the concept of social good, the judge must constantly balance the abstract code of the law against the stream of actual, all-too-human individuals who are brought before the law.

As the world's largest city, London posed certain common problems for both the city dweller and the judge. Fielding's sometimes garrulous narrator discusses these problems with his reader and makes them integral to the education of the reader his novels attempt. How should one evaluate the character of strangers? Why should we be skeptical about initial appearances? When should we extend sympathy to strangers? Out of Fielding's practice of literature and law there emerges the concept of society as a complex, interdependent totality. Such an idea is implicit in one of his practical solutions to the sheer scale and anonymity of London: the formation of a "Universal Register Office", where those needing services, and those providing services, could register and find each other.

It opened for business Feb 19, 1750, a year after the publication of Tom Jones. (Battestin, Companion, 197) Fielding's most systematic, nonnovelistic development of this idea is in a 1751 pamphlet, entitled, "An Inquiry into the Causes of the Late Increase of Robbers." Like numberless other enlightenment era pamphlets, Fielding seeks social improvement through a rational set of legal and institutional reforms. But what is most innovative about his analysis is the way Fielding interconnects the diverse causes for a recent crime wave. Insisting that this crime wave is symptomatic of a larger set of social maladies, Fielding attributes crime to the effect on the poor of the allure of luxury and the many diversions easily available in London, to the practice of drunkenness (intensified by the new prevalence of distilled gin), and to the rage for gambling. Luxury, drunkenness, and gambling not only motivate crime, they also expand the numbers of the poor, the chief source of the most hardened criminals. But rather than setting the poor against the middling and upper ranks of society, Fielding insists that the poor acquire these vices by emulating the rich. Fielding assures his reader he is no visionary, and would not think of trying to reform these pleasurable "fashions" of the rich. Besides, Fielding notes, these vices carry their own punishment to the great, in the ruin of their estates and families.

However, among the poor they lead to violent crime. This crime robs all Englishmen of the security needed to enjoy the liberty that they so much pretend to value. Further, these practices, by vitiating the health of the people, lead to a dangerous physical decay of the nation. In making his case for new laws, and new institutions to enforce old law, Fielding gives a new turn to the legal concept of the English constitution by making it the living soul of the body politic.

The constitution is dynamic and constantly changing because it is not simply its written and unwritten law, or the distributed power of its different political agencies (King, Lords, and Commons); it also comprehends the "customs, manners, and habits of the people." (Preface, 9) To conceptualize what gives coherence to the complex amalgam, Fielding has recourse to Greek philosophy: [The constitution is] something which results from the order and disposition of the whole; ... many of the Greeks imagined the soul to result from the composition of the parts of the body when these were properly tempered together; as harmony doth from the proper composition of the several parts in a well tuned musical instrument; in the same manner, from the disposition of the several parts in a state, arises that which we call the constitution.(Preface, 9-10; in William Ernest Henley, LL.D., The Complete Works of Henry Fielding, Esq., Vol. VIII, Legal Writings (United States: Barnes & Noble, 1967) Here, Fielding's analogy attributes the soul of the human body, the harmony of musical instruments, and the heath of the political constitution to the composition, or disposition, of parts "properly tempered together."

This is the alchemy that Fielding attempts in his magnum opus, Tom Jones, where the idea of society, as the necessary inter-relation of all its members, is given an early, and very influential, literary expression. Fielding constructs Tom Jones so that it offers an encyclopedic view of society, from country house to the road to the city of London, from high to middling to lower life, from a London Masquerade to Negate Prison. To incorporate this social diversity, Fielding privileges the picaresque locales of the public inn, the stage coach, and the road, places of unexpected encounter and unruly plurality, where different classes mix and converse. Adopting the formal conventions of epic, this literary construction requires an intricate plot that will bind all its events into one action. In this way, the reader can watch a host of characters, in ways dimly understood by the characters, and only gradually understood by the reader, come into a grand pattern of mutual interdependence.

This is the "truth" about human nature and human society to which Fielding's "great creation" hopes to give his reader access. The narrator of Tom Jones argues that the author who would actualize this idea, must, in contrast with the romance writers, have "powers of mind, which are capable of penetrating into all things within our reach and knowledge, and of distinguishing their essential differences," "a good share of learning," a "universal" "conversation" "with all ranks and degrees," and finally, he must have "a good heart, and be capable of feeling." The length of this catalog of traits is an index of the difficulty of comprehending the society in its totality. The necessity of doing so with a "good heart," suggests that the idea of the coherent interdependence of society is not just a theory that may or may not be true; it is also an ethical imperative toward which one should aspire. If both author and reader do so, they can then understand their own exchange as part of a worthy and enjoyable social conversation: "The author who will make me weep, says Horace, must first weep himself...in the same manner...I am convinced I never make my reader laugh heartily, but where I have laughed before him,..."(IX:1: 490-494)

The literary debt owed to Fielding by later novelists like Jane Austen, Charles Dickens and George Eliot, results in good part form his literary development of the idea of society is as a complex, mutually dependent totality.

Q3. How far is Fielding successful in presenting moral truths in Tom Jones.

Or

Q. Why do you think the author intrudes in the story?

Richetti states that eighteenth-century novels in England are "heavily didactic," and the writers of the period are "open in their championing of moral truths" (Richetti 35). This assertion is undoubtedly accurate for Tom Jones; however, Fielding is well aware that "novel-reading is gratuitous and that commitment to a text is provisional" (Sherman 232). Therefore Fielding, in order to procure and satisfy readers' desires, engages readers in a "literal contract" (Sherman 234).

> Narrative...depends on social agreements, implicit pacts or contracts in order to produce exchanges that themselves are a function of desires, purposes, constraints... It is only on the strength of such agreements [contracts] that narratives can exert their impact and produce change...No act of narration occurs without at least an implicit contract, that is, an understanding between narrator and narrate, an illocutionary situation that makes the act meaningful and gives it what we call a "point" (Chambers 4, 9)

Fielding realises, that in order to "produce change" in his readers' moral visions, he must "appeal to readily desire" and "earn the privilege to narrate" (Sherman 235). This realization of Fielding's is the major purpose of his authorial intrusions. While Fielding may describe his prefatory chapters as being "serious," and "dull," he knows, and we know, they are anything but serious (Fielding 184). Indeed, his prefatory chapters, narrative digressions, and chapter titles are as humourous and entertaining as anything narrated in Fielding's "comic" parts of the novel.

I submit that Fielding intended his prefatory chapters and narrative digressions to underscore one of the main themes in Tom Jones: the enormous difficulty of fully 'knowing' the people we interact with in society (or in novels). Fielding asserts that the only way to understand the characters of people is to be had through "conversation" (Fielding 425). However, this is not completely accurate, as Fielding gives us many examples of characters in his novel who were led astray by other characters that they believed they knew well. In the relationships between Blifil and Allworthy, Tom and Molly,

Sophia and Lady Bellaston, we see that 'conversation' is not always enlightening.

Likewise, Fielding-the-narrator deceives us through his 'conversation' with us throughout the entire novel. Although from the very beginning of the novel, Fielding shows himself as a person who may be 'feigning' at times, he still manages to achieve our trust as an 'honest' narrative voice. Though Fielding admits us "behind the scenes of this great theatre of Nature" in showing other characters' motivations (Fielding 285), in the end, we also are led astray by the narrator himself.

Q4. To what extent does the reader participate in Tom Jones?

Or

Q. Comment on Rationalism in Fielding's Tom Jones

Or

Q. Philosophical questions are not Fielding's main concern; even though they are among his favourite targets, discuss the issues in characters like Thwackum and Square.

Wolfgang User, developing his theory of reader participation and reader response, chose Fielding's Tom Jones and Joseph Andrews as his starting point.1 Fielding's novels, therefore, do not just serve User as examples to illustrate his theory but actually provide the patterns or substrata on which it is based. This inductive method, however sound in itself, requires close attention to what the text says. In this paper, I am taking issue with User because his reading of Fielding does not seem quite close enough.

According to User the reader of Tom Jones or Joseph Andrews is encouraged by the author-narrator to help constitute the meaning of the novel. He sees Fielding's offer of co-operation at certain places in the novels which he calls "blanks" or "gaps." The reader is meant to fill the "Blanks" (Tom Jones II.i.76), "vacant Spaces" (III.i.116) or "vacant Pages" (Joseph Andrews II.i.89) with the help of certain textual signs.

User's main contention is that the novel does not explicitly state its meaning, but that it is the reader who constructs its meaning on the basis of these signs. In other words, the author provides the reader with guidelines, "restructured by the written text." These guidelines are mainly found in the initial essays to the 18 books of Fielding's Tom Jones and the prefaces to his novels.

User interprets Fielding's theoretical essays and statements in an intellectual and epistemological sense. In this view he follows John Preston, who also claimed that Fielding aims at rational understanding and that the effect of his novels was "epistemological rather than moral." I cannot agree with either of these propositions but shall argue that Fielding's aim was a composite one, ruled by feeling.

[page 138]One of User's main stays is a passage from Tom Jones in which Fielding expands on "the vacant Spaces of Time." In Chapter Ibid. Fielding addresses his reader, attributing to him, as so often, "Sagacity".As nothing of importance has happened in the history of Tom Jones, so he tells the reader, he intends to pass over a long stretch of time. The reader, therefore, has a chance of intelligent participation, an Opportunity of employing that wonderful Sagacity, of which he is Master, by filling up these vacant Spaces of Time with his own Conjectures.

User comments this passage as follows:

The vacant spaces in the text, here as in Joseph Andrews, are offered to the reader as pauses in which to reflect. They give him the chance to enter into the proceedings in such a way that he can construct their meaning.

First of all, User does not meet the tone of the passage, but falls, to put it bluntly, into the trap of Fielding's irony. This is clearly indicated by the hyperbolic compliments concerning the reader's sagacity. Secondly, what Fielding calls "vacant Spaces" is hardly identical with spaces for a congenial interpretation leading up to "constructing" the text. He does not provide any spaces at all for readers to exercise their conjectural abilities but, on the contrary, he caricatures an altogether unwanted reader-participation.

> ... what Reader but knows that Mr. Allworthy felt at first for the Loss of his Friend, those Emotions of Grief, which on such Occasions enter into all Men whose Hearts are not composed of Flint, or their Heads of as solid Materials? Again, what Reader doth not know that Philosophy and Religion, in time, moderated, and at last extinguished this Grief?

The "capitation benevolent" is followed, first, by an example showing what might happen if the wonderfully sagacious reader really availed himself of the offer to fill in the "the vacant Spaces." He would produce the typical clichés of the dilettante. Fielding recounts purely conventional reactions and his irony—"... Flint, or... Heads of as solid Materials"—marks them as such. His approval of Bridget Allworthy's strict [page 139] observation of mourning as far as her garments are concerned points in the same direction. We should not, therefore, put too much trust in the reader's "Sagacity" nor in his ability to contribute intelligent conjectures or to participate in the construction of meaning.

This skepticism on Fielding's part is corroborated by some other comments on his readers. He distinguishes two types of readers, those of "the lowest Class" and "the upper Graduates in Criticism". Of course, everybody will identify with the "graduates," but it is just the epithet "upper" which should warn the discerning reader. The events or episodes which these readers are supposed to be imagining, the author assures us, are "of equal Importance with those reported by the daily and weekly Historians of the age," yet all these things are obviously not "worthy of a Place" in his history and therefore negligible. Of course, the reader is at liberty to conjecture whatever he likes, but Fielding would hardly regard this type of literary activity as very much worthwhile. He seems to have anticipated, ironically, Wittgenstein's famous phrase: "Whereof one cannot speak, thereof one must be silent." The reader should not talk of what the author is silent about.

After the ironic capitation benevolent Fielding then resorts to hysteron portion, expressing his conviction that the conjectures about the characters and their actions will exercise "some of the most excellent Faculties of the Mind." It would be much more "useful," indeed, to foretell "the Actions of Men in any Circumstance from their Characters" rather than to take the trouble to judge them by their actions. In the light of this ironic inversion of cause and effect it is not surprising that Fielding emphasizes the great difficulty of exercising this talent, assisted though it be by "Penetration" and "Sagacity," of course. The absurd flattery reaches its climax at the end of the chapter:

As we are sensible that much the greatest Part of our Readers are very eminently possessed of this Quality, we have left them a Space of twelve Years to exert it in; and shall now bring forth our Heroes, at about fourteen Years of Age, not questioning that many have been long impatient to be introduced to his Acquaintance.

Now we know what to make of the reader's attributed "Sagacity," warned by the assertion that most of the readers are "very eminently [page 140] possessed" of it. The ambiguity of the verb "possessed" is a special case of irony which allows Fielding to say and not say what he means. The very readers who are stupid enough to swallow his bait, "Sagacity," and believe (like the ass in the fable) to know better than the real craftsman, are the ones to whom the satirical epithet "possessed" applies. Perhaps the crowning absurdity in this passage is the offer of a twelve years' gap to be filled by volunteers. What they are offered is literally a stretch of twelve years in which to have their say. Discourse time and story time are inextricably mixed in the clause and sub-clause. The result is nonsense.

What User does not see or state clearly is that even "gaps" and "blanks" are a means of directing the reader. The gap is, if at all, the illusion of freedom to fill something in. The reader is confronted with schematized views and gaps between them, but they belong to schemes of textual presentation which aim at a particular reader-involvement.

In User's description of the reading process the terms "gap," "vacant spaces," and "missing links" are not ironical as they are in Fielding's (or in Sterna's) dialogue with the reader and their literal meaning is taken to be stronger than their function as metaphors. For User they seem to signal a deficiency. The reader is supposed to fill in what the author left out—on purpose and by necessity (the text cannot spell out its own meaning). But an author like Fielding does not leave out anything essential. The metaphors of space, if not used ironically, are rather unsuitable in a theory of reading as they suggest the author left out parts, almost in the way of a puzzie.

If Fielding's irony points to nothing else it points out that the activity of the reader depends on what the author actually put into words. His words create impressions in the reader's mind and subsequently cause imaginative activities. The reader reacts to the features of language, responds to its various aesthetic and rhetorical qualities as well as to its semantic aspects. Metaphors for these activities should have more positive connotations than those of "filling in," an expression which does not do justice to the richness of textual connotations, implications, references, and emotional appeals.

The reader's imagination is able to work on the text, not because of what the text does not say or leaves out, but because of what its words [page 141] suggest. Granted that we can only picture what we do not actually see, as User says, it does not make much sense to say "the written part of the text gives us the knowledge, but it is the unwritten part that gives us the opportunity to picture things." We imagine what the text says, precisely because the text is not picture but word, i.e. a sign which creates a picture in the mind. The contention that we "are not able to use our imagination" without the gaps in the text seems to ignore a fundamental function of language, especially literary language.

Throughout User's essays one encounters the notion that the reader is somehow competing with the author. This implies a wrong notion of the working of the imagination. User's interpretation of Virginia Wolf's comment on Jane Austen reflects this misunderstanding. The things which in Virginia Wolf's view Jane Austen offers to the reader are said to "expand" in the imagination. In other words, the reader's imagination builds on what the author provides, but this is different from saying that the reader does not get the whole story, that he creates the unwritten parts of the text. "The most enduring form of life" Virginia Woolf speaks about is not a material, quantitative, addition, not a background created by the reader, but a quality with which the author "endows... scenes which are outwardly trivial." It is Jane Austen who offers this to the reader's mind and imagination.

User understands the reader's role in a substantive sense, in spite of his protestations that he regards it as re-creative. The reader, however, is, and even ought to be, primarily an under stander—words convey first of all meaning—and where the imagination is concerned, the reader is a visualize. In the imagination the things signified come to life. Naturally, the author does not and cannot "give" that inner picture of the mind to the reader directly, but whoever would claim this to be the case? Therefore, the claim "no author worth his salt will ever attempt to set the whole picture before his reader's eyes" is either a truism or does not make sense. Fielding, at any rate, does not invite the reader to participate (or rather intrude), quite the contrary. The spaces he leaves out are not spaces for the constitution of meaning. Fielding's addresses to the reader primarily aim at the fanciful reading habits of dilettante readers. He exposes such habits by ironical praise and tells us more about how not to read than how to read. But, although Fielding makes it quite [page 142] clear how he expects a really intelligent reader to deal with a literary text, User sticks to his theory and takes those appeals to the sagacious reader for granted:

This typical appeal to the reader's "sagacity" aims at arousing a sense of discernment.... Here we have a clear outline of the role of the reader, which is fulfilled through the continual instigation of attitudes and reflections on those attitudes.

Though User mentions Fielding's irony in the "history" part of the novel, he fails to account for it in the addresses to the reader, whose activity he describes, without qualification, as a process of rational reasoning. Fielding's texts as well as the various philosophical treatises of the period demand an altogether different perspective. Rational self-righteousness, the supposed "Sagacity" of the dilettante, was nothing less than one of the targets of Fielding's satire. A reader reaching up to the author's ideal of participation would be a sensitive under stander, wary of ironic overtones and far from being willing to interfere.

The irony of "Sagacity" is obvious enough in the context of Tom Jones—even Squire Western boasts about his "Sagacity"20—but its poignancy becomes even more apparent when it is looked at in the light of John Locke's definition. In the Essay Concerning Human Understanding, "Sagacity" denotes the exercise of arriving at knowledge, not by intuition which is the highest form, but by "Demonstration," the use of "intermediate Ideas." In other words, sagacity is defined as an ability to arrive at knowledge through a process of "Reasoning," of using "intervening Ideas": "A quickness in the Mind to find out these intermediate Ideas... and to apply them right, is, I suppose, that which is called Sagacity." Locke is concerned here with that quality of judgment which is achieved through a process of reasoning alone. For Fielding this is just not good enough. His parody of sagacity suggests, rather, that he wants to question the possibility of arriving at any kind of true knowledge by this method at all. The reason for this ineffectiveness may be sought in the absence of wisdom, which is all the more apparent as it is present in "Sophia," the true end of Tom's journey. Keeping "Sagacity" and "Wisdom" so much apart, Fielding made it quite clear that he regarded the rationalist concept of sagacity as deficient. Tom Jones [page 143] much rather exemplifies Berkeley's view that "wit without wisdom... is hardly worth finding."

One of the reasons why User mistakes Fielding's "vacant Spaces" in his theory of reading may be his observation that Fielding rejected Richardson's overt didacticism. But in ridiculing outright didacticism, Fielding does not altogether dispense with teaching. On the contrary, he wants to teach in a less obvious and more effective way. He makes the reader learn on his own, not by telling him what he thinks is right but by letting him discover sense and nonsense for himself. To let his readers, i.e. us, achieve this aim, Fielding addresses the reader in the novel, makes him his confidant, an observer of his world. The actual reader, then, becomes a meta-reader who communicates with the author through the figure of the reader in the novel, a process reminding us of similar dramatic techniques, e.g. in Beaumont and Fletcher's The Knight of the Burning Pestle. In that play the audience on the stage, being the object of satire, serves to make the spectator aware of his own aesthetic and emotional expectations and reactions. Similarly, by exposing his reader's follies, Fielding is holding the mirror up to us, who are thus led to discover what he did not want to pronounce in a didactic fashion.

In his attempt to establish a place for reader participation, User knows only one alternative, either didacticism or vacant spaces, terbium non dater. But if we do not accept this alternative, the question remains: what is the function of Fielding's addresses to the reader?

One possible answer is that Fielding uses the weapons of irony and satire to expose the rationalist school of thought. As has been shown, the words "sagacious," "Sagacity" etc. indicate his opposition to and the ridiculing of Enlightenment rationalism. Fielding's irony is directed against the dogma of the animal rationale, the claim of the Cartesian school that we are human by virtue of our reasoning faculty only. However, Fielding counters this one-sided rationalism not on the level of philosophical discourse but in the context of an imaginative construction.

Fielding not only questions reading habits but also confronts the reader with his views on the nature of his novel as a work of art and the author as a creator. In the prefatory chapter of Book X he links the topics of reading and literary creation. Having tried from the very beginning [page 144] to create in the reader a real understanding of his role in relation to the history of Tom Jones, Fielding chooses, at this stage, to approach the subject by discussing the author's position with regard to the nature of his work, thus leading up to a more distinct outline of the relationship between the reader and the meaning of the novel. He defines the roles of the author and reader. One might say, he puts the reader in his place.

> Reader, it is impossible we should know what Sort of Person thou wilt be: For, perhaps, thou may'st be as learned in Human Nature as Shakespeare himself was, and, perhaps, thou may'st be no wiser than some of his Editors. (X.i.523)

As we can easily guess, Fielding takes no chances and decides to give the reader a few wholesome Admonitions; that thou may'st not as grossly misunderstand and misrepresent us, as some of the said Editors have misunderstood and misrepresented their Author.

Fielding stresses the primacy of the work and its own specific rules originating in the creative idea of the author. "This Work may, indeed, be considered as a great Creation of our own" (X.i.524-25). In the hierarchy of literary values Fielding puts all those categories in the first place which relate to the author as creator. Terms like "Design," "conceive," "Creation," the idea of the "Whole" and the "Parts" (524-25) suddenly abound and recall the fact that the idea of the poet as creator is an integral part of the epic tradition. Accordingly, the analogy between the poet as creator and creation as the art of God belongs to the tradition of poetic theory leading up to and culminating in the Renaissance. Placing himself within this tradition, Fielding seeks to affirm his control over his readers rather than open the way to reader participation. The prefatory chapters, just as the narrative reality in the novel, point to the unrelenting discipline of the author. Not surprisingly, therefore, Fielding asks the reader to refrain from passing judgment too quickly, because he may not have recognized the author's "Design."

It is not, however, Fielding's purpose to use this traditional metaphor in a merely affirmative sense.

> The Allusion and Metaphor we have here made use of, we must acknowledge to be infinitely too great for our Occasion, but there is, indeed, no other, which is at all adequate to express the Difference between an Author of the first Rate, and a Critic of the lowest. (X.i.525)

Fielding strikes a cautious note about his creative claim, after all. In the face of the older idea he sees himself and his role in the novel in an ironic light, particularly when he teasingly reminds the reader of his superior knowledge derived from "Inspiration" (III.v.135) or when he calls his work "prodigious" (V.i.209).

We should therefore take his assertion that he is "in reality, the Founder of a new Province of Writing" (II.i.77) with a pinch of salt. As an admirer of Cervantes, to whom he paid tribute for the kind of history he himself was composing, Fielding cannot but be ironic about his claim, the more so as he admits following a lost tradition, i.e. that of comic epic in prose, the definition of his comic romance.

Fielding, therefore, neither pleads the cause of the sagacious reader nor of the creator-author. This puts him in opposition to the intellectual as well as moralist demand for exemplary characters in literature ("in any Work of Invention," X.i.527), which, on the other hand, shows him to be an author who follows the classical doctrine of the mixed character. This, again, leads up to the real subject of the novel: the moral improvement of the reader.

> Indeed, nothing can be of more moral Use than the Imperfections which are seen in Examples of this Kind;... The Foibles and Vices of Men in whom there is great Mixture of Good, become more glaring Objects, from the Virtues which contrast them, and show their Deformity;.... (X.i.527)

The mixed character has a greater potential for improving the reader than an exemplary one, which is the reason why Fielding asks the reader to look closely at the differences between characters rather than to reduce them to popular literary types. The passage quoted is a seminal one for

Fielding's concept of reader participation. It indicates how the reader should or is likely to react.

Fielding's various claims, however sparkling with irony, are no mere intellectual vagaries but serve a purpose. He refutes those critics who [page 146] believe they have discovered eternal rules, said to be conforming to reason, and who are able to find fault, therefore, with authors like Shakespeare and, by self-ironic implication, himself. Fielding undermines these contemporary judges of taste and their dogmas by his travesty of the deus artier and, as he sets himself apart from the "jure divino Tyrant" (II.i.77), by a parody of another great paradigm of the past, the "rule by divine right" of the Stuarts. By asserting his position as a lord over his province, free to follow his own rules, Fielding puts himself on the same pedestal with established literary criticism and quite rightly challenges the validity of literary dogmas which deny their own origin in literary practice: "Who ever demanded the Reasons of that nice Unity of Time or Place which is now established to be so essential to dramatic Poetry?" (V.i.209-10) The danger, however, of undercutting his own position by mixing with such critical company is met by Fielding's assertion to "wave the Privilege" of demanding obedience for his own laws of writing and to provide reasons for them. Naturally this promise also belongs to the ironical exchange with the reader, who, in fact, has little choice but to accept the rules; Fielding obviously regards himself as the literary equivalent of the constitutional monarch, a Hanoverian King, as it were. These allusions to contemporary criticism and politics as well as Fielding's promise to provide the reader with reasons for his literary rules lead up to a new climax of self-irony:

> And here we shall of Necessity be led to open a new Vein of Knowledge, which, if it hath been discovered, hath not to our Remembrance, been wrought on by any ancient or modern Writer. This Vein is no other than that of Contrast, which runs through all the Works of the Creation.

Fielding raises the reader's expectations by his promise of "a new Vein of Knowledge," but instead of providing a real climax he pulls something very trivial out of his conjuror's hat which, like the hyperbolic and rather self-laudatory style, reveals the ironist at work. As a matter of fact, the claim to a new "Vein" is contradicted by the very ubiquity of it, which he sees "through all the Works of the Creation," and by the fact that it is the principle of any kind of perception, e.g. of beauty "as well natural as artificial". Even the arts serve to illustrate the principle. [page 147] Quite clearly, Fielding is not really au serious. As soon as he has assured the reader of what he "really" means, his example turns every idea of meaning into absurdity. While his criticism of contemporary comic practice on the stage is plausible enough—once again making the reader unaware of his ironic aim—at the end of the chapter he refers to "a late facetious Writer" (Sir Richard Steele) "who told the Public, that whenever he was dull, they might be assured there was a Design in it" (V.i.215), thus pointing out the evident absurdity of the very principle Fielding claims to have opened up.

In this Light then, or rather in this Darkness, I would have the Reader to consider these initial Essays. And after this Warning, if he shall be of Opinion, that he can find enough of Serious in other Parts of this History, he may pass over these, in which we profess to be labouriously dull, and begin the following Books, at the second Chapter.

I find it difficult to believe with User that Fielding has provided here for his novel a key named "Contrast" ("... at least it indicates clearly to the reader that this principle will provide him with a key to the narrative"). Even if Fielding were speaking quite in earnest, contrast is surely not a quality—structural or thematic—sufficiently specific to provide a key to plot or action. There is hardly any literary work that does not depend on contrasts.

And yet, Fielding's satire aims at the principle of contrast even quite specifically, because it is a rationalist commonplace. Seen from a skeptical point of view, the trust in the epistemological value of contrast has led into the darkness of absurdity. In the eyes of an ironist, skeptical of the absolute rule of kings as well as of reason, the light of reason and the rationalism of Enlightenment may be nothing but another version of darkness. Fielding makes use of the rationalist method of antithesis as the basis of thinking and knowing, i.e. of proving by contrast, in order to ridicule the rationalist ideal itself. What to the minds of rationalist critics appears as the brightness of reason turns out to be absolute nonsense when it has gone through the mill of Fielding's logic.

With his satire Fielding takes exception to a central issue of modern thought since Descartes, whose "Jed peens, don jet suis" marks the beginning of the epistemological separation between subject and object, [page 148] since the very act of consciousness constitutes an opposition between the subject thinking and the object of its thought. Historically Descartes opened the way to the rationalist subject-object difference, as well as to the scientific dissection of the world.

Though the image of light and darkness obviously links Fielding's discussion with the ideas of the Enlightenment, the link can be traced more specifically. In an epistemological context, the image of light and the idea of contrast both occur in Locke's Essay (after all the most notable document of rationalist philosophy in England). In the chapter "Of Knowledge and Opinion" Locke describes the method by which the mind arrives at the "clearest" kind of knowledge:

> The different clearness of our Knowledge seems to me to lie in the different way of Perception, the Mind has of the Agreement, or Disagreement of any of its Ideas.... And this, I think, we may call intuitive Knowledge. For in this, the Mind is at no pains of proving or examining, but perceives the Truth, as the Eye doth light, only by being directed toward it. Thus the Mind perceives, that White is not Black,... this kind of Knowledge is the clearest, and most certain,... This part of Knowledge is irresistible, and like the bright Sun-shine, forces it self immediately to be perceived,... the Mind is presently filled with the clear Light of it.

Locke here explains that the idea of contrast and the image of light are virtually interchangeable. What to the eye is light, contrast is to the mind. Both light and contrast lead to immediate perception and clear knowledge. Here light imagery is made to serve the rationalist foundation of knowledge, though it is nearly ubiquitous in the history of philosophy and therefore not characteristic as such. In the same way Pierre Bayle insists on the "natural light" of reason, as it provides the highest authority in the process of arriving at knowledge, any claim to knowledge having to submit to its rule. This rationalist dogma is ironically reflected in Fielding's "new Vein of Knowledge." It is precisely this philosophy whose light, in Fielding's eyes, leads into darkness.

As a "historian" concerned with "Human Nature" and not only "human understanding" Fielding points to pragmatic absurdities of the subject-object dichotomy, the principle of contrast and opposition. This has been exemplified in the figure of the author who assumes creator-like [page 149] supremacy, as well as in the pseudo-rational qualities of sagacity and judiciousness attributed to the reader. The absurd implications of the principle of contrast become even more evident when Fielding ironically applies it to the relation between the initial chapters and the history proper. Telling the reader that he might pass over these essays—"if... he can find enough of Serious in other Parts" (V.i.215)—he plays a rhetorical trick on him. Rather than deciding between what is supposedly important or not, serious or not, the reader is coaxed into recognizing that there is no such contrast. Fielding leaves him little choice but to read these chapters with particular attention, the more so as he ironically professes "to be labouriously dull." The author-reader relationship all but hides the author's omnipotence just as there is the unifying formal structure of the novel, even numerological organized, which symbolizes order in the apparent chaos of the world. This does not contradict but rather underlines the fact that Fielding displays a genuine concern for the reader, aesthetically as well as morally. It is the foundation of his kind of teaching.

Fielding's method is a case in point of the classic strategy of forensic rhetoric, namely to outmaneuver the opponent with his own weapons. Fielding's satirical attack against the rationalist principle of contrast employs the very means he attacks. The basis of satire, after all, is the perception of contrast. In other words, his weapon allows Fielding to turn the method against its rationalist proponents. His provocation, however, aims at more than just criticizing a principle, be it ethical (hypocrisy), aesthetic (reading), or philosophical (perception/knowledge); it aims at actually overcoming the discrepancies and contrasts laid open. Fielding, at least in the fictional context, does not accept the rationalist principle of contrast but establishes a dialectical method of using contrast to overcome it.

In the context of the philosophical arguments of the period, his "dialogue" with the reader questions basic tenets of rationalism. Like Richardson before him and Sterna after him, Fielding was sensitive to the limitations of a purely rationalist ethic. Harrison quite rightly pointed out that Fielding parts company even with Shaftsbury, because practical goodness can hardly be grounded on moral rationalism. This is what Fielding repeatedly holds against rationalist positions and their [page 150] spokesmen. He is not so much an anti-rationalist as that he looks upon rationalism as insufficient.

Philosophical questions are not Fielding's main concern, even though they are among his favourite targets, as characters like Thwackum and Square indicate. As a novelist he is, like Aristotle's dramatic poet, primarily interested in characters acting, in their motivation. Something other than intellectual principles or maxims are demanded, something Fielding does not name precisely, if for no other reason than to make the reader more attentive, but perhaps also to stay out of a merely communalist controversy:

> Mr. Jones had Somewhat about him, which, though I think Writers are not thoroughly agreed in its Name, doth certainly inhabit some human Breasts; whose Use is not so properly to distinguish Right from Wrong, as to prompt and incite them to the former, and to restrain and with-hold them from the latter. (IV.vi.171-72)

What Fielding regards as important is the spring of action, not a conviction only. In his "Essay on Knowledge of Characters of Men" he identifies this spring as "Good-Nature," the most important aspect of which is that it is an active principle.

> Good-Nature is that benevolent and amiable Temper of Mind which disposes us to feel the Misfortunes, and enjoy the happiness of others; and consequently pushes us on to promote the latter, and prevent the former; and that without any abstract Contemplation of the Beauty of Virtue, and without the Allurements or Terrors of Religion.

On the basis of this conviction, Fielding establishes a common ground between author and reader which remains untouched by doctrinal and communalist disputes. Here he finds a criterion on which to base the unity of knowing and doing. Given good-nature and disinterestedness, the rationalist dissection disappears in favor of a sympathetic relationship between author and reader as well as reader and fictional character. It is hardly surprising, then, that Fielding builds his moral teaching in the novel on this axiom. The reader is invited to identify with Fielding's mixed characters rather than to judge them from a moral distance.

> When we find such Vices attended with their evil Consequence to our favourite Characters, we are not only taught to shun them for our own Sake, but to hate them for the Mischief's they have already brought on those we love. (X.i.527)

In this explication of his moral teaching Fielding shows his skepticism toward rationalist objectivity. Fielding wants to excite "Compassion," "Admiration," and "Affection" in the reader. Though rational instruction might also be effective, the result of emotional response is far "more apt to affect and dwell upon our Minds," as Fielding says when he talks about the imperfections of characters. This way a different kind of reader-address becomes apparent, in which Fielding does not appeal to the reader's "Sagacity" but gives an advice familiar from the first sonnet of Atrophic and Stella:

Examine your Heart, my good Reader, and resolve whether you do believe these Matters with me. If you do, you may now proceed to their Exemplification in the following Pages; if you do not, you have, I assure you, already read more than you have understood;... To treat of the Effects of Love to you, must be as absurd as to discourse on Colours to a Man born blind;.... (VI.i.271)

Fielding now not only speaks in a new tone to the reader, but also appeals to another faculty, the heart. The words "Heart," "believe," and "understand" signify the level on which Fielding wants to establish the relationship between author and reader as well as his hierarchy of values. In a later "aside" Fielding coaxes the reader with the assumption: "thy Heart may be better than thy Head" (X.i.526). This points the way to overcoming the dichotomies of rationalism. If the reader cannot look into his heart, or if, to follow Fielding's way of thinking, he does not have one, he will never understand what love is, like the utilitarian philosophers to whom Fielding satirically attributes the opinion that "Love probably may... very greatly resemble a Dish of Soup" (VI.i.272); or, like Mr. Locke's blind man, who thought he could describe colours (IV.1.152).

In Fielding's eyes, then, the way which leads to knowledge is not rational analysis but empathy. This may also imply a possible explanation of Fielding's epistemological ideas. In Ivied, in which the author an[page 152]ounces the appearance of Sophia, we are able to observe Fielding's attempts to convey an "idea" to the reader, "the idea of Sophia," i.e. not the idea of beauty in the philosophical sense, but the notion of a particular beauty. As this is an example of a non-rational communication with the reader, the question arises how Fielding varies his technique in securing and directing the reader's participation. Fielding begins his announcement of Sophia with an atmospheric invocation drawing on myth and art to associate an image of beauty. Like Monticello's Primavera "the lovely Sophia comes," "bedecked with Beauty, Youth, Sprightliness, Innocence, Modesty, and Tenderness, breathing Sweetness from her rosy Lips, and darting

Brightness from her sparkling Eyes" (IV.ii.155). This allegorical vision then gives place to further examples of beautiful women in art and history and ends in an ironical remark to the reader about the naturalness of the effect of beauty: "If thou hast seen all these without knowing what Beauty is, thou hast no Eyes; if without feeling its Power, thou hast no Heart".

And yet, although the effects of beauty seem to allow no question, Fielding remains doubtful whether the images evoked have conveyed "an exact Idea of Sophia: for she did not exactly resemble any of them." The reader, then, is left with ideas and images of beauty and their power, none of which can do justice to Sophia. It seems the reader is led on to ever new expectations, only to be disappointed. Even Fielding's promise to describe Sophia's appearance sounds rather skeptical: "... we are sensible that our highest Abilities are very inadequate to the Task". Fielding is equally negative about his abilities to give an idea of Sophia's mind and again defers the reader's hopes:

> But as there are no Perfections of the Mind which do not discover themselves, in that perfect Intimacy, to which we intend to introduce our Reader, with this charming young Creature; so it is needless to mention them here: Nay, it is a Kind of tacit Affront to our Reader's Understanding, and may also rob him of that Pleasure which he will receive in forming his own Judgment of her Character. (IV.ii.157)

Ironically leaving it to the "Reader's Understanding," Fielding undercuts his description of Sophia's qualities by references to the inadequacy or superfluous ness of his words. What the reader finally gets from the author is neither a description which might convey an image of Sophia nor an adequate idea of her beauty, but a moral evaluation of her character, typically in the form of a negative compliment; she was not corrupted by the practices of the so-called polite circles or by the education of her experienced aunt.

> By her Conversation and Instructions, Sophia was perfectly well-bred, though perhaps she wanted a little of that Ease in her Behaviour, which is to be acquired only by Habit,

and living within what is called the polite Circle... and though it hath Charms so inexpressible, that the French... mean to express this, when they declare they know not what it is, yet its Absence is well compensated by Innocence; nor can good Sense, and a natural Gentility ever stand in need of it.

Fielding contrasts the corruptness of the very language of polite society—a kind of linguistic hypocrisy—with his moral norm. Ironically he reveals the emptiness and falseness of the words by applying the "je-ne-sais-quoi" of the aesthetic effect literally. As the terms are meaningless, so are the values they are supposed to denote. Sophia, however, untouched by such corruption, remains morally unstained as well. The fact that the "Absence" of that ominous social "Ease" rhymes with "Innocence" and "good Sense" explicitly points to its counterparts. This is what Fielding was aiming at: innocence, good sense, natural gentility. Sophia represents these moral ideals. Still, does Fielding convey an idea or a specific image or is this an instance of a "vacant Space" indeed, left open to be filled by reader-friends capable of the empathy Fielding wants to establish?

If we look at the chapter again, we notice that Fielding does not, like a Socratic teacher, make the reader ascend to an ever higher stage of cognition; on the contrary, he leads the reader to ever new impossibilities of knowing or forming the idea of Sophia. The "exact Idea of Sophia" resembles none of the beauties mentioned, nor does she represent an abstraction. Instead,

... she resembled one whose Image never can depart from my Breast, and whom, if thou dost remember, thou hast then, my Friend, an adequate Idea of Sophia.

On the one hand the pronoun "whom" syntactically refers to the image in the author's heart, on the other hand it points, logically, to the object of the reader-friend's memory. This does not make much sense from the commonsensical point of view, but it makes perfectly good sense from a Platonic perspective. The reader who is also an understander should be able to form an exact idea of her not because he has been told what it is like or because he derives it from abstraction and comparison—the rationalist steps to knowledge—but by looking into himself.

As it is in the heart that Fielding finds his true image, the reader can only participate by finding such an image in his own heart as well.

> How amiable sever the Picture of our Heroine will appear, as it is really a Copy from Nature, many of our fair Countrywomen will be found worthy to satisfy any Passion, and to answer any Idea of Female Perfection, which our Pencil will be able to raise. (IV.i.154)

The reader is not led to an ecstatic vision of the idea of beauty. On the contrary, Fielding introduces the passage with an ironical comment at the expense of his readers: "Indeed we would, for certain Causes, advise those of our Male Readers who have any Hearts, to read no farther". Nevertheless, he assures his readers that everyone is able to find his own image of "Female Perfection." In other words, everybody can remember the image that can never depart from his breast. Here, Platonic anamnesis takes the form of a sentimental memory.

In terms of contemporary ideas Fielding seems to side with those who claim that it is possible to arrive at the knowledge of abstract ideas through sense perception: "If thou hast seen all these without knowing what Beauty is, thou hast no Eyes; if without feeling its Power, thou hast no Heart" (IV.ii.56). For the artist, however, the different interpretations of sense perception which Locke and Berkeley debate are rather irrelevant. True knowledge lies in the heart, and without it there is only Lord Rochester's answer "to a Man, who had seen many Things" (IV.ii.155-56)—which is rude. Nevertheless Fielding is not engaging in an epistemological battle. His interest lies with his "Creation" and its effect. Whether one or the other philosopher is right remains unimportant, because in a work of art it is the author who makes the recipient [page 155] form an idea. Even his very personal experience, which is implied by Fielding's reference to the image in his breast, is not what the reader can draw on. The reader receives the ideas the author wants to convey in the work itself, in the "history" and is, therefore, enabled to form his own image and judgment. To quote again:

> But as there are no Perfections of the Mind which do not discover themselves, in that perfect Intimacy, to which we intend to introduce our Reader, with this charming young Creature; so it is needless to mention them here: Nay, it is a Kind of tacit Affront to our Reader's Understanding, and may also rob him of that Pleasure which he will receive in forming his own Judgment of her Character. (IV.ii.157)

The intimate acquaintance which Fielding promises to the reader is identical with the kind of reading Fielding wants the reader to practice. In that case communication between author and reader docs not take place on the level of rational demonstration, as Fielding implies in this chapter, but in a more immediate way. Fielding makes concrete ideas arise in the minds of his readers. Already in his "Dedication" he points out that the most effective method of communicating his intention ("to recommend Goodness and Innocence") will not be based on didactic preaching—though he will also appeal to his readers' "true Interest"—but on the immediacy of examples which are "a Kind of Picture". In these "Virtue becomes as it were an Object of Sight, and strikes us with an Idea of that Loveliness, which Plato asserts there is in her naked Charms". The narrative method suited to arrive at such objects of sight can hardly be the naming of an idea, which would be a rationalist understanding of the idea as an abstraction. This fear of abstract rationalism may be the reason why Fielding frequently makes use of periphrasis, in other words expresses his meaning by indirection, as though he distrusted the words. This would mean that communication works even beyond the level of denotative words when a sympathetic link has been established, in this case between author and reader.

Fielding, accordingly, is less interested in stimulating the reader to fill in gaps than in making him aware of the pitfalls of language, of clichés and hollow rhetoric, outright lies and linguistic insufficiency, [page 156] as well as hypocrisy. The relationship between words and meaning is just as dialectical as that between reason and sentiment. Meaning is conveyed as well as veiled by words. Fielding's irony is as much an indication of this as the hypocrisy he satirizes. Even in the case of an exemplary character like Mr. Allworthy words and meaning seem to be drifting apart when he starts "preaching," i.e. when he indulges in a fatal over-confidence in the affirmative effect of words. Inversely, Fielding's sympathy is with those characters who are discreet in their use of words, above all Sophia. She is not only reticent about disclosing her own true feelings but also puts more trust in Tom's goodness than in his protestations of love. It is only his goodness which finally convinces her of his love and makes her forgive him.

The problematical link between words and meaning reflects a certain distrust of words, but above all a trust in an indirect communication based on empathy. Certainly, Mr. Allworthy's rationalist beliefs are constantly proven wrong, just as his administration of justice is open to criticism and his long-winded speeches are ineffective. Yet he is the most positive figure and carries his name for the very good reason that he exemplifies what Fielding regards as necessary for true understanding, i.e. empathy and emotional identification. He practices solidarity from the very beginning when he takes in the foundling child. For Fielding feeling (and why shouldn't he have been aware of that paronomasia?) and doing are more important than rhetorical accomplishments or even the perfect administration of formal justice.

Fielding's exemplary characters show a sense of altruism, what he calls benevolence or what Square finally attributes to Tom, "Generosity of Heart... Capacity for Friendship... Integrity" (XVIII.iv.927). These characters obviously are not followers of pure rationality, but this does not mean that the basis of their thinking and acting is irrational. If benevolence and feeling are emphasized here as central to Fielding's ethical ideal, it has to be emphasized, too, that Fielding is surely not putting forward an ideal of mere irrationality and sentimentality. This can hardly be expected from an author who is so fond of intellectual teasing and whose favourite rhetorical strategy is irony. His exemplary characters are guided by reason, which, though not an end in itself, is necessary as a means to an end. But it is insufficient as a final aim, as [page 157] is most clearly expressed by the converted Square in his final letter from his death-bed (XVIII.iv).

Sophia symbolizes the true aim and ideal of wisdom in which reason and heart are united; that is to say, Fielding does not simply exchange the absolute rule of reason with that of sentimentality. Just as he expresses his belief in a dialectical unity of erotic love and charity, he equally looks to the unity of reason and feeling in wisdom. This is indicated by the great arguers in Tom Jones coming to naught or ending infamously, while those who think with the heart are rewarded. Tom himself is the best example that neither goodness of heart nor the impulses of feeling alone are a sufficient guide for getting safely through life, but he can be redeemed by the acquisition of wisdom, while his counterpart Blifil who affects reason and copy book virtue is left to his own corruption.

The kind of behaviour and communication realised in the novel mirrors Fielding's intentions with regard to the reader. He acknowledges that only on a common ground his aim of laughing his readers "out of their favourite Follies and Vices" may be achieved. Absolutely bad characters neither change for the better in his novels nor does he except this to happen in real life. If there were not a vestige, at least, of altruism, benevolence, and charity he could not convey "ideas" like Sophia's virtuous beauty or Parson Adams' excessive joy about the rescue of his son. What Fielding wants to "inculcate" in his readers is not so much an abstract ethical principle, but rather a basis on which he is able to communicate with them.

This shows that, in a moral sense, subject and object are not opposites but one and the same thing, in other words, sees est. precipice. A corrupted heart cannot understand. This is what Fielding held against the utilitarian philosophers, the followers of Hobbes and Mandeville. To him, their negative view of mankind reflected "the nastiest of all Places, A BAD MIND" (VI.i.269).

Fielding, to conclude, does not replace Richardson Ian didacticism with empty spaces for the reader to practice his intellectual faculty, nor does he advocate a sentimental ethic. Directly or indirectly, the author always guides the reader in a process of communication which achieves a fusion of irony and satire with empathy and charity. The participation [page 158] of the reader thus turns out to be a moral condition and an intellectual challenge, just as Fielding's epistemology proves to be inseparable from his ethics.

Q5. How does education of readers in Tom Jones removes the Mist that Dims the Intellect of Mortals?

In his dedication to George Lyttleton, Henry Fielding states one of his purposes in writing Tom Jones is to indicate that "virtue and innocence" cannot be "injured" but through "indiscretion". He then expands on this idea by relating that only through indiscretion do people fall into the "snares that deceit and villainy spread for them". How, then, can we reconcile Fielding's deceptive narrator to his aforementioned intention? In contrast to Samuel Richardson's didactic methods, Fielding prefers to teach his readers through the use of irony and satire; in his own words, to "laugh mankind out of their favourite follies and vices" (Fielding 6). To achieve his ends, Fielding "sometimes work[s] through parody, irony, and wit, tricking and shocking his readers, dissimulating and feigning" (Johnson 12). Fielding's prefatory chapters, while being witty and highly entertaining, nonetheless are didactic in design and integral to his overall design of the narrative. Fielding does not intend just to amuse his readers, but to educate them also.

Before Fielding can persuade his readers to embrace his philosophy of living properly, he must first convince us that he possesses the authority and knowledge to assert that his philosophy is the 'best' or 'true' way of living. By claiming narrative authority and instructing readers how to 'judge' his history, Fielding is manipulating us into then accepting his moral philosophy. This essay will examine how Fielding's didactic prefatory chapters complement the overall design of Tom Jones.

He uses his prefatory chapters in three ways: to assert his authority as narrator, to instruct on how to judge his narrative, and to teach us the proper mode of conduct. The division of these prefatory chapters into the three aforementioned categories is not to imply they have no connection to each other or the narrative proper. They are "indeed an integral and organically functional part of the novel" (Bliss 237). Whether being instructed on his style, or how to be a 'sagacious' reader, or on our value system, Fielding's rhetoric maneuvers readers into identifying with his "value universe...which is located in and around the concept of mutuality or empathy" (Bliss 238).

Q6. Why does Fielding states that: "It is Easier to Make Good Men Wise than to make a Bad Man Good?"

Explain in light to Tom's character.

Or

Q. Critically analyse the character of Tom.

Or

Q. How does Henry Fielding characterize the Hero in his novel?

Or

Q. How does Fielding changes the view of conventional hero?

Fielding's Tom Jones is the story of a foundling whom Nature has endowed with physical beauty and happy vitality. But the young Tom did not always act rightly, so that he seems to be something like an unumerichero. He acts on impulse, sometimes well, sometimes ill, and he lacks a settled kind of duty. It was a case of his seeing and approving the higher, and following the lower, impulses. His sexual escapades are morally outrageous.

But although Tom sins a number of times in the heat of his blood, his heart is in the right place. In his sexual adventures with Molly Saegrim, Jenny Waters and the lady of Bellaston, these women were the seducers and Tom the seduced. Besides, though Tom is a rake, Fielding finds Tom's happy animalist preferable to other graver sins like malice, cruelty, meanness and hypocrisy. Fielding genially comments that Tom the bachelor, in choosing to be a rake, probably thought one woman better than none, and that Moll probably imagined two men to be better than one! But though Tom confesses to being guilty with women, he claims that he has not injured or caused misery to any as a consequence.

Tom, thus, is not an anti-hero. If only Tom had prudence, he would not have involved himself in all his scrapes. Squire Allworthy is convinced that Tom has much generosity, goodness and Honour, and if only he would add prudence and religion to these, he would be happy. The novel is in part, an account of "how Tom learns to add prudence" which to Allworthy perhaps means practical religion.

Fielding directs us to Tom's generosity and compassion towards the dissolute Anderson family and to Tom's active and warm-spirited services on behalf of Nightingale and Nancy, and to Tom's rejection of Mrs. Hunts' offer of a comfortable marriage. He tells Mrs. Hunt that it would be dishonourable to accept her offer as he loves someone else, while admitting at the same time that he has little hope of ever winning Sophia.

Fielding states in his Dedication that it is easier to make good men wise that to make a bad man good. He presents Tom who is innately good in pursuit of wisdom which Tom finally attains in his union with Sophia. His exuberant nature has now matured to a wise discernment of virtue.

... So did this bowl of rack punch influence the fates of all the principal characters in this "Novel without a Hero," which we are now relating. (Thackeray, Vanity Fair 93)

Even before Thackeray's debunking of the central role of the fictional hero in Vanity Fair, the variety of heroes in British fiction was more subtle and often less obvious than many readers recognized. Henry Fielding may have written the first "novel without a hero" in Jonathan Wild (1743), and concluded his career in fiction with another, of a very different order,

Amelia (1751). From his first foray into fiction with Shamela (1741), Fielding continually experiments with the concept of the hero, writing novels with and without heroes over a century before Vanity Fair would specifically call attention to the issue. And he clearly uses as a structural basis of his works the counter play between "literary" and "real life" heroes.

Fielding himself lays claim to this formative position in the Preface to Joseph Andrews: "it may not be improper to premise a few words concerning this kind of writing, which I do not remember to have seen hitherto attempted in our language". Literary historians have given us an ever-widening picture of Fielding's premise and its influence on the shape of British fiction, noting his major influences not only on the form of the comic romance, but on techniques of characterization through which language expresses moral purpose. Many of these contributions have been studied in great detail, and a more complete picture of Fielding as conscious artist and pioneer has emerged during the past several decades. Yet in spite of the accumulation of knowledge, relatively little attention has been paid to Fielding's characterization of the hero as the central focus of his mission to establish and legitimize this new form of literature. Nor has there been much critical interest in how these heroes' relationship to Fielding's changing concept of the novel's rhetorical form and aesthetic purposes, as it developed in the intense world of mid-eighteenth-century literary activity.

Fielding's Heroes: The Traditional Moral View

The attention focused on Fielding's heroes has continually centreed on their relationship to the philosophical and religious climate of the age, especially the influence of latitudinarian philosophy. Fielding criticism has traditionally examined character—and especially the hero—as an integral aspect of the moral and social climate of the age, especially due to the pioneering and perhaps overly-influential work of Martin Battestin, whose 1989 critical biography of Fielding culminates this perspective. This is rightly so: Fielding was not only deeply aware of the complex relationship between literature and society, but helped define and formalize that relationship through the molding of narrative voice, particularly in Tom Jones. Heroic but fallible characters—Joseph Andrews, Tom Jones, and William Booth—all must learn the lessons of benevolence, charity, and Christian good nature provided by the supporting characters: Parson Adams, Squire Allworthy, and Mr. Harrison. To view characters as exempla of specific moral values is accurate, but does not give a complete picture of Fielding's achievement, and in the past has led to misinterpretation of the heroes. Ian Watt claims, for example, that the exemplary nature of characterization makes character less important than plot in Fielding's novels (Rise of the Novel, 268). This view may be somewhat helpful in reading Joseph Andrews, although incomplete even there; but it fails to take into account the absolutely interwoven relationship between character and plot, especially in Tom Jones, or between character and narrative method in Amelia.

Because so much critical emphasis has been placed on Fielding's heroes as examples of specific eighteenth-century moral and religious values, there has been little examination of their structural and rhetorical roles, the nature of Fielding's methods of characterization, or other ways these heroes reflect the time in which Fielding was writing (Hahn 20). Fielding's use of literary sources for his characters has been widely explored, but his debt to earlier literature is usually seen in more or less general terms—the novel as "comic-epic-poem in prose." There has been little careful study of how Fielding's conception of the hero changes through his career and how these changes affect the kinds of novels he writes. Indeed, while Fielding's conception of the character traits of the hero remain fairly fixed, the role of the hero in the rhetorical structure of the works changes radically.

Q7. How is Tom Jones a Character of Convention?

Or

Q. Fielding uses a rhetorical tool in the creation of a complex system of character contrasts and foils. Discuss.

Fielding continually reminds us at crucial points in the plot that the rhetorical movement of the novel is the recognition of Jones' heroic nature, not its formation. Two such crucial scenes are Jones' conversation with Lawyer Dowling on the road to London and his jailhouse "repentance" speech to Mrs. Miller. While Jones' philosophical statements are important manifestations of the system of beliefs in the novel, they are, in fact, purely conventional representations of latitudinarian Benevolence (straight out of sermons and tracts). They bear little relation to the individual thoughts of Jones himself.

To Dowling, Jones solemnly declares:

I had rather enjoy my own Mind than the Fortune of another Man. What is the poor Pride arising from a magnificent House, a numerous Equipage, a splendid Table, and from all the other Advantages or Appearances of Fortune, compared to the warm, solid Content, the swelling Satisfaction, the thrilling Transports, and the exulting Triumphs, which a good Mind enjoys, in the Contemplation of a generous, virtuous, noble, benevolent Action. (12.1;.)

It matters little to the conventional purpose of this passage that Jones does not choose "the solid Content" over "all the other Advantages," but has it thrust upon him by the machinations of others; nor, even less does it matter that Jones himself is hardly aware of this "swelling Satisfaction" in the context of the plot (and it is surely not accidental that the language here is usually reserved for the description of sexual rather than moral transports, adding to the comic irony of the passage).

Just as conventional is the language of Jones' prison "reformation":

I do not speak the common Cant of one in my unhappy Situation. Before this dreadful Accident happened, I had resolved to quit a Life of which I was become sensible of the Wickedness as well as Folly. I do assure you notwithstanding the Disturbances I have unfortunately occasioned in your House, for which I heartily ask your Pardon, I am not an abandoned Profligate. Though I have been hurried into Vices, I do not approve a vicious Character; nor will I ever, from this Moment, deserve it. (.;.)

Of course, it is precisely the "common Cant" of repentance that he does speak and every reader would recognize it as such.[7]

The Pattern of Contrasts

An even more important rhetorical tool is the creation of a complex system of character contrasts and foils, surprisingly not much examined in relation to the nature of the hero in Tom Jones. Critical attention has usually been focused on pairings of individual characters: Allworthy/Western, Thwackum/Square, Tom/Blifil, and Sophia/the string of other women in Tom's life.

A more important system of contrasts focuses on a series of individuals who represent more typical hero-types (moral, religious, romantic, and martial), against whom Jones is contrasted. Jones' heroism is delineated against false conventional notions, against the meaningless and destructive application of labels to human character, and against the failures of ideal role models. The narrator emphasizes the importance of contrast as the primary method by which we evaluate character in fiction: "The Vices of this young Man [Tom] were, moreover, heightened, by the disadvantageous Light in which they appeared, when opposed to the Virtues of Master Blifil, his Companion..." (.;.).

As exemplar of the father figure—the Ideal of the Christian good-natured man—stands Squire Allworthy, whose strength of character is contrasted with the weaknesses of behaviour in Jones on the one hand, and the failures of character in Western, Partridge, and the Man of the Hill on the other. But Allworthy would hardly make an appropriate hero of fiction (a mistake Richardson makes in creating Sir Charles Grandson). He is a "Favourite of both Nature and Fortune," with "an agreeable Person, a sound Constitution, a solid Understanding, and a benevolent Heart... " (.;.). He is "a

Man of Sense and Constancy" (.;.), for whom "Good-nature had always the Ascendant in his Mind" (.;.). He is, moreover, mightier than the "Sun; than which one Object alone in this lower Creation could be more glorious, and that Mr. Allworthy himself presented; a human Being replete with Benevolence, meditating in what Manner he might render himself most acceptable to his Creator, by doing most Good to his Creatures" (.;.).

Because Allworthy is the idealized spokesman for the Providence of a Benevolent God, his definition of the hero is one that Jones must strive to fulfill: "you have much Goodness, Generosity, and Honour in your Temper; if you will add Prudence and Religion to these, you must be happy; For the three former Qualities, I admit, make you worthy of Happiness, but they are the latter only which will put you in Possession of it" (.;.). But it is his very connection with the Divine that makes Allworthy himself inappropriate as a hero in the fictional world of Tom Jones.

Other father figures represent less ideal and less heroic models: Squire Western, Mr. Partridge, the Man of the Hill. And still other characters are grouped in sets that contrast with Jones: the negative models of middle-class complacency (Doctor Blifil, Captain Blifil, Thwackum, and Square); the litany of various romantic hero types, including Sophia Western, Mrs. Fitzpatrick, Nightingale, and Lady Bellaston. The group that provides the most important and most often used contrasts with is the military and martial hero, parodied and debunked in Northerton, Fitzpatrick, the gypsies, and various armies whose soldiers march in and out of the first half of the text.

Conclusion

Because Jones is Fielding's most fully-developed hero-model, he is naturally the central character in any study of Fielding's novels, and illustrates how Fielding's novels are always about the very nature of heroism in fiction. The plot of his journey to London and back to Somerset leads Jones to discover the value of prudence in self and the value of accepted standards and norms in society—a discovery that epitomizes Fielding's conservative view of human and social order. But as other parts of this study show, while Jones travels, Fielding shapes and defines his role in the larger rhetorical structure of the novel. Thus Jones' career as hero provides the model against which we can measure Fielding's other heroes. And, perhaps, even other heroes of th-century fiction.

Q8. Critically analyse Tom Jones as panoramic commentary on England.

Or

Q. Discuss the various character contrasts in Tom Jones.

Tom Jones the novel is a panoramic commentary on England in 1745 and it is also the story of Tom Jones and Sophia Western. Tom and Sophia are rebels revolting against the respectably accepted domestic standards of eighteenth century society. By such standards Sophia should obey her father and Tom should be what Blifil thinks him, an illegitimate become important suddenly who should be put firmly in his place. For the purposes of the plot Fielding makes Tom a gentleman.

Tom embodies Fielding's concept of benevolence and good nature, his generous personality reflecting Fielding's moral philosophy. It is from his impulsive and affectionate nature that many of his troubles spring.

Tom & Sophia fight conventional society embodied in the character of Blifil. They are not passive in their fight and that is why Tom Jones is not a tragedy but comedy. While Blifil is forever on the side of conventional respectability. Tom Jones has the vigour and spirit at spontaneity. He acts naturally and therefore the excesses into which his animal spirits lead him are forgiven. Here in the novel the natural man and the noble savage are pitted against each other. Tom's strength lies in the vigour and spontaneity of Tom's reactions.

Fielding's hero Tom Jones is shown as a young man of great health and spirits. He has so much life that it amounts for the effect of comedy.

Tom Jones is an attractive character quite the heroic. But his heroism is tinged with a recklessness of youth, which makes him get unintentionally into trouble.

Tom Jones cannot resist women and he has more than one affair. While his heart belongs to Sophia Western he constantly gives his physical self away to the pleasures of love.

But the goodness in his character pays him, in fact he is once again made the heir at Squire Allworthy's large estate. He even manages to marry Sophia.

The plot movement follows the curve of extreme high and low. Tom comes on the scene as a bastard, his reputation and his hopes are progressively blackened until he reaches his nadir in

London where he is accused of murder. There is further misinterpretation of his character, when he is accused of incest with his supposed mother Jenny Jones.

With the exposure of Blifil's malicious machinations and of Tom's true goodness his fortune sails to the Zenith of romantic happiness. He is proved to be of high birth and he marries the girl of his choice and he inherits wealth. At the end Blifil's treachery is revealed and Squire Allworthy realises rightly the good nature of Tom Jones.

Tom Jones gets married to Sophia eventually. The blustering careless Tom Jones converts into a responsible and faithful husband. He is one of the few heroes in English literature, who is represented realistically as having negative traits, as well as positive charms.

Criticism and Interpretation

Tom Jones is a daredevil: he does many stupid things, for example he gets drunk, he has sex with many different women, he is happy and impulsive, however he is good, honest and the narrator and the reader like him.

Mr. Allworthy loves him and he usually forgives Tom, but other characters like Blifil and Thwackum are against Mr. Jones and they are two hypocrites.

Sophia, who is good and virtuous, is different from the other women of her century: after falling in love with Tom, she runs away from home and she goes to London because she doesn't want to get married to Blifil. All the moralists that think to have many virtues are described as hypocrites. Tom, the hero, doesn't care about morality and philosophy: he is sincere, simple and good; his mistakes aren't characterised by malice and he is always ready to admit them.

Tom Jones was considered immoral by Fielding's contemporaries because of many events of the work: a woman gets pregnant after having sex with Tom.

However in Tom Jones there's a different morality that is connected with the philosophy of the 18th century: human nature is good. The sin can be forgiven when it is caused by imprudence and there is the desire of correcting his faults; the will of harming someone can't be forgiven.

Fielding doesn't like the hypocrites, in fact they pretend to be good and virtuous but they aren't. Those who are able to hide their bad plans thanks to their culture and astuteness are worse than hypocrites.

Contrasts in Varieties of Life

In Tom Jones there is a constant detail of contrast in the character relationships, scene relationships and even verbal relationships. By this novel, the full and direct artistic impact of son Quixote is felt.

Just as Cervantes Fielding uses the 'point of views' of the omniscient author. His world is populous and extensive in its spatial design. One character alone does not demand attention, the author's own humourous irony is itself one of the materials of the novel. In the 'head-chapters' a contrast is provided between intelligence focused 'on' the human situation he has created and the intelligence of the characters within the created situation.

Tom Jones, the central character contrasts with Blifil. The wicked Blifil, is indeed Tom's 'opposite' and the chief cause of his misadventures. Blifil is the antagonist of Tom.

The protagonist embodies tragic traits in his own passions and frailties, but he also has comical elements in his social behaviours. The conflict between hero and villain is propelled to a resolution.

In the end, the rogue (Blifil) who appeared to be a good man is exposed in his true nature as rogue, and the good man (Tom), who appeared to be a rogue is revealed in his true good nature.

The major contrast in Tom Jones - the novel is the conflict between natural, instinctive feeling and those appearances by which people disguise deny or inhibit natural feeling – intellectual theories, rigid moral dogmas, economic convenient doctrines of social responsibility.

This is the broad thematic contrast in Tom Jones. Form and instinctive feeling engage in constant eruptive combat. The battlefield is between with debris of ripped masks. It is shown in many occasions in Tom Jones that the animal or instinctive part of man is denied. Instead, a more formal appearance is adopted. The damaging uses of intelligence in human nature are depicted - in wicked Blifil's calculative shrewdness in Black George's rationalization for keeping Tom's money, in the absurd intellectual formulas, elaborated by Thwackum and Square. The disparaging effects can also, be seen in Allworthy's high minded ethics and in Tom's own idealism.

In the other hand intellectualized thoughts are the instinctive responses that are Tom's. Tom yields formidably and frequently to instinct, and in so doing, he exhibits the 'naturalness, and therefore the rightness of instinct as constituent of the personality.

Thus, he corrects the overemphasis on formal appearances which we see in other characters. But at the same time, Tom Jones shows a remarkable absence of that useful social sense which we call desertion, a lack which is damaging certainly to himself and a cause of confusion to others.

It is the incongruity between what a man might 'naturally' be and what he makes of himself by adopting a formulary appearance or mark, that gives ' human nature ' its variety and funniness and treacherousness.

Apart from the major contracts in characters, there are also prevalent many minor contrasts between what appearances are and what reality is. While Miss Brid get is the real mother of Blifil, this fact is hidden till the end. She is able to self righteously condemn the sexual indulgences of the lower classes, and at the same time preserve the fruit of her own indulgence. But finally we learn about the contrast between her appearance and her reality.

Q9. Discuss the theme of morality in Tom Jones.

"I have always thought love the only foundation of happiness in a married state... and in my opinion all these marriages which are contracted from other motives are greatly criminal... To deny that beauty is an agreeable object to the eye... would be false and foolish... But to make this the sole consideration of marriage, to lust after it so violently as... to reject and disdain religion, virtue and sense... is surely inconsistent... either with a wise man or a good Christian."

Although Fielding wrote many literary works I am going to deal mainly with his major novels, Joseph Andrews, Tom Jones, Amelia, and his shorter satirical work Shamela. All of these works contain a strong moral message, but the moral message is not entirely consistent, and is presented in various ways.

One of Fielding's main concerns was the question of marriage. His ideas on marriage are concisely summed up by Allworthy in his sermon on matrimony:

"I have always thought love the only foundation of happiness in a married state... and in my opinion all these marriages which are contracted from other motives are greatly criminal... To deny that beauty is an agreeable object to the eye... would be false and foolish... But to make this the sole consideration of marriage, to lust after it so violently as... to reject and disdain religion, virtue and sense... is surely inconsistent... either with a wise man or a good Christian."

Although this sermon mainly condemns marriage for reasons of lust, Fielding more commonly condemns marriage for reasons of financial gain or social elevation.

The way in which Fielding conveys his philosophy of marriage is different in all four works, and the virtuousness of the virtuous is variable. However, the basic message is fairly consistent.

Tom Jones is not presented as such a virtuous character, and is thus perhaps more credible. Tom and Sophia have many problems to overcome. Tom is illegitimate and wishes to marry above himself, which, at the time, would have meant the lady sinking to the social level of her husband. The fact that she is willing to suffer this consequence illustrates that she is marrying purely for love.

Although Fielding consistently condemns sex outside marriage, he does he not despise illegitimacy. This is made evident through Allworthy's words:

however guilty the parents might be, the children were certainly innocent

Fielding's belief that personal qualities are more important than social standing, and his admiration for characters who share his belief, are made clear through Sophia's description of Tom:

So brave, and yet so gentle; so witty, yet so inoffensive; so humane, so civil, so genteel, so handsome. What signifies his being base born, when compared with such qualifications as these?

As I have previously mentioned, however, Tom is not a perfect picture of morality. Tom is tempted and fails to resist. He is seduced by Molly Seagrim, but it is important to note that he stayed away from her for three months before succumbing because he did not like the idea of corrupting a young woman, particularly the daughter of a friend. This small fact is illustrative of Fielding's idea about which he writes in Works X1V [].

that very early and strong inclination to good or evil, which distinguishes different dispositions in children, in their first infancy.

However, he continues to write that although someone is basically good or bad they are also influenced by their passions, which can cause a lapse in a good person. This type of ruling by the passions did not occur for the virtuous characters in Joseph Andrews.

In both of Tom's yielding to temptation, he is portrayed to the reader as a victim. This is particularly notable in his liaison with Miss Waters. The aggressiveness with which she launches her seductive attack on Tom is described in terms of 'the fair conqueror' using her 'whole artillery of love' and the eventual unmasking of the royal battery, by carelessly letting her handkerchief drop from her neck.

Fielding makes it clear that he does not condone Tom's yielding to his temptations, but he does not entirely condemn it because it is so clear that he was a victim. Fielding excuses Tom's behaviour thus a single bad nut no more constitutes a villain in life than a single bad part on the stage

He obviously believes that in these instances Tom has been led by his passions rather than his basic nature, and so may be forgiven.

Tom is eventually rewarded with a happy marriage and financial security, despite the fact that Tom has not been as virtuous as he could have been and Sophia has defied her parents in their wish for her to marry Blifil. The important thing for Fielding is that Tom is basically a good person and Sophia defied her father out of love for Tom, as defying the wishes of parents is not an action of which Fielding would otherwise approve.

Their happy marriage is contrasted with other much less harmonious marriages in the novel, such as Squire Western's marriage to a pathetic woman whose father set up the marriage for financial gain. Western regards his wife as a servant and believes himself to be a good husband on the grounds that:

> he seldom swore at her (perhaps not above once a week) and never beat her.

Another more vivid example of an unhappy marriage as a consequence of avarice is the marriage between Bridget and Blifil. Blifil, like Western, sees his wife as a domestic utility. Their only pleasure within their marriage is derived from tormenting each other. The only factor which sustains Blifil in his marriage is the hope of eventually inheriting Allworthy's estate, however, Blifil dies prematurely, and so never inherits. Once again, Fielding ensures that a couple who married for the wrong reasons live and die miserable.

It thus seems that in Tom Jones the theme of marrying for love rather than gain remains, but it is presented realistically and the characters are allowed small slips without being entirely condemned.

Conclusion

To conclude, it would seem that Fielding's basic moral messages remained the same throughout these works. His main message is that marriage should always be for love, and this remains constant throughout. He also proclaims the benefits of chastity, but appears to attach less importance to this as his work progresses, and begins to believe repentance to be more important. He appears to become more tolerant of people's weaknesses and more willing to accept that people are sometimes ruled by their passions, which causes them to act in a way which is contrary to their basic moral code. Overall, Fielding conveys his moral messages in a subtle, entertaining and mainly consistent manner.

Q10. Discuss the eighteenth century society as presented in Tom Jones.

Or

Q. Discuss the society and its representation in Tom Jones.

The phenomenon of the "English gentleman" surfaced just prior to the eighteenth century, amid a centrifugal redistribution of power from town municipalities and guilds to the private person. The public sphere, long contaminated by monarchical hegemonies, began a cleansing process of contained, idealist self-fashioning. Of course, much of the impetus for change was couched in oligarchic self-interests, so "the private person" became the protagonist in the society.

British freedom, then, was secured by the central government's decision not to interfere with its bourgeoisie's rights and privileges, a remove that protected chartered corporations and instilled a rising confidence among all. A web of societies flourished that included salons, coffee houses, theatres, and literary, scientific, and philosophical associations, and all became important sites for reshaping identities and rethinking the rules of constitutions.

The Middle-class was the ruling class but also the leading one. In fact the ideas and the values of this class influenced all the society. For example the new "moral conduct" realised a great change in manners. For the first time in English history, there was an adoption of a specific code of social politeness.

The "gentleman" in Fielding's works is robust, learned and productive. He is a construct deemed invariably instrumental to the success of an emerging capitalist Britain.

Character and manners could explain why "the English nation, in little more than a century [...] since the happy revolution of 1688, has increased more in population, in knowledge, in grandeur and in political prosperity, than any nation, ancient or modern, has been able to do in many centuries."

If one is to disassemble such a construct, that is, unmask the eighteenth-century English gentleman and reconsider his tastes, pastimes, manners, and aspirations, one must first reveal the complexities that permit "gentleman" to figure prominently in Enlightenment England's socioeconomic relations and national identity.

The emphasis on an existential "to be" is deliberate here; after all, if one can construct oneself the "right way," then one's character cannot be fixed. This modern, dynamic ontology was for many something with which to be reconciled, for not everyone in eighteenth-century England was enthusiastic about dismissing the solidified self wrought through divine determinism. Fielding, for one, appears to have been unwilling to abandon the more conservative view that "character was fixed by God or nature, and that the seemingly unpredictable contingencies in which it expressed itself were equally predetermined".

The "stronger sense of the complexity of human psychology," at once underscoring Locke's table rasa and undermining Leibniz's devout determinism, had a direct bearing on the growing acceptance of "individual choice" rather than "inherited types and humours".

The decentring of power reached the countryside and had a tremendous effect on the nation's economic topography. According to some, the typical eighteenth-century Englishman was a villager, a "villager accustomed to meet men of various crafts and occupations and classes".

There is a "multiform and vigourous society, part agricultural, part industrial," in which the power of the squire "loomed large," "beneficent or tyrannical but always patriarchal.

There is no "class of men to whom the word 'Gentlemen' more emphatically applies, or who are more generally distinguished for their culture and refinement," the country squires of eighteenth-century England were very different people. According to almost unanimous testimony they were generally boorish and ignorant, mighty hunters, and hard drinkers, who swore oaths, and used in the drawing room the language of the stable. There are of course exceptions to the general description; and we have Squire Allworthy in 'Tom Jones,' and Sir William Thornton in the 'Vicar of Wakefield,' who are models of propriety".

Some one calls Allworthy the "typical squire".

Tom Jones, arguably the greatest novel of the eighteenth century, is in many ways a guide on how to be a gentleman.

Though Fielding certainly does not disown his class, he is, after all, a Tory through and through, his "instruction" on how to be in mid-eighteenth century England forces his reader to, at the very least, rethink "gentleman." Neither Squire Allworthy nor Tom is without fault, but both have enough redeeming qualities to become Fielding's gentleman, and that is the lesson. In Fielding's own words: "it is much easier to make good men wise, than to make bad men good".

Tom cannot take his place in the community, cannot be a gentleman if he is a foundling. But Fielding understands "gentleman" too—it is just that Tom, like many of his readers, is still on his way to becoming one. Fielding self-consciously tells his reader in his dedication that he should not find the work offensive, that there is nothing in the story that is "prejudicial to the cause of religion and virtue; nothing inconsistent with the strictest rules of decency, nor which can offend even the chestiest eye in perusal". What is more, he concludes "that virtue and innocence can scarce ever be injured by indiscretion; and that it is this alone which often betrays them into the snares that deceit and villainy spread for them". But "gentleman" is so entwined with production and with capital that Tom's desultory ways are perceived as a misrepresentation of the ideal. So one can see how Tom the flamer cannot possibly be Tom the gentleman, and that the novel overall might be antithetical to England's prosperity.

"Reason assisted nascent capitalism by permitting utility or usefulness to be calculated and objects and people to be identified, assigned categories, and controlled". The "gentleman" is one such category. The idea that he was being "controlled" may have been beyond the Enlightenment subject, including Diderot, who would situate man within a great creative process, a part within the whole. The capitalist collective, however, manifests a more tangible individual, now no longer for the benefit of a monarch, but for a privileged class.

This last distinction between the Enlightenment subject and the socialist self is certainly underscored if one considers how a good part of the former's construction arises from a

Locke an brand of individual liberty that does not include the poor or anyone thought to be of a "lower" race. Locke's belief that the right of private ownership is implied by natural law and justified by labour—a natural phenomenon belonging to the labourer—nonetheless excludes those doing most of the labour. Ironically, then, though man is not born immoral, as Hobbes had suggested, Locke's discriminatory liberalism would make him so anyway. Such conflicting ideologies fuel the eighteenth-century, and if one attempts to trace a path from rationalism to empiricism to scepticism one ultimately finds that the Enlightenment is never any one thing. Rather, it is a period that both prefigures Modernism's autonomous self and denies its plausibility.

Q11. Discuss the major themes in Tom Jones.

General Comments

Fielding influenced the main tradition of the English novel through the eighteenth century and the nineteenth century (Dickens shares Fielding's talent for humour and eye for the grotesque; Eliot also writes on the differences between country and city life). With the character Tom Jones, he introduced a new kind of fictional hero-a good hearted, well intentioned, generous young man with ordinary human weakness, one who yields to temptation with women and to make errors in judgement. From Fielding's point of view art is artifice or the deliberately crafted (this view contrasts with modern theories of realism as a "slice of life"). Fielding as well as Richardson and Sterna was regarded as startlingly realistic and widely admired by contemporary readers on the continent. Fielding believed, as did most eighteenth century writers and educated readers, that the purpose of art is to create pleasure which is both civilized and civilizing. Coleridge declared the plot of Tom Jones was one of the three perfect plots in all literature. In its "preface" Fielding stated: "the excellence of the entertainment consists less in the subject than in the author's skill in well dressing it up...we shall represent human nature at first to keep appetite of our reader, in that more plain and simple manner in which it is found in the country, and shall hereafter hash and ragout it with all the high French and Italian seasoning of affectation and vice which courts and cities afford". The introductory chapters that preface each of the novel's 18 books involve the reader in a way that had never been used before.

Names

Many of the key characters possess allegorical names. Mr. Allworthy is said to be very fair, true and compassionate. Thus, he appears to be worthy of all. The narrator always describes Mr. Thwackum "thwack"-in Tom, and so, he earns his name. One sees Mr.Square as being very philosophical and the slang term of "square" fits his disposition as well as being his given name. Also, Sophia Western and Harriet Fitzpatrick create nicknames for each other which illustrate their personalities. Harriet calls Sophia "Miss Graveairs", and Sophia calls Harriet "Miss Giddy". This shows Sophia's tendency to be serious and Harriet's tendency to be the opposite.

Narration and Audience

The narrator enters the novel from the beginning and rarely leaves for an extended length of time. He explains every nature of the story, both the plot and the method of writing. He shows how the plot thickens with each added character and explicates why he utilizes a specific form of writing in one instance rather than in another (such as the use of a quasi-epic style). Also, every book begins with a formal introduction from the narrator.

He also does exactly what he says, such as ending a chapter directly when he says he will end it. The chapter closes and the next opens. This humour and literal-mindedness of the narrator mirrors Sterna's in his Tristan Sandy. The narrator openly communicates whit the audience, to the point of dictating exactly who makes up the audience at specific times. Sometimes the audience is wise, and other times, foolish. Sometimes the narrator speaks only to a feminine audience; other times, to a masculine one, and others, to a combination of the two.

Touchstones

In Fielding there are many touchstones (= quotes) from Pope, Swift, Homer, Francis, Shakespeare, and others. These touchstones take the form of both verse and prose as well as Latin and English. Fielding will translate the Latin, sometimes literally and sometimes by quoting another author who says the same general concept but uses a different terminology. Another aspect of this contains the "battle of the books", also known as the "classics" versus the "moderns". Fielding stays along the middle of the two sides of this "battle" because he mentions both the "classic" (Homer etc.) and the "modern" (Pope etc.). Thus, he has the ability to appeal to both sides of the argument.

Heteroglossia

Finally, Fielding fills the novel with heteroglossia. He uses different types of texts which include English, Latin, French, cant phrases, and different forms of English accents. These generally appear through the entrances and exits of various characters and Fielding's use of touchstones.

Critical Verdict of the Audience

When you're reading Tom Jones the author himself seems to draw his armchair into the room "and chat with us in all the lusty ease of his fine English". Samuel Johnson disapproved of Tom Jones's libertinism in the strongest possible terms. Fielding is regarded with a mixture of acceptance and contempt, as a worthy boy who did the basic engineering for the novel because he invented the clockwork plot, but tiresomely boisterous, "broad" to the point of being insensitive to fine shades, lacking in any temperament of the higher aspirations, and hampered by a style which keeps his prosy commonsense.

Fielding and the Theatre

The stage taught Fielding how to break the monotony of flat, continuous narrative scenes do not ramble on and melt into each other. They snap past, sharply divided, wittily contrasted, cunningly balanced...only a theatre man's expertness in the dramatic...could cover the packed intrigue of the narrative. The theatre taught Fielding economy. The fact that Fielding had worked in the theatre before becoming a novelist influenced his narrative technique, especially in the use of lively dialogue and the choice of characters. Tom and Sophia are round characters but Mr.Western and Mr. Allworthy have some characteristics borrowed from the stock characters of drama.

The influence of drama on Fielding's novels was in formal structural elements. For example, he employs concrete "visual" symbols such as Sophia's muff to anchor the reader and focus his attention in a way similar to the use of stage properties. The most obvious influence of drama on Tom Jones is in the intricacies of the plot, which are the typical confusion of comedy.

Omniscient Author

The most original and memorable element of Tom Jones, however, is the narrative voice informing the action and discoursing on the philosophy of writing to the reader in the introductory chapters. Fielding controls the reader's response thorough the urbane, tolerant presence of the figure of the omniscient author, a polished and rational gentleman with a pronounced sense of the ridiculous who emerges as the true moral focus in the novel. While this technique sacrifices to a certain extent the sense of identification and verisimilitude provided by the first-person or epistolary forms used by Defoe and Richardson, the reading experience is enriched by the analysis of the all-knowing 'author.' On the other hand, the wry narrative voice accounts for various comic effects Fielding achieves in this remarkable novel; it is often the detached description which transforms a melodramatic situation into a comic one.

Humour

The humour is primarily a high comedy, as illustrated by hyperbole and double meaning. There is a good example of hyperbole in Tom Jones. Partridge's fears as they are travelling to London are exaggerated to the point of being a vice. The exaggeration of normally acceptable qualities to vices should teach us not to take fear, the want of order and bragging about oneself to extremes.

Hypocrisy in the Religion

Reverend Mr. Thwackum is an obvious sadist who enjoys beating religion into young Tom. Thwackum does his best to try to portray Tom in a bad light to Mr. Allworthy, eager to make him hate Tom. Fielding creates more inhospitable Christian characters. Mrs. Wilkins insists that it would not be "Christian" to protect the foundling that Mr. Allworthy finds on his bed, and tells him to leave him at the churchwarden's door. From the point of view of Mrs. Wilkins this is infinitely more Christian than protecting the child of a "strumpet who lays her sins at men's doors". When Mr. Allworthy is dying, Mrs. Wilkins, Mr. Thwackum and Mr. Square hypocritilly pretend like they care when they are angry at what is being left to them in Mr. Allworthy's will. Fielding loves portraying Christianity as violent.

Chapter 8

Fielding's Changing View of the Fictional Hero

Fielding offers his own early definition of the hero in "An Essay on the Knowledge of the Characters of Men," in 1743, and two poems, "Of True Greatness" and "Of Good Nature." Heroes, in life and literature—and I reiterate Fielding's emphasis on the combination—"should have stood up the Champions of the innocent and undesigning, and have endeavored to arm them against Imposition" (I.153). They should be good-natured rather than good-humoured (I.158). Their actions rather than their words should reveal the truth of their character (I.163), and, while religious, they should act against hypocritical sanctity (I.167). They are observant and watch the "Actions of Men with others" (I.175) in order to judge other men's characters.

By the publication of Tom Jones in 1749, however, Fielding had ameliorated his view, first by asserting that the unalloyed idealized hero is no longer a viable character; and second, by moving toward a more inward, less active view of the hero: First, the movement away from idealization:

For in this Instance [meaning the novel, Tom Jones], Life [in the novel, not in the world] most exactly resembles the Stage, since it is often the same Person who represents the Villain and the Heroes; and he who engages your Admiration To-day, will probably attract your Contempt To-morrow.... A single bad act no more constitutes a Villain in Life, than a single bad Part on the Stage. The Passions, like the Managers of a Playhouse, often force Men upon Parts, without consulting their Judgment, and sometimes without any Regard to their Talents. (8.1;I.327) Secondly, in the Dedication to Tom Jones Fielding moves toward a more inward definition of the hero's qualities:

... no Acquisitions of Guilt can compensate the Loss of that solid inward Comfort of Mind, which is the sure Companion of Innocence and Virtue; nor can in the least balance the Evil of that Horror and Anxiety which, in their Room, Guilt introduces into our Bosoms.

Fielding does not deny the possibility of the heroic life in the real world—a life Ralph Allen, Fielding's close friend and patron, most clearly exemplifies. But he is now distinguishing between heroes of fiction and heroes of life, rather then lumping them together.

This change in the rhetoric of the hero moves Fielding away from both the materialistic self-serving picaresque of Defoe and the moralistic self-centreed sentimentalism of Richardson's epistolary technique. This difference is reflected not only in the kind of hero Fielding creates, but more importantly in the relationship of the hero to the narrative structure He cannot, for example, except in the special case of Shamela, rely on internal characterized narration as Defoe often and Richardson always does. Since Fielding's heroes must learn to act within the range of possibilities sanctioned by society, the reader needs an observer-narrator to define the values of that society and to differentiate between the appropriate expression of those values and their corruption and misuse.

Since individual characters in Fielding's novels, such as Parson Tulliver or Squire Western, are often corrupters of those values, the narrator is necessary to provide the appropriate evaluation for the reader (which, of course, is pretty standard formal analysis). Where I differ from other readers is to suggest that Fielding's choice of narrative method is dictated by the rhetorical needs of the hero, not by the moral/social paradigm of his world (which for Fielding is always defined by the ideals of latitudinarian Benevolence).

Tom Jones: Definition of the Hero

More overtly and intentionally than in his other fiction, Fielding develops character and plot in Tom Jones to dissect and define the nature of the hero in the rhetorical structure of the newly-emerging novel form. Jones acts the role of traditional hero (discussed at length in an earlier section of this study) in relation to other characters and a new kind of hero in relation to the structure of the novel. Although critics have always emphasized the importance of Jones' life as a moral fable, we must remember that Jones is primarily the exemplary hero of fiction not of the real world—the hero of a comic novel, not of a rational world, whose method of characterization is primarily objective and external.

We are hardly ever permitted the intimacy of Jones' mind, heart, or soul. At moments when we might expect this intimacy—when he repents in prison, for example—Jones feels and speaks in eighteenth-century clichés, not in the language of personal individual experience. Nor does Jones himself change in any fundamental way during the course of the novel, as we might expect from a character that is learning important moral lessons. Instead, the complexities and conventions of the plot and rhetorical structure lead the reader through a process of changing notion of the heroic (guided by the narrator).

The same character who acts the very fallible non-Christian hero of the comic novel that is the beginning of Tom Jones is the worthy ideal hero of the idealized romance that is the conclusion. The plot of the novel rewards Jones for his recognition and acceptance of the true value of Prudence and the appropriate place of Benevolence in a world of Divine Providence. But the rhetorical structure of the novel tells us that this world is a fiction, and the rewards come only in romance not in life (please recall my earlier comments about Fielding's putting distance between literature and life).

Errors in Reading Tom Jones

Serious attempts to place the moral nature of Jones himself at the structural centre of the novel have also led to creative but misleading schemes. Tiltyard, for example, suggests that the unifying feature in Tom Jones is Fielding's conception of Jones as a hero of chivalry "who pledges himself to serve the commands of his lady". While this is a striking character metaphor, it is clearly contradicted by the text itself in a number of ways: Jones will serve the commands of almost any lady, from Molly Seagrim to Mrs. Waters to Lady Bellaston; the language and process of Jones' education is an ironic reversal of the education and quest of the chivalric knight.

Shoehorn goes even farther field when he seeks a parallel between Jones and Christ, a view that even common sense easily refutes: "It was his [Fielding's] answer to one of the most difficult problems he faced, how to make his unnatural protagonist a representative of mankind, how to give some kind of other, and moral dimension, to his comic hero". Of course, Fielding's solution is actually more simple, elegant, and effective—we don't need the Holy Spirit hovering over the text when we have the charming, authoritative, and intrusive narrator.

Chapter 9

Narrative Technique of Tom Jones

The Voice of the Narrator

Tom Jones uses a variety of rhetorical methods to define and exemplify the nature of its hero, the most obvious and pervasive being the voice of this intrusive narrator. Although this narrator is often a moral bully and social propagandist, he is also (like Thackeray's later narrator), a master showman. We do not mind his bullying and manipulation, because he is (with one or two minor exceptions), open and direct with the reader, never pretending to be anything other than the controlling force behind the action.

Abstraction and Generalization

One major technique is the narrator's use of abstractions and generalizations as the common vocabulary of description of the hero. And this generalizing is not merely typical of 18th-century thought, but carefully calculated for effect. For example, although Jones's appearance is a large part of his charm, we are not given any specific physical description of Jones until well into the middle part of the novel. And even then the language is abstract and general rather than detailed and specific:

Mr. Jones, of whose personal Accomplishments we have hitherto said very little, was in reality, one of the handsomest young Fellows in the World. His Face, besides being the Picture of Health, had in it the most apparent Marks of Sweetness and

Good-Nature. These Qualities were indeed so characteristically in his Countenance, that while the Spirit and Sensibility in his Eyes, though' they must have been perceived by an accurate Observer, might have escaped the Notice of the less discerning, so strongly was this Good-nature painted in his Look, that it was remarked by almost every one who saw him.

It was, perhaps, as much owing to this, as to a very fine Complexion, that his Face had a Delicacy in it almost inexpressible, and which might have given him an Air rather too effeminate, had it not been joined to a most masculine Person and Mien; which latter had as much in them of the Hercules, as the former had of the Adonis. He was besides active, genteel, gay and good-humoured, and had a Flow of Animal Spirits, which enlivened every Conversation where he was present.

Hardly a walking likeness. In spite of Fielding's disclaimers about the importance of concrete and specific language and detail, he hardly follows his own advice. In Book 10, chapter 1, the narrator provides a lengthy treatise on the nature of characterization in drama and fiction, claiming it is the sign of the greatest artist to be able to differentiate nuances of behaviour and characteristics among the many seemingly similar types that abound in life and on the stage: "Every Person, for Instance, can distinguish between Sir Epicure Mammon, and Sir Fooling Flutter, but to note the Difference between Sir Fooling Flutter and Sir Courtly Nice, requires a more exquisite Judgment... " (2.525). Fielding may admire this "Judgment," but his narrator hardly displays it in his descriptions of the hero in Tom Jones.

The introduction of Sophia (Fielding's notion of the hero is gender neutral) provides another example of abstract presentation: "Thus the Heroes [Sophia] is always introduced with a Flourish of Drums and Trumpets, in order to rouse a Martial Spirit in the Audience, and to accommodate their Ears to Bombast and Fustian, which Mr Lock's blind Man would not have grossly erred in likening to the Sound of a Trumpet" (4.1;1.152). Among the many purposes of this passage—

including the notion of female heroism—lie two particularly significant characteristics of the narrator's rhetorical strategy. First, it focuses not on the description of the heroic character being introduced (Sophia), nor even on the abstract qualities of the Hero in general (as in the description of Jones above), but solely on the method of presentation evidenced through language ("the Heroes is always introduced... "). Secondly, the passage points out that the hero will be developed throughout the text by contrast with other characters, particularly the military and pseudo-martial ("Flourish of Drums and Trumpets"). A similar passage occurs not much later in the text when the narrator defines the characteristics of the hero, again not through description of action, but through Sophia's (and by comparison, all sensible women's) responses to Jones' bravery: "The Generosity of Sophia's Temper construed this Behaviour of Jones into great Bravery; and it made a deep Impression on her Heart: For certain it is, that there is no one Quality which so generally recommends Men to Women as this" (4.13;1.201).

Irony and Contrast

Fielding's narrator further reminds us of the nature of true heroism through its ironic contrast to the more common uses of the word—the difference between label and reality. When Sophia first contemplates marriage to Blifil she is enamored of her heroic role in accepting his hand: "Sophia was charmed with the Contemplation of so heroic an Action, and began to compliment herself with much premature Flattery..." (7.9;1.360). The word and the deed do not belong together. But the criticism and irony is gentle and directed more against the false Idea of the heroic than against Sophia herself.

Jones' argument with Northerton over the toasts to Sophia (7.12) is a more serious instance of the difference between label and reality—in this case the Gentleman is no Hero and the Hero is no Gentleman. When Jones reaches London, the false heroism of the foppish aristocracy and its imitators, "Men of Wit and Pleasure about Town" (13.5; 2.700), will be ironically contrasted with Jones's more modest behaviour.

Character Commentary

Character commentary often corroborates the narrator's point of view. The corroboration is offered in a number of ways:. the use of indirect discourse, which may give us the thoughts of the character, but clearly gives us the words of the narrator;. the direct presentation of contrasting views of heroism from unreliable characters; and. the direct presentation of positive examples and definitions from morally reliable characters.

Indirect discourse. Fielding often uses indirect discourse to present both contrasting and corroborative definitions, such as this view of Squire Western's admiration for Tom's "heroic" qualities:

[Tom] had so greatly recommended himself to that Gentleman, by leaping over five-barred Gates, and by other Acts of Sportsmanship, that the Squire had declared Tom would certainly make a great Man, if he had but sufficient Encouragement. He often wished he had himself a Son with such Parts; and one Day very solemnly asserted at a drinking Bout, that Tom should hunt a Pack of Hounds for a thousand Pound of his Money, with any Huntsman in the whole Country. (3.10;1.149)

Western's view of heroism—not untypical of his time and social position—defines heroism as qualities of physical strength, courage, and determination in activities of drinking and hunting. Western's views are, furthermore, both comparative and materialistic: heroism is measured in comparison to the actions of others (not to any clearly defined moral or other standard), and it is worth its weight in money. While Western's views of Tom are positive from his own perspective—they are only positive in a limited sense since they do not make him a proper candidate for son-in-law.

Contrasting Views

That not everyone shares the narrator's view of heroism is evident through the direct commentary of other characters. That heroism is a matter of class and social position rather than individual behaviour and merit is reflected by such people as the Barber and Landlady who would have behaved quite differently to Jones had they known he was a gentleman's son (8.4;1.417). The opposite extreme, which sees the hero as an idealized character out of myth and romance, is expressed by Partridge directly to Jones: "Certainly, Sir, if ever Man deserved a young Lady, you deserve young Madam Western; for what a vast Quantity of Love must a Man have, to be able to live upon it without any other Food, as you do.

Chapter 10

Critical Essays

Eighteenth-century opposition between "Principle and Appetite"

In one, Bernard Harrison suggests that a major merit of Fielding's Tom Jones is that it takes issue with a commonplace eighteenth-century opposition between "Principle and Appetite", and so counters a pervasive philosophical culture of systems of fixed, dualistic "conceptual oppositions" — Good/Evil, Reason/Passion, and so on—in favor of a more flexible, dynamic and challenging moral universe. In crucial episodes "appetite wields the scepter of Principle, passion turns out to lie at the heart of goodness". Readers are encouraged to revise their mental maps in the light of Fielding's radical course in moral orienteering, with the novel's ironies, paradoxes and deceits stimulating them to be "sufficiently intelligent and candid" to recognize that their habitual cultural assumptions are under review. Harrison uses this argument to attempt a partial rehabilitation of Wolfgang User's readings of Fielding. This seems curious, in that User's readings are distinguished by an inveterate reliance on dualistic forms, whether this be the "polarity" of the two elements of Abraham Adam's name, the "two negative poles" of Adam's behaviour versus that of the world, "two sides of a contrast"1 in Book V, chapter I, Fielding's disquisition on his [page 137] "new Vein" of "Contrast," or many others. "Terbium non dater," as Luther Corny remarks laconically, "didacticism or vacant spaces". User's only third or modifying term is the imagination of the reader, which is why he seems to me incapable of conveying the sense of flexibility for which Harrison wants to argue.

But in the preceding article Andrew Varney describes the same period in wholly different terms. He brings forward an array of examples of early eighteenth-century aesthetic discourse, and of material prefatory to fictional and factual narratives, in order to show that such discourses negotiate freely between apparently opposed categories such as moral and appetitive, didactic and sensational, factual and romantic. Even Robert Hooker, Secretary to the Royal Society, is not above advertising Robert Knox's informative tome An Historical Relation of the Island Ceylon (1681) in terms of the transporting "rapture of the reading experience". Readers and writers of fiction collude knowingly in a sophisticated game in which the audience agrees to pretend to be persuaded by protestations of moral beauty which legitimate the more basic, tastier pleasures—savory and unsavory—of the texts. Varney caps his argument by noting how Fielding "sardonically unpicks" this "collaborative tissue" woven by previous readers and writers, by reworking the metaphor of taste in the first chapter of Tom Jones, where the reader's appetite for the story and the subject is made to sound almost as voracious as, later, does that gross appetite "commonly called Love".

Harrison's Fielding wants to teach, to present a case. Varney's is a bully, and wants the reader to share his own rather scathing attitudes. One wishes to rework dualisms creatively, the other to satirize others' casual or hypocritical manipulations of such dualisms. And unlike Harrison's good reader of the novel, Varney's is merely "complicit and ductile", like Ian Bell's account of John Presto's "deferential, remarkably passive" reader, who is intelligent only insofar as he or she is alert to the sense that they will be "led by the nose" through the novel's shifting codes and systems, towards whatever gap, stumbling-block or ha-ha, or up whatever garden path the author has in mind. "To reject irony is uncoil, and to miss it is worse". One wonders what User, whose readings of Fielding's higher ironies are often, to quote Bream Hammond, "touchingly naïve", would have to say to this.

Two different Fielding's, two different visions of the eighteenth century. The editors of Connotations. were clearly trying to turn the number into an imaginative fiction by creating an Iberian "gap" between the two articles and inviting readers to transform the resulting met text into an "aesthetic object" by filling in the gap with their own version of the unwritten truth that might lie between. Or perhaps, as Imlay says, "inconsistencies cannot both be right, but... may both be true," especially where a mind as unusual as Fielding's is concerned.

There are two preliminary questions. How can both these visions of the nature of eighteenth-century thought be true? And how can Fielding subscribe to or embody both of them? As regards the first, one might point out that Harrison's description of Fielding's method is reminiscent of Cashier's initial description of Enlightenment thought in general, at the start of The Philosophy of the Enlightenment:

> [it] again and again breaks through the rigid barriers of system and tries, especially among its greatest minds, to escape this strict systematic discipline.

This hint might be taken further: suffice it to say that Harrison's account of the wider eighteenth century may be contestable beyond a certain point. Varney's scenario, if pushed further, would yield a two-fold conclusion; firstly, that early eighteenth-century advertisers and readers of fiction were pre-empting some aspects of this intellectual revolution by practicing and favoring discourses that negotiated subtly between categories which were, to culturally normative moral thought, dualistically opposed; and secondly, that Fielding had reservations about such free negotiations. All this may be true, although it is possible to scale down the first part of that conclusion, because Varney is dealing with a different kind of discourse. As far as reading of or attitude to Tom Jones is concerned, this turns out to be the main point of difference between the two positions.

Both Varney and Harrison assume that Fielding makes readers engage with patterns of thought inherited from some aspect of their cultural heritage. Harrison's assumption is that in Tom Jones such "fore-understandings" derive mainly from the discourse of moral philosophy (Luther Corny questions Fielding's rationalism from a similar [page] general premise in Connotations 2.2, while he makes clear in 3.3 that engagement with philosophical language does not make Fielding a moral philosopher). Varney's answer, though he does not argue the case through, would be that such patterns also derive from the separate but related discourses of aesthetics, taste, and competing attitudes to the nature and function of literature. These and moral philosophy are not mutually exclusive categories of discourse—literary criticism is moral criticism, in this period, and moral philosophy is also often social philosophy—but their emphases and characteristic modes of expression and tones of voice differ, and readers would have identified and listened to them in different ways. It would be useful, in dealing with the still vexed questions concerning Fielding and his readers, to have as full a sense as possible of what those readers would have felt to be the origins and areas of association of his fictional modes of address. There is also the possibility that the two cases above do not exhaust the options: Czerny's assertion in 3.3 that Fielding is more like a poet than a philosopher is arresting, and will be worth pursuing.

The well at the bottom of which the truth is hiding is, I suspect, on the border between Varney's broader cultural plain and Corny/Harrison's loftier philosophical hills, with the water in it tending, as water should, to the lower level. To test this supposition, I wish briefly to re-examine Book V, chapter I of Tom Jones, which treats of the split between serious prefatory chapters and comic history in terms of darkness and its opposite, light, and which raises the question of the relations between philosophical and aesthetic discourses in a particularly striking way. It is also valuable because it deals explicitly with dualisms, day/night, comic/serious and light/ darkness, and because it is one of the chapters relating to the question of the "sagacious reader" (XENIX and elsewhere) which have emerged by consensus as cruxes in this debate. Properly so, as the sagacity or otherwise of the reader reflects on a historiographical level two of the central difficult abstractions of the novel as history, that "true Wisdom" of which Allworthy is said to be a "Pattern" and the dullness, "Darkness" and folly which are, or should be, its opposites. But there is the second preliminary point to consider: does Fielding characteristically express himself in such a [page 140] way as to reflect both of the incompatible attitudes to conceptual categories suggested by Varney and Harrison, and if so how?

He does. A main feature of his mind is that when dealing with the languages of taste, criticism, aesthetics and literature he tends to think differently to the way he thinks when dealing with other matters, public, professional and documentary. This will have implications for the highly mixed discourse of Tom Jones, but it seems wise first to illustrate these differences with reference to Fielding more widely.

On the one hand, it is easy to find Fielding passing critical comments that seem to reflect caustically on some of Varney's earlier examples and hence tend to validate his approach to Tom Jones. The example of Robert Hooker, for instance, calls to mind Fielding's mordant procedure in Volume Two of the Miscellanies, where the "editor" tells us that the stationer who found the manuscript of the fabulous Journey from This World to the Next had offered it to, among others, the Royal Society, but that "they shook their heads, saying, there was nothing in it wonderful enough for them." The most notable example of Fielding's taking issue with what he finds to be a dubious conflation of imaginative excitement and moralism in the reading of fiction is his incorporation, in Parson Tickle text's encomium of Pamela at the start of Shamela, of parts of the commendatory letters included in the first and second editions of Richardson's novel. Only very brief effusions from the ductile Tickle text are required in order to create the ionizing context:

"The Author hath reconciled the pleasing to the proper; the Thought is every where exactly clothed by the Expression; and becomes its Dress as roundly and as close as Pamela her Country Habit; or as she doth her no Habit, when modest Beauty seeks to hide itself, by casting off the Pride of Ornament, and displays itself without any Covering"... —Oh! I feel an Emotion even while I am relating this: Methinks I see Pamela at this Instant, with all the Pride of Ornament cast off.

One would think from this that Fielding would systematically disdain making effects that relied on insouciant marriages of moralism and salacious enticement, but a reading of his pamphlet The Female Husband; or, The Surprising History of Mrs. Mary, alias Mr. George Hamilton, written as he was engaged on Tom Jones, would dispel such an idea. The [page 141] pamphlet records and dramatizes the sensational career, trial and punishment of the gold digging Methodist lesbian Mary Hamilton, who had managed a creative enough subversion of a supposedly fundamental dualism (man/ woman) by marrying, bedding and acquiring the assets of more than a dozen "wives" under her alias. As Donald Thomas says, it is a classic of its kind, "praise of 'virtue and religion' mingled [in the introductory material] with promises of 'unnatural lusts' and 'vile amours' as the reader's reward to come... sexuality and sensationalism [combined] with moral finger-wagging."

So the prefatory material to Shamela establishes ironic relations not merely with a Richardson text and its contemporary readership but also with another Fielding text and its readers. It is as though Fielding did not mind, in some circumstances, being a potential target for his own satire. And in prefatory material to other fiction he is not above engagement with figures of speech that deal in quasi-Tickletextian negotiations between the moral and the visual-nude: the "Dedication" to Tom Jones offers the opinion that fiction offers examples that are like pictures "in which Virtue becomes as it were an Object of Sight, and strikes us with an Idea of that Loveliness, which Plato asserts there is in her naked

Charms" (1: 7). Plato as moral teacher presumably trumps Tickle text, but the image as rendered still harks back to Varney's gallery of examples.

As well as these textual examples, which suggest a picture rather different from Varney's, some episodes in Fielding's career would tend to add weight to Harrison's argument about the way that Tom Jones revises the relationship between categories. Readers familiar with Fielding's life will recall his final major public achievement of ridding the London streets of violent gangs in four months in late 1753. This created, out of the blue, what is now known as Criminal Intelligence, and involved as radical a revision of the relationship between two more conceptually opposed categories—criminal/judicial—as did anything in his fiction. Having obtained the relatively small sum of £ 600 from the Privy Council, Fielding used the money to advertise and implement a policy of paying criminals to shop their colleagues, at the same time offering the informants freedom from prosecution as far as possible. That criminals and the judiciary might work together for their mutual benefit, [page 142] with the legal rewarding the illegal and so colluding in a morally green area and both taking on as a result the quality of mixed characters rather than the Good and the Bad, had never been considered. "As a method of enforcing law it was revolutionary." Order is restored through the breaking of dualistic decorum's: turning the world upside-down intellectually ameliorates it socially, turns it the right way up.

So there are two Fielding's, and if there were "gaps" in his fiction they might have something to do with a gap in him: a psychological or internalized version, perhaps, of the Bauhinia dialogic imagination with its "internal contradictions and volatility," which is responding differently to different aspects of its conditioning historical ambience. In short, Fielding's attitude to the manipulation or reworking of oppositional categories tends to depend on the context. If the ends to be gained in the real world seem worthwhile, then the benefits of those ends may outweigh the tackiness that may be involved in the expression of the means. In The Female Husband, impressionable readers can be warned about the outrageous forms that duplicity can sometimes take; in the almost equally sensational pamphlet called Examples of the Interposition of Providence in the Detection and Punishment of Murder (1752), a superstitious horror of being found out may be instilled into an audience that Fielding must have thought of as akin to the credulous Partridge in Tom Jones; the London streets may be cleared of systematic criminal terrorism. But where imaginative literature and its supporting discourses are concerned, the response is often more satirical, a more Augustan reaction to the perceived absurdities of a literary-moral world that must be imagined as already "topsy-turvy," where "whales now perch upon the sturdy oak" and Pamela can be advertised by breathless clergymen as the naked image of virtue and a clear moral example. Here literary means and moral ends are almost identical, and it takes the sharper clarity of satire to make the point.

The corollary of this split for a reading of Tom Jones, which synthesizes many different modes—historic and romance, history and historiography, serious and comic, satiric and comic, aesthetic and actual—would be that there is no philosophical stability in the novel, but instead a restless maneuvering between kinds of language and systems of value, the "constantly fluctuating activity" and "original intellectual force" that [page 143] Cassirer talks of as characteristic of the best minds of the period. Rather than there being a moral case in Tom Jones which builds up "like Euclid," or rather than "Fielding, the poet" simply being "under no obligation to be philosophically consistent", there is a powerful Hyracoidean flux of contexts and attitudes, an active process which affects and may actively constitute that case.

This can now be put to the test by looking at the example of Book V, chapter I, where Fielding opens his important "new Vein of Knowledge," which is "Contrast", by waiving his authorial "Privilege" of saying nothing at all (a privilege he very rarely exercises) and explaining to the reader why the comedy of the story is interspersed with such "Serious" prefatory essays.

Disdaining the small gesture, he first invokes the universe, "all the Works of the Creation," in which the contrasts and reverses of day and night, winter and summer, may generate "the Idea of all Beauty, as well natural as artificial." Referring to this solemn dualistic hyperbole as "too serious an Air," he then shifts the figure towards that of the brilliance of a jewel being set off by its setting, its "Foil," illustrated in turn by the beautiful woman who chooses a plain companion for public display. Women ("at Bath particularly") even contrive to be their own foils, by trying "to appear as ugly as possible in the Morning, in order to set off that Beauty which they intend to show you in the Evening" (:). Everyone their own contrast: seen comically, the binary opposition dissolves, or is made ridiculous, by the kaleidoscope of frames of reference.

The metaphor then shifts again as Fielding accounts for the structural principles of the venerable form of the "English Pantomime" in terms of contrasts, in this case between comic ("Duller") and serious ("Dullest") elements (:). Only the stygian gloom of the serious—mythical—parts of the entertainment could ever make the insipid English Harlequin, that dullest of brilliants, seem bright and funny. From this now well-shaded tour of light and dark the discussion returns, via Pope and a dig at Steele, the "late facetious Writer, who told the Public, that whenever he was dull, they might be assured there was a Design in it," to the present case. What is "Serious" is now what is dullest, darkest and most soporific. "In this Light then, or rather in this Darkness, [page 144] I would have the Reader to consider these initial Essays." Readers may sleep while the author is dull, except for those who have noticed that this author is dull in the same sense that darkness is light. The comedy of visual metaphor is then subtly extended into the next chapter, the subtitle of which promises "some fine Touches of the Passion of Love, scarce visible to the naked Eye" (:). The dark-adapted eye of the somnolent reader must, it seems, be instantly exchanged for the trained and focused beam of the microscopic investigator. Poor readers, led not just by the nose but by the optics. No wonder some are dazzled.

Corny focuses on the antithesis of light and dark, and analyses the chapter's absurd quality in terms of Fielding's supposed desire to burlesque Locke and "the rationalist method of antithesis.... What to the minds of rationalist critics appears as the brightness of reason turns out to be absolute nonsense when it has gone through the mill of Fielding's logic" Harrison demurs, apparently sensing no dislocation between a philosophical framework of ruptured oppositions and an aesthetic method based on retained contrasts, and opines that Fielding is not being ironic about his "new Vein," but boasting about his invention. And User, to whom as usual binary oppositions are powerful stimulants, notices that Fielding uses them in the early paragraphs, and provides an account in which "the text... only sets up two sides of a contrast."

None of these readings seems wholly to the point, because the philosophical, logical and antithetical elements of the prose are clearly subordinate to others. These constitute a vividly metaphorical, witty medium, part of the function of which is to play with another area of the language of taste to which Varney points, the relation between literary qualities and the world of the senses in the form of light. It is mock-Spectator chiaroscuro, reflecting on the statelier mode of Addison's well-known papers on the "Pleasures of the Imagination", which express literary pleasures in terms of "Light and Colours" as well as Varney's taste and "Relish." In these papers the great principle of imaginative pleasure is not blunt contrast—"what a rough and unsightly Sketch of Nature should we be entertained with, did all her Colouring disappear, and the several Distinctions of Light and Shade vanish?" —but the mind's power of "comparing" the works [page 145] of Nature with those of Art. In Fielding this modulation between "natural" and "artificial" beauty is carefully destroyed early on, the conceptual opposites coarsely lumped together in an overriding stylistic flourish in order that the rest of the chapter should carry the mock-assumption that all manifestations of

"Contrast," on whatever level, are part of the same grand principle.

Some of the energies here are satirical, subtly mocking Addison's universalizing and new-philosophy solemnity—"when we survey the whole Earth at once, and the several Planets that lie within its Neighbourhood, we are filled with a pleasing Astonishment" once again the Royal-Society mentality ["survey"] and the mild aesthetic gasp ["Astonishment"] coalesce, with the genteel "Neighbourhood" making the solar system sound like a sort of cosmic Twickenham). But it is only the manner that comes within range, with the seediness of Fielding's later paragraphs pointing up the inappropriateness of Addison's mandarin tones for the more rumbustious social world of Tom Jones. The brutalizing of Addison's elegance implicit in the reduction of his structure of argument to simple contrast smacks of self-mockery, and of mockery of the reader who accepts the early hyperbole at face value. If anything, it all defers implicitly to Addison's superior, more flexible, form of argument. Then, when the chapter blows itself up at the end in the comic conflation of light and dark, the fun seems too tricky and good-natured to be at all satirical. The chapter bears out Harrison's thesis in that the apparent antithesis comic/serious has been remodeled, but it also bears out Varney's sense that Fielding often plays with aesthetic discourse for his own ends. The metaphorical nature of the passage has somehow extended to a figure that can bridge the gap between the two positions and the two Fielding's, critical and reconstitute.

But sagacious readers have not really learnt anything about moral philosophy, nor about aesthetics or taste. Instead they have been made to pass through a highly specific and energetic process of figuration in which things at first appear philosophically clear and then become comically clouded. In other words the passage is per formative at a much higher level than it is argumentative, and readers learn to the extent that they "see" this process by experiencing or sensing it, not by "seeing" [page 146] the point. It is not about chiaroscuro, it is chiaroscuro, and the method is not argumentative prose or mock-aesthetic satire but poetic wit: Fielding is partly serious when he talks about comic epic-poems. This appears more clearly when we consider Fielding's source, for (naturally enough in per formative chiaroscuro) the "new Vein" is in fact new in the same sense that darkness is dark. His whirling paragraphs are expanded from hints in the burlesque couplets near the start of Matthew Prior's Alma, or The Progress of the Mind (1718), as Dick replies to Mat's digression in praise of Butler's variety of effect with another brilliantly furbelowed reduction of at picture poesies:

> As Masters in the Clare-obscure,
> With various Lights your Eyes allure...
> Or as, again, your Courtly Dames,
> (Whose Cloths returning Birth-Day claims,)
> By Arts improve the Stuffs they vary;
> And Things are best, as most contrary...
> So you, great Authors, have thought fit,
> To make Digression temper Wit.

Again there is a comic split between the case argued, the message about contraries, and the medium, the rapidity and variety of the similes. These digressive darts do not temper the heat of wit with the coolness of extended illustration (a single word gives yet another "contrary"); they embody and perform it, and so both express and destroy the argument-by-contraries in a "Clare-obscure" of their own. Mat appreciates this in his reply—this being a supposed dialogue, we have a trustworthy example of the proper response of the sagacious reader/auditor—

> RICHARD, quota MAT, these Words of Thane,
> Speak something sly, and something fine.

As with Fielding, the passage manages both to burlesque itself and to express a central value of the work at large; or at least it does if Tom Jones is, like Alma, a comic-metaphysical hymn to variety and relativity of perception. The good reader of the novel is, perhaps, the good reader of a certain kind of Augustan poetry.

In a less obtrusive form this shunting of the reader through metaphorical processes of shifting contexts, frames of reference, languages and attitudes is fundamental to Tom Jones, especially where the language of value, such as wisdom or sagacity, is concerned. In XENIX, at the end of which readers are exhorted to use their "Sagacity" to uncover the mysterious authorial "Meaning", this apparently abstract value of sagacity has been coloured firstly by the discussion between the landlord of the inn and his wife, the landlord having been introduced as long ago as chapter ii as having the character, "among all his Neighbours, of being a very sagacious Fellow". This elegant conversation ("you are always so bloodily wise") ends with the landlord claiming to have talked Sophia into giving him money, which he has not, and with his wife joining in "the Applause of her Husband's Sagacity". They are a well-suited couple. There is then an effusion from the narrator-as-pseudo-aesthete on landscapes natural and artificial, and on those who ride through the former. This effusion contrasts "the ingenious" and responsive "Traveller" with the "sagacious Justice," who, together with the other "numerous Offspring of Wealth and Dullness", ride without attending to the view. From this the transition to the "Sagacity" of the reader is immediate; as in Vs., the good, ingenious reader is the one who senses and perhaps follows the process through novelistic interlude, supposedly serious digression, and direct address.

But the tour de force of these processes comes in Visio, iii and iv, which present the "wonderful Sagacity" of a gallery of characters, Squire Western and his sister Did, the wisest of the three countrymen pursuing the Wiltshire thief, and eventually Blifil, in order to shade and throw into relief the blunt definition of Allworthy as a "great... Pattern" of "true Wisdom" near the end of chapter iii. This quality is here defined as "Moderation... the surest Way to useful Wealth", the golden mean, control and reasonable indulgence of a variety of passions, but only five paragraphs later we hear that Blifil too has very "moderate" appetites. Wisdom or sagacity is very slowly and surreptitiously redefined by contact with different contexts until it approximates to the lesser prudence which is the cunning and perspicacity of Western as "Politician", Did Western as shrewd but inadequate observer of Sophia's one passion of love, the wisest but unreflecting countryman, [page] and the toad like hypocrisy of Blifil. Everyone is wise: Allworthy's "Wisdom" is undercut as subversively by the narrator as it ever is by Blifil. The character in the episode who is closest to being a fool, according to Fielding's definition ("the Fool sacrifices all the rest [of the passions] to pall and satiate one") is Sophia, whose great passion is her love for Tom, which she cannot properly disguise; and Sophia's name, in Fielding's emblematic technique of naming, means moral wisdom. When the fools and knaves are "wise," it may be wise to be a fool.

This is the great benefit of considering the novel as a network of metaphorical relations of the kind suggested; it ionizes and energizes its emblematic systems, and invites the reader to consider the novel as a play of forces rather than a moral system per se. Put more simply, it forces the wit and the seriousness closer together. To take as a final example, Tom's appeal to the "Image" of Sophia's face in the mirror when Sophia asks him, in XVIII.iv, why she should believe him when he says he is sincere in his rather exorbitant professions of love, sincerity and constancy. Reading this as philosopher will yield Battestin very beautiful point that the passage, like others, demands

To be read on more than one level: Sophy Western's image in the glass is the literalizing of the Platonic metaphor, the dramatization of Fielding's meaning in the broadly allegorical scheme of the novel. Ultimately, her true identity is ideal, an abstraction.

One can hardly demur. At the same time, it is very lucky for Tom that his tactic can be interpreted with this degree of seriousness. His outrageously flattering rhetorical gesture is, to put it mildly, a brilliant way of blurring the issue and of converting defence into attack. Tom inadvertently manages a "Clare-obscure" of his own, and Sophia's reaction is a little like Mat's to Dick in its combination of admiration and suspicion, though she is less sure of her reading. Can he be serious in his conflation of the ideal and the actual, or is he being cunning and opportunistic with aesthetic language? (Has Fielding taught him his own two "personalities," as Nightingale teaches him to write duplicitous letters to temper his constitutional urge to tell the truth?) Sophia blushes, half smiles, forces herself to frown, but is eventually won over to the extent that she promises she will marry him one year later. Like Sophie, [page] the reader feels the pull of two readings, one philosophical and abstract, the other skeptical, dramatic and suspicious. These mirror or stand opposite to each other, creating a double mirror and a double metaphor: the skeptical reading would carry no force were the other context not also present. There is not necessarily a "gap"; there is, again, a per formative process to be gone through which creates, marries and resolves contraries in the reading rather as Tom and Sophia are married in the history. But if there is a single reading, or just "two sides of a contrast," gaps there may well be.

The Interpretation of Tom Jones. Some Remarks

Luther Czerny's essay on "Reader Participation and Rationalism in Fielding's Tom Jones" has triggered a lively discussion, to which Bernard Harrison and Leona Taker have made substantial contributions. As some of my statements regarding reader response have been focused on and indeed attacked in this debate, it may not be inappropriate to highlight the implications of Czerny's claim that he knows what Fielding really meant when using the word "sagacity" in Tom Jones. Although "sagacity" is differently contextualized in Fielding's novel - to which Leona Taker has drawn attention - it nevertheless has a fixed meaning for Corny, and he sticks to this assertion in spite of the fact that he once quotes Wittgenstein, from whom he might have learned that the meaning of a word is its use which, of course, varies. Shades of meaning, however, are not Czerny's concern, perhaps because they might subvert his claim to know exactly what was in Fielding's mind.

Such a type of interpretation calls for scrutiny, and as I do not want to provide another interpretation of Tom Jones, I should like to raise a couple of issues that seem to have been overlooked in Czerny's essay: namely, why interpretation is frequently a matter of dispute, and what the difference is between methods of interpretation and theory.

Every interpretation transposes something into a different register that is not part of the subject matter to be interpreted. Therefore, each interpretation is an act of translation, in the course of which something is shifted into what it is not. In the case under discussion, a literary text is translated into a cognitive discourse, which makes any such act into a two-tiered operation. The literary discourse is the subject matter, and the cognitive discourse provides the parameters within which it is to be understood.

Comprehending Tom Jones could be directed towards ascertaining what the novel is about, what it means, what it intends, what it represents, what impact it exercises, what responses it elicits, what its representation aims at, and so on. There is a wide potentiai range of registers into which the literary discourse may be translated. Such a two-tiered operation brings the inherent duality of the register to the fore. All the viewpoints listed - and one can think of many more - decide what is important for the respective interpretation. As the viewpoints are selective, they give each interpretation a particular slant. The problem, however, is that the cognitive terms of the register are partial, and so the register actually molds the subject matter to the shape of its own interest.

This inherent duality makes it impossible to claim full knowledge of the text to be interpreted. Hence any such claim can only mean - in the case under consideration - to identify Tom Jones with the stance adopted for grasping the novel. This is strikingly illustrated by what Corny claims to have found - namely, the intention Fielding is supposed to have pursued in Tom Jones, summed up by the statement: "Just as he expresses his belief in a dialectical unity of erotic love and charity, he equally looks to the unity of reason and feeling in wisdom." How can "unity" be the guiding intention of someone who announces in his "Bill of Fare to the Feast" that the "Provision" for him "is no other than H U M AN N A T U R E, " whose importance is emphasized by spaced capital letters, and which is of "such prodigious Variety, that a Cook will have sooner gone through all the several Species of animal and vegetable Food in the World, than an author will be able to exhaust so extensive a Subject."

Interpretation is bound to go awry when the following considerations are not sufficiently heeded: First, the ineluctable partiality of the terms set by the register, and second - even more importantly - the space opened up by any act of interpretation between the subject matter and the register into which the latter is transposed. This space cannot be ignored, but has to be negotiated; otherwise the inherent stances of the cognitive discourse are just superimposed on the literary discourse. Now, Czerny's claim that "unity" is to be considered the hallmark of human nature clearly shows the partiality of his interpretation: a set of assumptions is elevated to the status of reality. Negotiation, however, implies going back and forth between one's assumptions and the text, thus developing a hermeneutic circularity that acknowledges the space opened up by any interpretation, and simultaneously brings under scrutiny one's assumptions which, when focused upon, will not stay the same.

This is almost exactly the kind of repair that Harrison carries out on Czerny's claim to know that Fielding strove for "unity"; he highlights the interplay between "Reason" and "Appetite", whose oxymoronic relationship - according to Harrison - Fielding unfolds in kaleidoscopically shifting patterns, which both shatter and rebuild reader expectations. "He has constructed, with extreme detail and verisimilitude, an array of cases in which Appetite wields the scepter of Principle, passion turns out to lie at the heart of goodness, morality turns out to demand worldliness (in a certain sense) of us, and unwieldiness (in a certain sense) stands under moral condemnation. All this may indeed stagger the reader; but if it does, the expectations it staggers are not introduced for the first time to the reader through his hermeneutic struggles with the text, but ones insinuated by presumptions, fore-understandings, which while they are not, in fact, essential to the preservation of a common understanding of terms in the language in which the text is written, are sufficiently engrained and habitual within the cultural milieu addressed by the text as to seem so."

In the final analysis, a claim to knowledge is alien to interpretation, which would be redundant if one knew the 'true' nature of the matter to be explored. For interpretation is an attempt to understand what is beyond knowing. Therefore negotiation is the guiding principle of interpretation, not least because any claim to knowing colonizes the very space between object and register that interpretation it has opened up.

Why someone who 'knows' what Fielding's enterprise should was, deem it necessary to debunk the statements of those who are not in line with his thinking? Why should he pay any attention at all to those who are wrong, especially if he 'knows' that they started out from false presuppositions anyway, and thus were bound to go astray?

Well, no premises of interpretation are self-evident in view of what it is meant to achieve. The short cut to justifying one's own premises, therefore, is to single out opponents and tear them to pieces, implying, of course, that this is already sufficient evidence for the validity of one's own assumptions. The more vehement the attack, the more the assumptions depend on constant reminders of the opponent's failure. If the opponent has to be caricatured to the verge of simple-mindedness, the effect can only be to divert attention from the premises on which the attack is based. It is, after all, no proof of strength to say that the position attacked is weak.

Czerny's interpretive strategies make one thing quite clear: he does not consider his premises to be a heuristic assumption; assumptions initiate and develop trial runs, and since they can never cover all eventualities, some of their features must be exposed to change. Furthermore, Corny does not reflect on what is inherent in his premises - and why should he, in view of his certainty that he is right? Such an attitude is sadly reminiscent of those outmoded brands of explanation which laid claim to a monopoly on interpretation. The proponents of such claims inspected only other people's premises, but never their own, which for them had a self-proclaimed authority. However, they too were dependent on opponents, whose different starting points had to be distorted in order to provide negative support for the would-be indisputable.

I have obviously also been tailored in such a manner, and thereby converted into a foundational element of Czerny's interpretive enterprise. That he needs me urgently is borne out by the fact that even when replying to Harrison's criticism, he calls me up as his whipping-boy. It is flattering to be so indispensable, though a little disconcerting to be seen as simple-minded. I am used to my work being regarded as too abstract, sometimes too difficult, even too complicated, but now suddenly, according to Corny, it is simplistic: "In his attempt to establish a place for reader participation, User knows only one alternative, either didacticism or vacant spaces, terbium non dater." If only I had known this earlier, I could have saved myself hundreds of pages. My Carnelian mask of simplistic did not last long, as both Bernard Harrison and Leona Taker swiftly pulled it off. Harrison explained very succinctly the phenomenological conceived text processing that I had advanced, and even stressed the fact that in the reading process the "noetic-noematic constitution" requires a "continuous adjustment of anticipations in the light of their fulfillment." Of course, this adjustment will apply to the text-processing of Tom Jones, as each reader brings different anticipations to bear, just as each interpreter has preferences for his or her chosen assumptions. Corny bridles this, and begins his rebuttal of Harrison's criticism by stating: "He (Harrison) has given us, in fact, a theory of reader response which he, rather too modestly, claims to be a modification of User's theory only." Well, why not? And isn't modification integral to our common pursuit of exploring issues and addressing problems in literary criticism? At least it is more productive than the currently fashionable victim discourse.

Leona Taker has given an exhaustive analysis of my attempts to conceptualize the different lacunae in the text, thus providing an impressive demonstration of why the register of any interpretation should be examined first, as it forestalls a rush to judgment in the conflict of interpretation. "Reading the Instructions" - as she puts it - means inspecting the register into which the subject matter is translated. Such an inspection is all the more pertinent as the register not only molds the subject matter, but also translates it into a contemporary context. In other words, the register is conditioned by the context out of which it has arisen, and its fashioning of the subject matter is essential if the latter is to be translated into terms of contemporary understanding. In the two-tiered structure of interpretation, the register itself is dual by nature, as it simultaneously gives a perspective to the subject matter, and transmits it into the parameters of a particular intellectual environment.

This is a basic reason why interpretation has to come under scrutiny. For a long time, it was just an activity carried out without much attention to what it actually entailed. It was tacitly assumed that interpretation was something that came naturally, not least as human beings live by constantly interpreting. However, what does not come naturally are the forms interpretation takes. And as these forms structure the acts of interpretation to a large extent, it is important to study them, not least as the structures will reveal what the respective interpretive agenda is designed to achieve.

This is all the more essential with a prevailing type of interpretation that predicates and judges what in actual fact has to be understood. Understanding entails opening up the issues to be explored, whereas predication and judgment provide closure, thus pointing to a transcendental stance which decrees what the subject matter has to be. The critic, however, as T.S. Eliot once remarked, "must not coerce, and he must not make judgments of worse or better. He must simply elucidate: the reader will form the correct judgment for himself." Otherwise, we might add, interpretation is merely decision-making, and as such stands in need of deconstruction, since it reifies either individual or contingent preferences, which more often than not block the road to an historically and situation ally conditioned understanding.

There is a final point to be touched upon briefly: the distinction between method and theory of which, to put it mildly, Corny seems unaware in his magisterial interpretation. He starts out his first essay by saying: "Fielding's novels, therefore, do not just serve User as examples to illustrate his theory but actually provide the patterns or substrata on which it is based." and he has another dig at me in his second essay, maintaining that "a theory" cannot "be convincing which does not really meet its chosen empirical subject." Irrespective of whether a theory is convincing or not, it is certainly not a method of interpretation.

In the past I have already tried to explain the difference between theory and method, and for argument's sake, I am afraid I have to quote myself: "Theories generally provide premises, which lay the foundation for the framework of categories, whereas methods provide the tools for processes of interpretation. Thus the phenomenological theory, for instance, explores the mode of existence of the artwork; the hermeneutic theory is concerned with the observer's understanding of himself when confronted with the work; the gestalt theory focuses on the perceptive faculties of the observer as brought into play by the work. Distinctive assumptions are made which reveal a particular mode of access to the work of art, although they do not represent a technique of interpretation. Theories must undergo a definite transformation if they are to function as interpretative techniques. Thus the bases laid down by the three theories above must be transformed into (a) the strata model, (b) question-and-answer logic, and (c) the concepts of schema and correction. There is, in fact, a hermeneutic relationship between theory and method. Every theory embodies an abstraction of the material it is seeking to categorize. If the degree of abstraction is the precondition for the success of categorization, then, clearly, the theory tends to screen off the individuality of the material, whereas it is the central function of interpretative methods to bring out and elucidate this very individuality. Thus the theory provides a framework of categories, while the method, in turn, provides the conditions whereby the basic assumptions underlying the theory will be differentiated by the results emerging from individual analysis."

A theory of aesthetic response, as I tried to conceive it, follows the very same lines, i.e. it has to be transformed, if a method of interpretation is to be derived from it. However, when a theory is taken for a method of interpretation, either confusion or redundancy ensues: Confusion insofar as the comparatively abstract frameworks of a theory tends to distort the text when used as guidelines for interpretation; redundancy insofar as texts are turned into documentation when used to bear out a theory that really does not need such evidence. In each instance, the hermeneutic interrelationship between theory and method is lost to view. If theory furnishes the focus for a method, the latter in turn can feed its findings back into the theory, which is thus fine-tuned.

At a historic juncture in literary studies, this circularity became paramount in order to dispel the smokescreen arising from an impressionistic type of interpretation that took the emotion aroused by the art work for its intrinsic structure. This is reason enough for observing the distinction between theory and method, and this is exactly what Leona Taker has stressed in her contribution, to which, by way of conclusion, I can unreservedly subscribe. "A literary example can partially illustrate but not bear out a theory, since, as noted above, a literary text is a testing ground rather than a tribune for ideas, a field which only partly overlaps with the theory one superimposes on it. It is richer than a theory in some ways and poorer in others (less numerous); and it will necessarily indicate the insufficiencies of this theory while failing to do justice to its extensions."

A Double Standard for Men and Women in Tom Jones

For this project, I will be summarizing three different articles that pertain to the argument that there is an apparent double standard for what is acceptable behaviour in men versus women in Tom Jones. In addition to summarizing these articles, I will also be adding my own views and comments throughout this paper.

The first article is by April London, entitled controlling the Text: Women in Tom Jones. London begins by stating that Fielding uses a metaphor between property and women throughout the text in Tom Jones. She states that "Fielding plays with the multiple meanings of property, undercutting the equation of female and helplessness, to offer versions of power unconstrained by gender which are... contradicted by... Sophia's subordination [at] the novel's happy ending". London argues that although Fielding seems to put aside the gender bias, he actually enforces it by the way his character Sophia changes at the end of the novel. I think this is an interesting observation that has some merit. London does a good job of providing examples to reinforce her argument.

London claims that throughout the novel Sophia steps over the bounds of authority in order to maintain her own integrity, something rather uncommon for women to do back in the 18 th century. The most outright example of this, of course, is when Sophia refuses to marry Blifil and runs away after her father locks her in her room, intending to keep her there until the day of the wedding. London says that "the structure of authority... arose from property" and that Sophia is testing her father's power of acquisition of that property. Because she decides to place herself in her aunt's care, Sophia takes control of her own life.

According to London, throughout most of this novel, the female characters sort of control the plot and course of action, which is really unusual for its time. Furthermore, a few of them, Lady Bellaston in particular, actually demonstrate assertiveness and determination, which is again, unusual for the time period. London states that "female power, although most richly evoked in negative terms as an expression of carnality, also has its positive embodiment in the person of Sophia".

This seeming rise of feminine power stops abruptly, however, with Sophia's concession and marriage to Tom. According to London, "Sophia... is correspondingly diminished as she becomes part of the property relations that now define her husband". She goes on to say that this development brings the 18th century values concerning land (and women through the use of the property metaphor) back into line: symmetry, stability, and continuity. London finishes by stating that in all of Fielding's novels, including Joseph Andrews, Amelia and Tom Jones, women are given power only so that they can later give it up through the ceding of their property to their male counterparts once the men have "revealed themselves as prudential". She argues that "Relinquishing the possibilities of character, they are absorbed into the ethic of property relations, becoming metaphoric attributes of the constitutional order Fielding defends".

It is apparent that while Fielding does attribute a certain power to the women of this novel, he finishes by adhering to the traditional views of the time and almost implies that Sophia was really a means to an end: she ultimately cedes her property and wealth to Tom, which allows Tom to establish himself and his position in society.

The Mitigated Truth: Tom Jones's Double Heroism by Peter J. Carlton is the second article. Carlton argues that Tom gets away with a variety of actions, especially illicit sex, with very little punishment and even less guilt. Tom's actions are always minimized by the actions of other characters, very often female characters, as well as by the convenient surrounding circumstances. For example, Tom is involved with Molly Seagrim, but his involvement is minimized by a character sketch of Molly that Sophia's maid Honour shapes when she states that Molly was always a forward, willing wench and that when wenches are so coming, men are not so much to be blamed, for it's only natural to act on this forwardness. This double standard is actually stated and "justified" by another woman, which accurately highlights the way of thinking in the 18th century that Fielding evidently recognized.

Later, when Molly is found to be pregnant, Allworthy lectures Tom much in the same way he lectured Jenny Jones years ago, but according to Carlton, Fielding "minimizes its impact in Tom's case". These two instances are a few of many examples of this double standard for men and women. Carlton sums up the view of women when he states,

> Fielding relies on... the traditional view of women, implicit in the fact that it is always the woman who is the aggressor in Tom's affairs... women are perceived as either "purer" than they are or more sexually ravenous than they are (the familiar 'virgin/whore' polarization), but never simply as they are. At one extreme, they are seen as semi divine beings... at the other, women are portrayed as insatiable sinks of lust.

Sophia and Lady Bellaston seem to represent these two extremes precisely. Sophia is often referred to with heavenly and divine inferences, while Lady Bellaston is the instigator of an on-going affair with Tom. Tom is viewed as an innocent bystander who falls victim to 'an evil temptress' of sorts.

Carlton tells us that another critic, Battestin, remarks that "at a time when the double standard was widely accepted, Fielding strove to define the morality of sexual relationships for men as well as women". Carlton refutes this, however, by saying that rather than trying to make an ideal judgment about sexual behaviours of men and women, Fielding simply compares Tom's actions to those of Nightingale and Will Barnes and demonstrates that Jones's behaviour is not as loose in morals as is his peers.

Carlton goes on to discuss the depiction of heroism in Tom, most of which does not apply in the scope of this paper. However, he does argue that one facet of Tom's heroism is a "Cavalier heroism, a dashing blend of sexual and martial prowess" which seems to excuse Tom's promiscuous behaviour and even adds to his attraction. While the women involved in these affairs are looked upon as evil and tempting, Tom is actually looked upon as a dashing cavalier hero. This development speaks volumes about the double standard apparent in Tom Jones.

To further support these arguments is a third article by Gene S. Koppel entitled Sexual Education and Sexual Values in Tom Jones: Confusion at the Core? Most of this article talks about the sexual education and lack thereof in Tom, focusing on inconsistencies throughout the novel. Again, most of this is not within the scope of this paper, but Koppel does make one statement that completely supports the double standard argument. He says, "After all, it is quite obvious that Fielding accepted, at least partly, the traditional Western 'double standard,' which considered males to be sexually 'grosser' than females and allowed them (unofficially, at least) more sexual freedom than it permitted women".

Again, Fielding seems to maintain a double standard for what is acceptable behaviour in men versus women. This is highlighted through endless examples and situations throughout the novel which would provide formidable arguments for anyone who sought to argue otherwise.

Although Henry Fielding (1707-1754) wrote many literary works I am going to deal mainly with his major novels, Joseph Andrews, Tom Jones, Amelia, and his shorter satirical work Shamela. All of these works contain a strong moral message, but the moral message is not entirely consistent, and is presented in various ways.

One of Fielding's main concerns was the question of marriage. His ideas on marriage are concisely summed up by Allworthy in his sermon on matrimony:

I have always thought love the only foundation of happiness in a married state... and in my opinion all these marriages which are contracted from other motives are greatly criminal... To deny that beauty is an agreeable object to the eye... would be false and foolish... But to make this the sole consideration of marriage, to lust after it so violently as... to reject and disdain religion, virtue and sense... is surely inconsistent... either with a wise man or a good Christian.

Although this sermon mainly condemns marriage for reasons of lust Fielding more commonly condemns marriage for reasons of financial gain or social elevation.

The way in which Fielding conveys his philosophy of marriage is different in all four works, and the virtuousness of the virtuous is variable. However, the basic message is fairly consistent.

Joseph Andrews

Of the works mentioned, Joseph Andrews contains the most virtuous and idealized couple; Joseph and Fanny, even if they are somewhat unrealistic. Joseph is tempted by both Lady Booby and Mrs Slipslop and refuses the advances of each of them, remaining constant in his chaste devotion to Fanny. The chastity of their love is constantly emphasized and admired by Fielding, and they are rewarded for their virtuousness with eternal happiness (it is heavily implied). Fielding writes of their union thus:

Joseph remains blessed with his Fanny, whom he donates on with the utmost Tenderness, which is all returned on her side.

As well as maintaining their spiritual happiness, their financial problems are solved by Mr Booby's 'unprecedented generosity' in giving Fanny a gift of two thousand pounds.

Their blissful life is contrasted with the life of Lady Booby who married for financial gain. She obviously has little or no affection for her husband, which is indicated by the fact that she attempts to seduce Joseph at the beginning of the novel, and it is reiterated by Fielding at the end of the novel in these words:

As for the Lady Booby, she returned to London in a few days, where a young Captain of Dragoons, together with eternal parties at cards, soon obliterated the memory of Joseph.

This also suggests that her lifestyle is now rather banal and tedious in comparison to the married idyll of Joseph and Fanny.

Tom Jones

Tom Jones is not presented as such a virtuous character as Joseph, and is thus perhaps more credible. Tom and Sophia have more problems to overcome than did Joseph and Fanny; the worst that the latter couple had to cope with was the brief scare that they may be brother and sister. Tom is illegitimate and wishes to marry above himself, which, at the time, would have meant the lady sinking to the social level of her husband. The fact that she is willing to suffer this consequence illustrates that she is marrying purely for love.

Although Fielding consistently condemns sex outside marriage, he does he not despise illegitimacy. This is made evident through Allworthy's words:

However guilty the parents might be, the children were certainly innocent

Fielding's belief that personal qualities are more important than social standing, and his admiration for characters who share his belief, are made clear through Sophia's description of Tom:

So brave, and yet so gentle; so witty, yet so inoffensive; so humane, so civil, so genteel, so handsome. What signifies his being base born, when compared with such qualifications as these?

As I have previously mentioned, however, Tom is not such a perfect picture of morality as Joseph Andrews. Tom is tempted and fails to resist. He is seduced by Molly Seagrim, but it is important to note that he stayed away from her for three months before succumbing because he did not like the idea of corrupting a young woman, particularly the daughter of a friend. This small fact is illustrative of Fielding's idea about which he writes in Works X1V.

> That very early and strong inclination to good or evil, which distinguishes different dispositions in children, in their first infancy.

However, he continues to write that although someone is basically good or bad they are also influenced by their passions, which can cause a lapse in a good person. This type of ruling by the passions did not occur for the virtuous characters in Joseph Andrews, but is relevant to Booth in Amelia, so this could be regarded as an inconsistency in Fielding's morality. He does not acknowledge temporary lapses in Joseph Andrews, whereas in the later novels, he does, possibly for the sake of more realistic and rounded characters.

In both of Tom's yielding to temptation, he is portrayed to the reader as a victim. This is particularly notable in his liaison with Miss Waters. The aggressiveness with which she launches her seductive attack on Tom is described in terms of 'the fair conqueror' using her 'whole artillery of love' and the eventual unmasking of:

> The royal battery, by carelessly letting her handkerchief drop from her neck.

Fielding makes it clear that he does not condone Tom's yielding to his temptations, but he does not entirely condemn it because it is so clear that he was a victim. In Joseph Andrews he seems to suggest that yielding to temptation even once is sinful, but this is only alluded to by the fact that neither Joseph nor Fanny fall from their path of morality. Fielding excuses Tom's behaviour thus:

> A single bad nut no more constitutes a villain in life than a single bad part on the stage

He obviously believes that in these instances Tom has been led by his passions rather than his basic nature, and so may be forgiven.

Like Joseph, Tom is eventually rewarded with a happy marriage and financial security, despite the fact that Tom has not been as virtuous as he could have been and Sophia has defied her parents in their wish for her to marry Blifil. The important thing for Fielding is that Tom is basically a good person and Sophia defied her father out of love for Tom, as defying the wishes of parents is not an action of which Fielding would otherwise approve.

Their happy marriage is contrasted with other much less harmonious marriages in the novel, such as Squire Western's marriage to a pathetic woman whose father set up the marriage for financial gain. Western regards his wife as a servant and believes himself to be a good husband on the grounds that:

He seldom swore at her (perhaps not above once a week) and never beat her.

Another more vivid example of an unhappy marriage as a consequence of avarice is the marriage between Bridget and Blifil. Blifil, like Western, sees his wife as a domestic utility. Their only pleasure within their marriage is derived from tormenting each other. The only factor which sustains Blifil in his marriage is the hope of eventually inheriting Allworthy's estate, however, Blifil dies prematurely, and so never inherits. Once again, Fielding ensures that a couple who married for the wrong reasons live and die miserable.

It thus seems that in Tom Jones the theme of marrying for love rather than gain remains, but it is presented more realistically than in Joseph Andrews and the characters are allowed small slips without being entirely condemned.

Amelia

Amelia differs from the two novels previously mentioned in that it does not deal primarily with the problem of courtship and pre-marital resistance to temptation, but rather with problems within marriage. Previously, the reader has been left at the end of the novels with the impression that the couples will live in peace and harmony and fidelity for the rest of their lives, having already overcome their various problems, whereas in Amelia the marriage is clearly not trouble-free.

Amelia and Booth, like Tom and Sophia, have to deal with the problem that they are of different social standing. Similarly, it is once again the parents rather than the couple who object to the discrepancy in class, so Fielding continues the idea that that defiance of parents is allowable if it is a necessity for personal happiness.

Amelia is a similar character to Joseph, in that she is tempted but never yields. She is pursued by Bacillary and James, spurns them both and suffers in silence. Her constant fidelity causes Booth's liaison with Miss Matthews to be seen by the reader as particularly reprehensible. However, Amelia forgives him, as both Sophia and Fielding forgave Tom for his wrongdoing. It must however be noted that Booth appears virtuous compared to the villains of the novel such as James and Trent, and so receives less harsh judgment from the reader.

Once again Fielding brings unhappy marriages into the novel, but in this instance they do not create such as dark contrast as in the previous novels because the marriage of Amelia and Booth is far from idyllic. James and Miss Booth are married for reasons of lust on his side and monetary gain on hers, James soon realises his foolishness and grows to hate his wife more each day. Mrs James even agrees to act as her husband's procuress in his attempts to seduce Amelia in order to avoid being banished to the country by her husband, which adequately shows both her lack of morals and lack of affection for her husband. The marriage does not last and James returns to Miss Matthews whilst Mrs James, like Lady Booby, immerses herself in the trivial world of card-playing.

In contrast, Amelia and Booth eventually sort out their problems, Booth becomes a Christian and Amelia's inheritance is restored. Their happiness appears to be a reward for Amelia's virtue and tolerance and Booth's repentance. Booth has 'sinned' more than Tom and yet is still forgiven. As Fielding progresses in his literary career, he appears to become more aware of and more tolerance to human foibles.

Shamela

Shamela contains a similar moral message but it is presented in an entirely different way, and also deals more directly with hypocrisy than with motives for marriage. Hypocrisy and feigned virtue had been touched on in previous novels through characters such as Mrs. Slipslop, but it is in this work that Fielding deals with it most comprehensively. Fielding wrote Shamela in opposition to Richardson's recently-published Pamela, in which the heroine is held up to be admired as a perfect model of virtue. However Fielding's idea of virtue clearly differs greatly from that of Richardson. Richardson appears to consider virtue to consist mainly of chastity, which Pamela retains, but she uses her chastity and front of virtuousness in order to gain her master for her husband and elevate herself socially. Pamela does not marry for love. The letters of Shamela effectively expose the fact that Fielding did not see Pamela as a virtuous woman, but rather as a calculating conniving creature.

Throughout the novel the key words used by Shamela in her letters are 'feign', 'act' and 'pretend'. Shamela continually tempts her master but pretends to be doing so unwittingly, thus retaining her virtuous image. She resists his advances, but only for the sake of appearing virtuous and hoping to lure him into marriage, rather than for moral reasons. Her false virtue is particularly evident in letter V1 in which she writes to her mother mentioning that Squire Booby had offered to 'touch her under-petticoat'.

Sir, says I, you had better not offer to be rude; well, says he, no more I won't then; and away he went out of the room. I was so mad to be sure I could have cried.

Fielding also makes evident the fact that her 'affections' fluctuate between Squire Booby and Parson Williams according to which is more convenient and advantageous for her at the time. In the true Fielding tradition, she eventually suffers for her lack of morals and for marrying for financial gain. At the end of the novel the letter to Parson Oliver concludes:

P.S. since I writ, I have a certain Account, that Mr Booby has caught his wife in bed with Williams; hath turned her off, and is prosecuting him in the spiritual court.

The presentation of the clergy in this work could be seen as inconsistent with the other novels. Parson Williams is a corrupt man who writes to Pamela:

For I purpose to give you a sermon next Sunday, and shall spend the evening with you in Pleasures which though' not strictly innocent, are however to be purged away by frequent and sincere repentance.

This Parson provides a great contrast to Abraham Adams who is described thus:

He was besides a man of good sense, good Parts, and good Nature... he was generous, friendly and brave to an Excess.

Adams appears to be the realization of Fielding's perfect clergyman, whilst Parson Williams is the exact opposite. It is difficult to understand why Fielding chose a parson to be a character of vice in Shamela, as previously he has not criticized religion. It is possible Fielding chose a parson merely to make his corruption appear more shocking to the reader.

Conclusion

To conclude, it would seem that Fielding's basic moral messages remained the same throughout these works. His main message is that marriage should always be for love, and this remains constant throughout. He also proclaims the benefits of chastity, but appears to attach less importance to this as his work progresses, and begins to believe repentance to be more important. He appears to become more tolerant of people's weaknesses and more willing to accept that people are sometimes ruled by their passions, which causes them to act in a way which is contrary to their basic moral code. Overall, Fielding conveys his moral messages in a subtle, entertaining and mainly consistent manner.

Bibliography

A Journey From This World To The Next, 1743.

Amelia, 1751.

An Apology For The Life Of Mrs. Shamela Andrews, 1741.

Collected Works, 1882, 1902, 1967.

Don Quixote In England, 1734.

Love In Several Masques, 1728.

Pasquin, 1937.

Proposal For Making Effective Provision For The Poor, 1753.

The Coffee-House Politician, 1730.

The Historical Register, 1737.

The History Of Mr. Jonathan Wild The Great, 1743.

The History Of The Adventures Of Joseph Andrews, 1742 - Joseph Andrews - *Film 1976, Dir. By Tony Richardson, Starring Peter Firth, Ann-Margret.*

The History Of Tom Jones, A Foundling, 1749 - Tom Jones - *Film 1963. Dir. By Tony Richardson, Written By John Osborne, Starring Albert Finney, Susannah York.*

The Journal Of A Voyage To Lisbon, 1755.

The Modern Husband, 1732.

The Tragedy Of Tragedies: Or, The The Life And Death Of Tom Thumb The Great, 1730.

Works, 1766.